Why the Religious Right Is Wrong about Separation of Church & State

Why the Religious Right Is Wrong about Separation of Church & State

Second Edition

Robert Boston

Prometheus Books
59 John Glenn Drive
Amherst, New York 14228-2197

Published 2003 by Prometheus Books

Inquiries should be addressed to
Prometheus Books, 59 John Glenn Drive, Amherst, New York 14228–2197
VOICE: 716–691–0133, ext. 207; FAX: 716–564–2711
WWW.PROMETHEUSBOOKS.COM

07 06 05 04 03   5 4 3 2 1

Library of Congress Cataloging-in-Publication Data

Boston, Rob, 1962–
Why the religious right is wrong about separation of church & state / Robert Boston.—2nd ed.
p. cm.
Includes bibliographical references and index.
ISBN 1–59102–114–6 (pbk. : alk. paper)
1. Church and state—United States. 2. Conservatism—Religious aspects—Christianity. I. Title.

BR516.B664 2003
322'.1'0973—dc21

2003040514

Printed in the United States of America on acid-free paper

Contents

To my parents,

Robert E. and Alice R. Boston,

with love and gratitude

Introduction

Virtually the first thing I did after becoming Executive Director of Americans United in 1992 was to write an introduction for Rob Boston's just-completed book on how wrong the Religious Right is about the concept of real religious freedom in America.

Rob told me that he was fed up with the increasing erroneous history and constitutional analysis cropping up in right-wing books, pamphlets, and videos about the principle of church-state separation. It was this nonsense that motivated him to write a book for general audiences to correct the record.

The result was *Why the Religious Right Is Wrong about Separation of Church & State*. The volume you hold in your hands now has the same title but is in many ways substantially different. This second edition is updated and expanded, and it contains plenty of additional information. Indeed, every chapter has been rewritten with new material included. The appendix dealing with common Religious Right myths about church-state separation is longer, and two new appendices have been added: the text of Thomas Jefferson's famous 1802 letter to the Danbury, Connecticut, Baptist Association (along with the text of the Baptists' letter to Jefferson) and the complete text of James Madison's 1785 "Memorial and Remonstrance against Religious Assessments."

But one thing hasn't changed: The Religious Right is still spreading misinformation about church-state separation, and this book still debunks those calumnies. During the past decade, even some prominent right-wing revisionists have had to concede that some of their own work was based on data and documents which literally did not exist. They had merely repeated completely fabricated polls, letters, and speeches.

In the decade that Rob and I have worked together, plenty of things have been in flux. Presidents have come and gone. Congressional leadership has shifted through elections and personal scandals. The Supreme Court has issued important rulings that have reshaped what its majority believes religious freedom means. (At the Supreme Court, as in baseball, the side with just one more run or vote wins.)

Religious Right leaders and groups have come and gone too. As I look at the landscape now, I see many Religious Right groups in a state of transition. Pat Robertson has severed official ties with the Christian Coalition, and Jerry Falwell says he wants to spend more time building a compound containing a church, law school, retirement community, and other structures in Lynchburg.

None of this means that the Religious Right has lost its punch. Indeed, the Religious Right wields considerable clout with national political leaders in the White House, in Congress, and in among state lawmakers. The Supreme Court and lower federal courts have also handed down decisions lately that have greatly pleased the Religious Right—such as the June 2002 ruling upholding the constitutionality of vouchers for private religious schools.

Religious Right groups may rise and fall—but the movement is in this for the long haul. When I started my career in civil liberties, Jerry Falwell's Moral Majority was all the rage. Falwell no longer heads a national organization with a multimillion-dollar budget, but he remains a staple on the airwaves—both through his own program and his frequent appearances on Fox News Channel, MSNBC, and other television news outlets.

Furthermore, there's always somebody else eager to become the Religious Right's new leader. TV preacher D. James Kennedy broadcasts virulent propaganda that attacks church-state separation nationwide. Radio counselor Dr. James Dobson heaps abuse on Thomas Jefferson's wall of separation for his millions of daily listeners. From its multimillion-dollar office building in Washington, D.C., the Family Research Council maintains a roster of "talking heads" that are dispatched with regularity through the media and to assail church-state separation on numerous fronts.

The influence of antiseparationist thinking on public policy is easy to see. "Faith-based initiatives" proliferate in the federal government and in the states. Voucher bills abound. School prayer amendments continue to menace our Bill of Rights. In local communities around the nation, advocates of religious liberty and good science education must constantly fend off well-funded creationist groups. Efforts are even under way to allow houses of worship the special privilege of endorsing or opposing candidates for public office, all while remaining tax exempt.

We are seeing more local officials who advocate the use of "biblical" law in making legislative decisions, and even find a few judges who seem to think that their view of "sin" is an appropriate basis for citation in legal opinions.

Whenever and wherever we see and hear Religious Right arguments against church-state separation, they tend to be the same. Claims are made that church-state separation is hostile to religion, that it is unhistorical, that the United States was founded to be a "Christian nation," that the Founding Fathers never really intended to build a wall of separation between church and state, and that religious values are the only legitimate basis for making moral decisions.

Rob Boston's book uses everyday, nonlegalistic language to explain why all of that is wrong. Ten years ago, few people ever heard of the word "theocracy," a government run along narrow sectarian lines. Today, most people can see the dangers of such an arrangement—but they persist in believing it can't happen here. They persist in thinking that the Religious Right is yesterday's news, even while activists with this movement affect our political system and the courts, leading to a steady chipping away of our basic rights.

It has been a great honor to work alongside Rob for the past decade, and I look forward to the years ahead. Rob brings a rare combination of passion and precision to every article he writes, every speech he gives, and every debate he has with a Religious Right leader on a television news program.

That spirit is reflected in this book. Rob and I believe that the first step to responding to invidious efforts to undermine the Constitution is to arm yourself with the facts. This second edition of *Why the Religious Right Is Wrong about Separation of Church & State* is designed to be your first line of defense. Please use the information in it to defend church-state separation in your own community. Then take the next step: get involved, speak out, spread the word. The future of religious liberty depends on it.

—Rev. Barry W. Lynn
November 2002

Preface and Acknowledgments

I wrote the first edition of this book in 1992–93. A lot has happened in the church-state world since then.

The Supreme Court has handed down several major cases dealing with church-state issues. In addition, the political landscape in the country has shifted. Legislative proposals that would have likely died in Congress in 1992 get hearings today and sometimes even pass.

Much has happened with the Religious Right as well. In 1992, TV preacher Pat Robertson was just getting his Christian Coalition off the ground and trying to build it up as a major political force in the nation. When he launched the Coalition, Robertson outlined a series of ambitious goals: He wanted to have a Congress controlled by politicians who share his views, and he wanted a conservative Republican in the White House.

Robertson has largely achieved these goals. His Coalition has also had a significant impact on state and local politics. Throughout the 1990s, the organization sought to elect its supporters to school boards, city councils, and other local offices, with the aim of changing the political system from the bottom up.

It is true that in December 2001 Robertson stepped back from the

Coalition and severed his ties to it. However, the Coalition still exists under new leadership, and other Religious Right organizations, such as Focus on the Family and the Family Research Council, are working alongside the group. The Religious Right remains a powerful force in American politics and enjoys great influence in the nation's capital. After the election of George W. Bush to the presidency in 2000, the *Washington Post* went so far as to declare Bush the new leader of the Religious Right in America.

One thing has not changed: The Religious Right and its political allies are still attacking the separation of church and state and spreading misinformation about that constitutional principle. If anything, the attacks on separation by the Religious Right have only grown more intense and mean-spirited. As I was working on this update, Joyce Meyer, a TV preacher now connected with the Christian Coalition, called church-state separation "a deception of Satan" during a Coalition meeting that took place in Washington, D.C., on October 12–13, 2002. Robertson continues to insist that church-state separation was conceived by Communists in the former Soviet Union.

In my preface to the original edition of this book, I stated that Religious Right propaganda against church-state separation is not only wrong, but dangerous. I still believe this. I am now even more convinced that it is vital that Americans understand how separation of church and state came to be in the United States and how the courts have interpreted the principle.

Separation of church and state needs defenders. The principle is being attacked by the Religious Right, by national politicians, and even by academics. As I worked on this update, Harvard University Press issued a book by a law professor asserting that separation of church and state is somehow anti-Catholic. This assertion has been made even though without church-state separation, the Roman Catholic Church would never have flourished as it has done in the United States.

No matter the origin of the attack on separation—from a Religious Right magazine or a high-toned academic press—it must be answered, and it must be answered with force and gusto. Separation of church and state is America's contribution to the world. Other nations had experimented by expanding freedom of the press and freedom of speech before the Bill of Rights was penned. No nation had dared to separate church and state.

The results of America's experiment in separation speak for themselves: We have a vibrant, multifaith religious society that, with the exception of a few fundamentalist Muslim states, is admired all over the globe. We have a degree of interfaith harmony unmatched in the world. Our government is legally secular, but our culture accommodates and welcomes a variety of religious voices. New faiths take root here without fear. People leave, join, and form congregations as they see fit. Americans remain greatly interested in religion and things spiritual—unlike their counterparts in Western Europe, where religion is often state subsidized but of little interest to most people.

Under America's separation policy, we have striven for a meaningful balance between the rights of the believer and the responsibilities of the state. By and large, we've got it right. Children are no longer forced to pray in school or read from religious texts against their will, yet they are free to engage in truly voluntary religious worship whenever they feel the need. The important task of imparting religious and philosophical training to youngsters is left where it always belonged—with each child's parents or guardians.

Under that balance, Americans are free to worship as they see fit, and the government does not make value judgments among religions. Some European nations have passed so-called anticult laws aimed at curbing the rights of unpopular new religions. Such laws would not be acceptable in the United States or permitted under the First Amendment. Adults, our Constitution declares, have the right to make their own decisions about religion.

Like its predecessor, this book defends the separation of church and state and does so without apology. Advocates of church-state separation have no reason to apologize. We are defending a concept that has made the United States a model for religious liberty and given its people more religious freedom than any other nation.

This book says it's time to get back to basics. Thomas Jefferson and James Madison got it right. Their wisdom should today be venerated, not criticized. Jefferson called for a "wall of separation" between church and state. Some modern-day commentators may believe Jefferson's wall is too extreme. Many of the people who live in countries where there is no wall, such as repressive Islamic theocracies or nations with stale and sterile state-established religions that no longer fill spiritual needs, would probably beg to differ.

My purpose in this book is to correct the historical errors about church-state separation that proliferate and help readers understand what the courts, especially the Supreme Court, have said about leading church-state issues. This is not a legal tome or a dry historical recitation. I am neither an attorney nor a history professor. This book is for the layperson. It's a type of "Church-State 101," if you will. It is written for the reader who has little or no prior knowledge of the subject but who wants to learn more. Those who want to continue their study of the subject can then move on to more academic tomes, of which there is no shortage.

I will begin by setting the stage. The opening chapter looks at why church-state controversies are so compelling and commonplace. Subsequent chapters examine church-state relations in ancient times through the modern era. Chapters after that take a look at contemporary church-state issues, with special emphasis on what the Supreme Court has really said about controversies like school prayer, government aid to religion, and religious free exercise. Appendices that follow debunk common Religious Right myths about church-state separation and reproduce two key documents in church-state history: Thomas Jefferson's 1802 letter to the Danbury Baptists and James Madison's 1785 "Memorial and Remonstrance against Religious Assessments."

As the title indicates, this book is critical of the Religious Right. I have worked at Americans United for Separation of Church and State for fifteen years and am more familiar with this religopolitical movement than I ever expected to be. I read Religious Right publications, watch TV preacher broadcasts, and regularly visit Religious Right Web sites. Over the years I have attended dozens of Religious Right conferences in Washington, D.C., and other cities. (Some of my experiences at these events are chronicled in my 2000 book, *Close Encounters with the Religious Right: Journeys into the Twilight Zone of Religion and Politics*.) I know what this movement is saying about the separation of church and state. I also know why what is being said is false. My purpose in writing this book in 1992 was to share that information with readers, and that remains my goal ten years later.

I wrote the first edition after I had been working at Americans United for about five years. Ten years have passed, and I've learned a few more things. Thus, this second edition is expanded as well as updated. It contains more history, more background, and more information.

And now a few caveats: Although I disagree with the Religious Right, I do not mean anything in this book to be critical of theological conservatives or political conservatives. Many moderate and conservative Republicans disagree with the Religious Right. Many theological conservatives do as well. I define the Religious Right as a movement that blends theological conservatism with far-right politics and hostility toward church-state separation. A movement must have all three elements to be part of the Religious Right. Thus, someone who believes that the Bible is inerrant does not automatically belong in the Religious Right camp. Some people who believe this about the Bible have moderate political opinions or support church-state separation.

I also believe that separation of church and state deserves a strong defense, and I do on occasion speak forcefully in this book. I believe that Religious Right leaders like Pat Robertson and Jerry Falwell, who have led the attack on Jefferson's wall of separation over the years, have done much damage to America. Of course they have the right to speak their minds—but their views are controversial and should not be left unchallenged. And when their views are challenged, they must be challenged with strength and clarity of purpose. Our First Amendment deserves nothing less.

I am thankful for many scholars and writers who have taught me much since 1987. Books that I have found especially helpful include *Church, State and Freedom*, a classic work by the late Leo Pfeffer; *The Establishment Clause* by Leonard Levy; *Under God* and *James Madison* by Garry Wills; *The Godless Constitution* by Isaac Kramnick and R. Laurence Moore; Edwin Gaustad's books on Roger Williams; *James Madison on Religious Liberty*, edited by Robert S. Alley and other books and writings by Professor Alley; the writings of Prof. Gregg Ivers at American University and *Toward Benevolent Neutrality* by Ronald B. Flowers and Robert T. Miller, a casebook that contains the text of the Supreme Court's most important church-state rulings, with commentary. I recommend all of these works for anyone interested in further study.

The Separation of Church and State Homepage (http://members.tripod.com/~candst/index.html), run by Jim Allison, Tom Peters, and Susan Batte, has been extremely helpful. I enthusiastically recommend this site to all readers. It's packed with information and can help you respond to any other Religious Right myths you might encounter. It's also easy to use with a good search engine.

I also owe a debt of thanks to members of the staff of Americans United for Separation of Church and State. Special thanks go to my colleagues in the AU Communications Department: Joe Conn, Steve Benen, Susan Hansen, and Donya Khalili. I'm thankful to Steven K. Green, former legal director at Americans United, whose writings have taught me a lot. I'd also like to thank the Rev. Barry W. Lynn, executive director of Americans United, whose support has helped make this new edition possible.

Lastly, I must thank my wife, Carol, for her patience, her always-wise counsel, and her support, and I want to thank my children, Claire and Paul, for their regular infusions of love and energy. I want my children to grow up enjoying the benefits of church-state separation. My hope is that this book will, in a small way, make that possible.

Robert Boston
October 2002

1

Setting the Stage: Separation of Church and State under Attack

The separation of church and state has given Americans more religious freedom than any people in world history. In light of this success, it's hard to understand why anyone would criticize the separation model or actively oppose it.

Yet some Americans do exactly that. In the late 1970s, a political movement known as the Religious Right began to gather steam. Led by television preachers and far-right political leaders, this movement asserted that separation of church and state was never the intent of the Founding Fathers and insisted that separation harmed religion in America.

Popular belief holds that the Rev. Jerry Falwell formed the first Religious Right group, the Moral Majority, in the late 1970s. In fact, such movements had existed before in American history. In the section of this book that deals with the nineteenth century, I discuss the National Reform Association, a coalition of conservative Protestant ministers who sought to add a "Christian nation" amendment to the U.S. Constitution during the post–Civil War period.

The modern Religious Right was created more for political reasons than religious ones. During the waning years of the presidency of Jimmy Carter, some Republican political strategists began to theorize about ways to get Southern white Protestants out of the Democratic Party and into the GOP. They decided the way to do this was to emphasize what we now call "culture war" issues—abortion, gay rights, school prayer, and so on.

Falwell neither conceived nor created the Moral Majority on his own. The idea was handed to him by political strategists with the New Right—a largely secular movement of conservatives led by direct mail wizard Richard A. Vigeurie; Paul Weyrich of the Free Congress Research and Educational Foundation; Terry Dolan, a fund-raiser for the far right; and Howard Phillips, who had served in the Nixon administration.

Weyrich had already been working with the Rev. Robert Billings, a former public school principal who in the late 1970s was traveling the country lecturing to fundamentalists about the dangers of "secular humanism" in education. Weyrich had brought Billings to Washington to do some lobbying and decided that he should be the first executive director of the Moral Majority. It was Weyrich, not Falwell, who came up with the name.

Ed McAteer, a former salesman turned New Right activist, knew Weyrich and recommended Falwell as the man to front the Moral Majority. Weyrich and Phillips traveled to Lynchburg, Virginia, where Falwell was headquartered, to pitch the idea. Although Billings held title of executive director, Falwell quickly became the most visible manifestation of the Moral Majority. He was soon traveling the country giving speeches and appearing on television programs. Falwell also penned a few books.[1]

With heavy evangelical support, Ronald Reagan defeated Carter in 1980. But Reagan, while he talked a good line to the Religious Right, seemed more interested in pursuing conservative economic and military policies rather than making social changes. Reagan did back a tuition tax credit bill and a school prayer amendment, but both died in Congress. In other areas, his actions angered the Religious Right. For example, Reagan nominated to the Supreme Court Sandra Day O'Connor, a moderate who voted to keep abortion legal.

As the '80s progressed, Falwell's star faded and he became less and less visible on the national scene. In 1989, Falwell announced that he was shutting down the Moral Majority. He spent a few years focusing his energies on Liberty University, the fundamentalist school he founded. In 1992, when Democrat Bill Clinton was elected, Falwell began working to regain the spotlight. Although his public profile is not as strong today as it was in 1979, Falwell still broadcasts his *Old Time Gospel Hour* television program to millions every week and publishes a monthly newspaper. In his broadcasts, printed materials and Web site, Falwell attacks separation of church and state constantly.

Falwell's Moral Majority had always been more of a direct-mail operation focused on Washington than a real grassroots organization that emphasized state and local politics. As Falwell went into eclipse, another Virginia TV preacher, Pat Robertson, began building a Religious Right group with a real grassroots presence. That organization, the Christian Coalition, dominated the Religious Right and exerted considerable influence over the Republican Party throughout the 1990s.

As the decade wound down, the organization went into decline. High-profile staffers jumped ship, membership declined, and the Coalition's budget dropped. Robertson was forced to prop up the organization with money from his own personal fortune. In 2001, he cut his ties to the organization, but the Coalition still exists.

Robertson really doesn't need the Coalition to keep his profile high. His *700 Club* television program, a mix of Pentecostal Christianity and far-right politics, airs every weekday on Fox Family, a cable channel. Robertson, a millionaire many times over, enjoys significant influence in the Republican Party and has millions of followers nationwide. Like Falwell, Robertson continually attacks church-state separation on the air, in his books, and through the World Wide Web.

Alongside Falwell and Robertson there exists a plethora of other national Religious Right organizations. Largest among them are the Family Research Council and Focus on the Family, two related organizations founded by radio counselor and fundamentalist psychologist James C. Dobson. Dobson, also a vociferous critic of church-state separation, broadcasts to millions every day over the radio from his headquarters in Colorado Springs.

Some political commentators have argued that the Religious Right no longer needs outside groups like the Christian Coalition because it is so engrafted into the conservative leadership in Congress and the White House. It is a chilling thought.

The Religious Right has had its political ups and downs, but it has left a legacy. That legacy is a well-funded, sustained attack on church-state separation that persists today. Robertson has stated that church-state separation is a "lie of the left" and a "myth." There is nothing in the U.S.

Constitution, Robertson says, to require church-state separation. He has gone so far as to call church-state separation an invention of Communists in the old Soviet Union. (For a longer list of Robertson's attacks on church-state separation, see my 1996 book, *The Most Dangerous Man in America? Pat Robertson and the Rise of the Christian Coalition.*)

Falwell has made similar attacks against church-state separation. In recent years, Falwell has boldly stated that he does not believe in church-state separation and has called the concept unhistorical. Dobson's organization, which has an annual budget in the tens of millions, produces books, pamphlets, and videos attacking church-state separation.

A host of lesser known TV preachers and right-wing political operatives have made similar charges. Separation of church and state, a concept that once enjoyed near universal support in America, has been badly battered.

Is there any truth to the attacks on church-state separation launched by the Religious Right? Is the separation concept unhistorical? Why do certain religious and political groups oppose church-state separation?

Separation: The Origins

To answer these questions, it's important to have an understanding of what separation of church and state really means and how that concept manifests itself in the U.S. Constitution. This book is designed to do that; it examines the history behind the evolution of church-state separation in the United States and looks at how the Supreme Court has interpreted the principle over the years.

I take it as a given that the Constitution does create a separation of church and state. The term was used by key Founding Fathers like James Madison and Thomas Jefferson. An examination of the history of colonial America underscores why some of the framers were so adamant about instilling church-state separation in the Constitution. They saw implementation of that principle as the only way to guarantee religious freedom.

Chapter 2 begins the historical survey by looking at the relationship between religion and government in ancient and medieval times. But before we do that, it's necessary to step back and cover some basics. It's never safe to assume that Americans know what the First Amendment says. Many people can list at least some of the freedoms in the First Amendment but cannot recite the actual wording. Even fewer know how we got the First Amendment.

The First Amendment guarantees freedom of religion, speech, press, and assembly. Since this book deals with church-state separation, we need only consider the portion of the First Amendment that outlines religious freedom. That part of the First Amendment reads, "Congress shall make no law respecting an establishment of religion, or prohibiting the free exercise thereof."

The first portion of that phrase—"Congress shall make no law respecting an establishment of religion"—is often call the "establishment clause" (sometimes the "no establishment clause") by judges, attorneys, and legal scholars. This is simply a legalistic way of saying that this part of the First Amendment is concerned with stopping the establishment of religion by government. (We'll examine later what the framers meant by "establishment.")

The second of the religion clauses—"Congress shall make no law . . . prohibiting the free exercise [of religion]"—is often called the "free exercise clause." This means that this portion of the First Amendment guarantees every American the right to freely exercise the religion of his or her choice, without undue government interference.

The religious freedom guarantees of the First Amendment are only sixteen words long. It's unlikely that any politician today could express a fundamental human right in a mere sixteen words. Yet that is exactly what the Founders did. As we'll see in the next chapter, early American leaders did argue over the language, but at no time did they consider a lengthy amendment that attempted to spell out religious freedom rights in great detail. They opted for an economy of words.

Sixteen Words and Decades of Battles

Those sixteen words have sparked thousands of legal battles over the years. When does the government "establish" religion? How far can "free exercise" of religion be extended? The records of the debate over the First Amendment and the Bill of Rights (the first ten amendments to the Constitution) are sketchy, so it's impossible to know how much the framers argued over questions like this.

We do know that most church-state battles have taken place in modern times. In fact, church-state cases were rare at the Supreme Court in the eighteenth and nineteenth centuries. The twentieth century saw an explosion of them. Why did this happen? The Religious Right says it's because the courts in the modern era for some reason suddenly became hostile to religion and tried to curb its influence. That's nonsense. Here are the real reasons why church-state conflict has escalated in modern times:

- **Increasing religious diversity in the United States:** For many years, the United States was an overwhelmingly Protestant nation. That began to change with an increase in Roman Catholic immigration around the middle of the nineteenth century. The trend continued from there on, largely due to immigration. Soon significant numbers of Jews, Muslims, Hindus, and members of other non-Christian faiths were also living in America. For many years most members of these religious minority groups feared rocking the boat and challenging the dominant Protestant majority. But as they grew in number, their confidence also increased. It was inevitable that sooner or later they would begin to use the courts to secure their religious freedom rights.
- **Increasing diversity among Christian denominations:** As non-Christian faiths grew in number in America, a related trend occurred within Christianity: It became more diverse. Today, some Christian denominations are fundamentalist in approach, while others are moderate or liberal on theological questions. As a general rule, moderate and liberal Christian bodies are more likely to support church-state separation. (This is true only as a general statement. Many theological conservatives support church-state separation.) American Christianity does not speak with one voice on the issue of church-state separation. Thus, an effort by government to give preferential treatment, aid, or support to a certain Christian denomination can spark protests and legal action from other Christian groups.
- **The passage of the Fourteenth Amendment:** Astute readers will note that the First Amendment begins with the word "Congress." As originally written, the First Amendment was a limitation on Congress—the federal government—only. This is no longer the case. After the Civil War, Congress passed the Fourteenth Amendment, a provision designed to make it impossible for the Southern states to force African Americans back into a state of slavery. One of the ways the Fourteenth Amendment accomplishes this is by binding the entire Bill of Rights on the states—a process known as "incorporation."

Although passed in the post-Civil War period, the Fourteenth Amendment was more or less ignored by a succession of ultraconservative Supreme Courts in the latter half of the nineteenth century. The High Court simply refused to acknowledge what Congress had done. Finally, after the turn of the century, the legal tide began to change. The Supreme Court began to acknowledge the incorporation doctrine. In a church-state case from 1940, *Cantwell* v. *Connecticut*, the High Court ended all doubt and firmly embraced incorporation, declaring that states must abide by the entire Bill of Rights.

The Supreme Court's acceptance of the incorporation doctrine meant that people with civil liberties cases who had formerly been limited to state courts could now seek redress in the federal court system. And they did so. Thus, there was a dramatic spike in church-state cases and other types of civil liberties disputes in the federal courts after 1940.

- **Liberation movements:** The 1960s saw the struggle for racial equality, led by African Americans. In the 1970s, the women's rights movement took hold. During the 1980s, gay Americans demanded their rights.

As these movements were going full steam, a quieter struggle was under way. Members of religious minorities were demanding their rights as well. Jews and Catholics grew weary of their children being forced to recite Protestant prayers in public schools. Jehovah's Witnesses fought for the right to preach in public places. Nonbelievers battled religious qualifications for public office.

Liberation movements usually have two components: a public education component that is designed to help the public understand why the group in question is oppressed and deserves its rights, and a legal component. Members of the minority group file lawsuits seeking to advance their cause in the courts. These two components often work side by side.

This was certainly the case with religious minorities. They filed several church-state cases from the 1940s until the present day. Many of these lawsuits were successful, spurring even more litigation as the groups sought to build on their victories.

- **The rise of legal defense groups.** The American Civil Liberties Union (ACLU) was founded in the 1920s with the goal of defending the Bill of Rights in the courts. Prior to that, there was no national organization with a coordinated legal strategy to defend constitutional rights.

Other organizations copied the ACLU's model. In the 1980s, several Religious Right groups that disagree with the ACLU's views were created. These organizations sponsor their own litigation. People who believe their rights have been violated are no longer on their own. They can turn to national organizations for legal representation and assistance. These groups seek to shape the law by filing cases that will set legal precedent. Naturally, this has led to more church-state cases in the courts.

Religious Right legal groups have spawned much church-state litigation. In some cases, minor problems are blown out of proportion or exaggerated for fund-raising purposes before being rushed into court.

Some Religious Right groups have filed church-state lawsuits they know cannot be won in court. Several Religious Right organizations, for example, have filed lawsuits on behalf of public school teachers who want to pray with students in class or teach creationism alongside of or instead of evolution.

These cases have not been successful. No judge in this country, no matter how politically motivated, is likely to accept the Religious Right's argument that a teacher in the classroom has a constitutional right to ignore school policy as well as prior Supreme Court rulings and include religious activity in the classroom.

Similarly, prior to the Supreme Court's 2002 decision upholding vouchers, some pro-voucher groups filed lawsuits seeking to force states to provide voucher assistance to low-income parents. These lawsuits were rejected. Creation of a voucher program, the courts ruled, is a matter for the legislature, not the judiciary.

Lawsuits like this, it seems, are filed to attract attention and get the sponsoring organization's name in the newspaper. They certainly are not serious legal efforts. Nevertheless, they add to the amount of church-state litigation in the courts.

- **Society is more litigious.** Finally, it's a fact of life that Americans today are more litigious than they have been in the past. Americans are quicker to turn to the courts for resolution of problems. In recent years there has been an upswing in all kinds of legal cases. It's not surprising that church-state cases would increase as well.

All of these factors and others have led to an increase in church-state legal disputes in courts of law and courts of public opinion. Religious Right groups argue that there is more church-state conflict because the Supreme Court "invented" the separation principle in recent times. This is simply not the case. Rather, church-state separation is more contentious today due to a confluence of social, demographic, and legal trends.

Does Separation Harm Religion?

Religious Right groups make serious charges against church-state separation. For example, they frequently assert that America's policy of separation discriminates against or somehow harms religion.

The most extreme leaders and members of the Religious Right posit a conspiracy theory—that church-state separation is used by members of a type of secret society called "Secular Humanists." These Secular Humanists hate religion and seek to destroy it in the United States, especially the dominant faith, Christianity. According to this conspiracy theory, whose main proponent these days is the Rev. Tim LaHaye, author of the popular "Left Behind" series of apocalyptic potboilers, Secular Humanists run the federal government, the public education system, the public libraries, the colleges, the media, and the entertainment industry in the United States. They also supposedly have many churches under their control.

It's hard to believe that any adult could believe such folderol, but LaHaye has sold millions of books expounding on this conspiracy theory. A large number of gullible people apparently believe his ideas.

There are Secular Humanists in the United States. A national organization, the Council for Secular Humanism, is headquartered in Amherst, New York, and was founded by Dr. Paul Kurtz, a philosopher and former university professor. A separate group, the American Humanist Association, has offices in Washington, D.C.

But Secular Humanism, which holds that there is no God and thus humans must learn to solve their own problems by working together and accepting their differences, has never been a large movement in the United States. The handful of Humanist, freethought, and atheist organizations in America might collectively have a membership of perhaps 200,000. The overwhelming majority of Americans say they believe in God. To accept that a small number of people have managed to seize control of all major institutions is to suspend reason. The scenario is too fantastic for any thinking person to believe. Indeed, if you read LaHaye's books and the fund-raising mail issued by the Religious Right organization his wife, Beverly, founded, Concerned Women for America, you will see that LaHaye defines "Secular Humanism" to be essentially any expression of religion or philosophy that conflicts with his rigid fundamentalism. The millions of Americans that LaHaye calls "Secular Humanists" are actually Methodists, Presbyterians, Roman Catholics, Jews, Unitarian Universalists, Lutherans, and so on.

What do Americans really believe about religion? Our government is secular, but is our culture as well? Numerous public opinion polls have examined Americans' attitudes toward religion. The question has been studied extensively, and the polls tend to converge on certain points. It's worth mentioning a few broad conclusions:

- The vast majority of Americans believe in God. Gallup polls have never shown a large number of nonbelievers in America. There simply are not that many. In a 2001 Gallup poll, 90 percent said they believe in God. Only 2 percent said they do not. Seven percent said they were not sure, and 1 percent had no opinion.
- Belief in Heaven and angels is very high. Eighty-three percent of Americans believe in Heaven; 79 percent believe in angels.
- Fifty-seven percent of Americans say religion is "very important" to them. Twenty-eight percent say religion is "fairly important" to them. Only 15 percent say it is "not very important."
- Sixty-three percent say they believe religion can answer most of today's problems. Twenty-two percent say religion is too old-fashioned to do this. (A separate study conducted by Zondervan Publishing in 2000 found an even higher number, 80 percent, saying that religion can answer most of today's problems.)
- Forty-nine percent believe that the Bible is the inspired word of God. Twenty-seven percent believe it is the actual word of God, to be interpreted literally. Only 20 percent say the Bible is largely a human document composed of fables, stories, and ancient history.[2]

Americans tend to hold a favorable opinion of religion and members of the clergy overall. In some years, the public's respect for religion has dipped slightly, but this usually occurs when a religion-related scandal has been in the news. Public respect for religion soon rises again as soon as the story fades from the headlines. The public's confidence in religion, for example, dropped in 1989, a year when many scandals erupted involving TV preachers. It soon climbed back up again. Public confidence dropped again in 2002, in light of the ongoing child-abuse scandal in the Catholic Church, which dominated headlines for weeks.

U.S. Religiosity High

The fact is, the United States is one of the most religious nations in the world. In Western Europe, nonbelief or skepticism about religion is much more prevalent—even though many Western European nations retain officially established churches, church taxes, and other forms of government support for religion.

To Western Europeans, Americans seem obsessed with religion. Fundamentalism is very rare there, and TV preachers are practically unheard of. The idea of religion playing a political role, as it does in America, is thought absurd. Politicians do not routinely end their public pronouncements with a plea for God to bless the nation at hand. Culturally, Western European nations are much more secular than the United States, although legally they may have closer ties between church and state.

Although the United States is overwhelmingly religious, Religious Right groups continue to criticize the nation for not being religious enough. Why do they do this? One reason is that Religious Right groups are often not happy with the type of religiosity many Americans choose.

Recent polls have shown religious diversity on the upswing in the United States. Although most people still belong to Christian denominations, the number of Muslims, Buddhists, Hindus, Wiccans, and others is growing slowly but surely. Most Americans welcome such diversity; to the Religious Right it is an ominous trend.

Polls also show that most Americans are not dogmatic. Large majorities believe that there is more than one path to Heaven. They believe that salvation and eternal life can be found in many denominations and spiritual paths. Most Christians tells pollsters they believe even non-Christians can go to Heaven.

This bothers the Religious Right. Fundamentalist theology holds that only certain believers will be saved—and that certainly non-Christians are not going to Heaven. Many in the Religious Right feel confident that those who fail to interpret the Bible exactly as they do are bound for eternal damnation. To fundamentalists, people who believe otherwise are not taking religion seriously.

Other polls taken in 2000 and 2001 indicated that many Americans feel comfortable about switching religions or merging elements from different traditions together. Many other Americans, while they have a strong interest in religion and identify with certain groups, rarely attend formal services. These trends, too, are anathema to the Religious Right.

People feel free to make these types of decisions about religion only when there is a maximum amount of religious freedom. Some scholars, notably sociologist Rodney Stark at the University of Washington, have proposed that the United States has created a type of "religious market place." Drawing an analogy from economics, Stark asserts that believers are consumers of religion, and religious groups are offering the product. The "consumers" choose their "product" on the basis of a type of cost-benefit analysis.[3]

Stark's theory has its critics. Some are offended by the notion of reducing religion to the level of an economic exchange. However, there can be little doubt that in a multifaith society such as the United States, a type of religious marketplace does exist. Religious groups that aggressively seek converts, such as the Mormons and the Jehovah's Witnesses, are well aware that people in the United States are able and even willing to change their religious beliefs. To these groups, it's well worth it to enter the marketplace and advertise their goods. Lots of people might buy them.

Stark argues that because the U.S. government is secular, religious groups are left to contend for members based solely on their own initiative. They create a free marketplace of religion that spurs competition and a vigorous religious life. This explains why the United States, which maintains church-state separation, retains a high degree of religiosity among its people.

Church-state separation, under this model, is the defender and protector of religion. The government refrains from endorsing one particular faith, thus allowing them all to prosper. One can easily see why such a system would anger the Religious Right. Many fundamentalist Christians and traditionalist Roman Catholics are convinced that their denomination or particular mode of belief is the only "true" one. It makes sense to them that the government would want to back the one "true" religion. They are disturbed at seeing their "true" religion put on the same level with so many "false" faiths.

The more sophisticated and perceptive believers realize that the separation principle is a boon to their faith. They see danger in any attempt by government to decide which religion is true and which is false. They know that a faith that is in favor with the government today can be out of favor tomorrow. These believers are thankful for the free marketplace of religion and the secular state that makes it possible. They understand that the way to get new members is through persuasion, not government aid.

Why Support Separation?

People have many other reasons for supporting the separation of church and state. Some do not want religion to be imposed on them, in any form. Others believe that government attempts to help or aid religion either financially or symbolically will corrupt religion and detract it from its spiritual mission. Other church-state advocates say only separation will guarantee real religious diversity and pluralism. Still others cite the lesson of history. They note that throughout history, unions of religion and government have tended to foster oppression, not freedom. Some people note that church-state separation is a uniquely American phenomenon and should be celebrated as our nation's gift to the world.

Whatever their reasons, most Americans do support the overriding theory of church-state separation. Public opinion polls show that. But these same polls indicate a disturbing trend: Large numbers seem to have difficulty putting the separation theory into practice. Thus, they back things like official prayer in public schools, the teaching of creationism in public school science classes, having the government keep tabs on "unpopular" religious groups, and government display of the Ten Commandments and other religious symbols.

The Religious Right has been quick to exploit these sentiments, trying to turn people away from the principle of church-state separation entirely. This disinformation campaign has had results. Egged on by misinformation from the Religious Right, many Americans have come to believe in the myth of a systematic war against religion waged by some sort of sinister cabal or band of Humanists who have infiltrated our schools, courts, government, and other public institutions.

To understand the church-state issue better and see why the Religious Right is wrong, it is necessary to take a step back and look at religious freedom in history—in the United States and other nations. The next chapter begins this brief historical survey.

Notes

1. For more on the early history of the Religious Right, see Perry Deane Young, *God's Bullies* (New York: Holt, Rinehart & Winston, 1982) and Flo Conway and Jim Siegelman, *Holy Terror* (New York: Dell Publishing, 1982).

2. "The State of American Faith & Culture," *Religion Matters!* (July 2001).

3. For more on Stark's theory, see Toby Lester, "Oh, Gods!" *Atlantic Monthly* (February 2002).

2

In the Beginning: Church-State Relations before America

Religion has always been a prominent aspect of human life, predating the development of the first governments. Neanderthal Man buried his dead, which some anthropologists believe is a sign that these early people believed in an afterlife. When, thousands of years ago, people began to live together in organized societies, creating the first proto-governments, it was inevitable that these two institutions—religion and state—would interact.

Unfortunately, that interaction has too often taken on a negative cast. For as nearly as long as humans have been participating in religion—be it monotheism, polytheism, or something else—governments have assumed the power to regulate, suppress, foster, or otherwise control aspects of this relationship. State-sponsored religion existed alongside the earliest forms of government and persists until the present day in many parts of the globe.

The birth of the United States as a political unit saw the creation of a radical experiment in government and religion—the concept of the separation of church and state. The ratification of the U.S. Constitution marked the first time any nation had dared to put a formal distance between these two institutions.

Like any other great concept, separation of church and state did not rise in a political vacuum. The men who wrote and ratified the Constitution were astute observers of the political scene of their times and were students of history. They had read about and seen the dangers of church-state unions both in Europe and colonial America. Many had witnessed state-sponsored religious persecution up close and were determined that unions of church and state would find no safe haven in the new country.

But placed in perspective of world history, the United States is a relatively young country with a short history. Civilizations flourished in the Near East, Western Europe, Asia, and Africa long before the settlement of North America by Europeans. These nations had their own experiences with religion and state—and again the interaction was all too often negative.

Early Church-State Relationships

Ancient Egypt, for example, saw conflicts between religion and government, often brought about by that society's powerful priests. Ancient Egyptian society was polytheistic in nature, meaning the people worshipped many gods. An attempt by the pharaoh Amenhotep in 1379 B.C.E. to force the people to accept monotheism and worship one god—the Sun god—nearly resulted in disaster.

There were occasional instances of more enlightened thinking. In 270 B.C.E. Asoka, one of greatest rulers of the Maurya Empire, what is now India, accepted Buddhism and encouraged his followers to do the same. Though Asoka became a devout believer in Buddhism and sent missionaries to nearby lands, he insisted on religious toleration for everyone. Spurred by his beliefs, he urged his followers to show greater charity toward their fellow citizens.[1]

The spread of Islam in the Middle East around 600 C.E. also demonstrated some fairly progressive thinking on religious toleration—progressive for that time, at least. Many early Muslims were warriors who lived to win new lands, but most did not force conversion on to those they conquered. People living in areas conquered by Arab armies were given the option to either accept Islam or keep their current religion and pay an annual tax. By the standards of the time, when forced conversions and government-sponsored religious persecutions were common, this was a leap forward.

But sadly, these types of events are the exception. More commonly, early history is filled with stories of religiously based persecution and forced conversion. In the year 800 C.E., for instance, the emperor of what is today China, alarmed by the growing wealth and power of Buddhist priests, launched a program of persecution against Buddhists. Nearly 5,000 monasteries were destroyed, and more than 250,000 monks and other religious figures were forced to renounce their vows. In 988 C.E. Vladimir, emperor of Kiev Rus, a kernel of what became Russia, converted to Christianity, ordered all pagan statues destroyed and commanded all of his subjects to accept Christian baptism.

Church and State in Europe

These early struggles between religion and government, while interesting, are sidelights to our story. To understand what took place in the United States and why it happened, it is necessary to look more closely at the experience of Ancient and Medieval Europe, the power of the papacy and the Protestant Reformation. Developments that unfolded during this period eventually led to the creation of the church-state arrangement put into effect in the fledgling United States. Therefore, it is important to look at this history in a little more detail before examining the colonial period in North America.

Please note that this chapter is not meant to be an exhaustive overview of this period. Scholars have written thousands of books about the history of Europe and the Middle Ages. For the purposes of this volume, we will only touch on the highlights. This is a fascinating area of study, however, and I recommend that anyone interested in the subject read Morris Bishop's excellent 1968 book, *The Middle Ages*, which is a good introductory history of the period designed for a general audience.

Bishop's book begins with the fall of the western Roman Empire. To set the stage for our story, we'll step back a bit to the rise of that mighty empire, which laid the foundation for much of Western civilization.

The Roman Empire

Much of what is today known as Western Europe was once part of the Roman Empire. For most of its existence, as a republic and during the imperial period, the empire was officially pagan. There was no division between religion and government. During the imperial period, the emperor often assumed the title of *pontifex maximus*—supreme ruler of the state religion. Paganism and its series of complex rituals were considered a unifying factor in the empire, and participation in the rituals became a way for Roman citizens to express a sense of patriotism. Scholars have debated the extent to which the average Roman actually believed in the existence of every god in the pantheon. It is not really relevant to this discussion. What is important is that the Roman state religion played an important role in the function of the state and government as well—a role that would remain unchallenged for hundreds of years until the rise of Christianity.

The Romans were aggressively expansionist. At its height, the Roman Empire included Italy, Spain, Portugal, France, Greece, most of Great Britain, much of the Balkans, and Eastern Europe as well as Middle Eastern regions, Egypt, and other parts of northern Africa. When the Romans conquered new lands, they usually allowed the inhabitants to keep their own religion. Often Romans adopted local gods and inducted them into the pagan pantheon. At death, emperors were customarily deified, although actual worship of emperors as gods was not common except in certain far-flung portions of the empire.

Jesus Christ was crucified under the reign of the emperor Tiberius, who ruled from 14 to 37 C.E. Thus began the slow but steady growth of Christianity. Unlike other religions, Christianity could not be assimilated into the Roman state religion because its adherents insisted that there was only one true God. (Jews felt the same way, and, since much of the region we now call the Middle East was under Roman control, they often came into conflict with the government.)

As their numbers grew and Christianity came to be seen as a new, distinct religion—as opposed to just a new sect of Judaism—Christians became objects of persecution at different points in the empire's history. Persecution was especially severe under the reigns of the emperors Nero (54–68), Marcus Aurelius (161–180), Valerian (253–260), Trajan Decius (249–251), and Diocletian (284–305). It was during Diocletian's reign that the last and most severe persecution—known as the "Great Persecution"—occurred.

Roman persecutions of Christians waxed and waned depending on a number of circumstances, including the character of the man occupying the emperor's throne. During the reign of the emperor Trajan (98–117), Pliny the Younger, an administrator in the province of Bithynia, wrote to

Rome to ask how he should deal with the Christians in his area. Trajan replied, "They are not to be hunted out. Any who are accused and convicted should be punished, with the proviso that if a man says he is not a Christian and makes it obvious by his actual conduct—namely by worshipping our gods—then, however suspect he may have been with regard to the past, he should gain pardon from his repentance."[2]

Trajan seemed to have little interest in assuming a proactive anti-Christian stance. But other emperors were determined to have Christians hunted down and destroyed. Christians could be convenient scapegoats. During Nero's reign, a great fire destroyed much of central Rome. Nero blamed the fire on Christians, perhaps hoping to divert attention away from rumors that he himself had started the blaze to clear space for a luxurious new palace.

During the Roman persecutions, Christians were often given the opportunity to renounce their faith by swearing allegiance to pagan gods and offering a small sacrifice—usually a pinch of incense. Facing torture and death (which included being devoured by lions and other wild animals in the Coliseum of Rome), some did recant. Others refused and became martyrs.

In 303 C.E. the Emperor Diocletian undertook what turned out to be the final persecution. Its goal was the complete destruction of the Christian faith. A series of edicts was issued forbidding Christians to assemble, ordering their churches and sacred books to be destroyed, and demanding that their clergy sacrifice to pagan gods or face arrest.

For a number of reasons, the Great Persecution failed. Diocletian himself voluntarily gave up the throne in 305, abdicating and retiring to an estate. The persecution, however, lived beyond his reign—at least for a few years.

Diocletian had reorganized the Roman Empire and appointed co-emperors to rule with him. This system, called the Tetrarchy, remained in place for a few years beyond Diocletian's abdication in 305. One of these co-emperors, Galerius, vigorously supported the new persecution. But in 311 Galerius fell seriously ill, probably with stomach cancer. Ancient historians write that his flesh melted away and worms emerged from his bowels. Christians believed this sickness was God's way of punishing Galerius for persecuting Christians. Galerius may have agreed. On his deathbed, he and his fellow emperors issued an edict lifting the persecution of Christians.

Under the new edict, Christians were given freedom of worship but were commanded to "entreat their God for our well-being and for that of the State and for their own."[3] It took three centuries, but official persecution of Christians in Rome had come to an end.

What happened next is even more remarkable. Under the rule of Constantine the Great (306–337), Christians underwent an amazing reversal of fortune. Not only did state-sponsored persecution stop, but also within the space of a few years Christianity began receiving government favor, and many Christians were appointed to high office. Christianity became the empire's semi-official religion and later its official one.

Historians who study the Roman Empire disagree on why Constantine became such an aggressive proponent of Christianity. There is some evidence that his mother may have been a Christian and that she influenced him. Another story, this one related by the ancient historian Lactantius, a contemporary of Constantine, is much more dramatic. It is said that Constantine had a vision (or perhaps a dream) of a giant cross in the sky surrounded by the words "With This You Will Conquer" the night before he faced a rival emperor named Maxentius in battle at the Milvian Bridge in 312 C.E. Constantine supposedly ordered all of his soldiers to put a Christian symbol, the chi-rho cross, on their shields. In battle, Constatine's outnumbered forces routed Maxentius' army, which had supposedly sacrificed to pagan gods before battle.

Historians of the ancient period debate the accuracy of the tale. Lactantius, the primary source for it, is generally not considered reliable because he was a fellow Christian convert and nonobjective biographer who flattered Constantine shamelessly. Also, the dichotomy of the "good Christian" army facing off against the "bad pagan" army is a little too neat. In fact, much of Constantine's army was undoubtedly still pagan at the time of the battle. The military was one of the last Roman institutions to accept Christianity. Even the story of Constantine's famous vision is suspect. Constantine was something of a mystic and experienced weird visions earlier in life, while still a pagan.

Speculation about why Constantine adopted Christianity is interesting but less than relevant to the development of church-state relations. What matters is that the new faith, boosted by the power of the state, rapidly took hold in Europe. Although he is often credited with Christianizing the Roman Empire, Constantine did not officially establish his new faith as the empire's state religion. He was aware that most Romans were still pagans and knew that any attempt to force Christianity through state action might bring about his downfall. Rather, Constantine gave Christianity certain favors, including government-funded churches and generous subsidies. While Constantine ended many of the privileges paganism had enjoyed, he did not attempt to stamp out the old faith. There was, in other words, no reverse persecution.

Constantine's real legacy is that he took an active role in shaping still-emerging Christian doctrine. At this period in history, as the Christian church emerged from a period of persecution, many doctrines that seem familiar today remained nebulous or had yet to be established as dogma. For example, a long-running debate occurred over the nature of the Trinity, especially the relationship between God and Jesus Christ.

One view, held primarily by a bishop named Arius, maintained that Jesus was somehow subordinate to God and that the two, while of like nature, were distinct entities. (This belief today is known as the Arian heresy.) Other Christians strongly disagreed, arguing that Arius was in fact promoting polytheism. God and Jesus, they insisted, were of the same substance and in fact the same entity.

Such a debate may seem esoteric today, but it occupied the attention of many bishops, emperors, and even laypeople for decades. Roman emperors often took sides. Constantine was an opponent of Arianism, but his son and successor, Constantius II, was a fierce advocate of that view. Arianism also took hold among many of the Germanic "barbarian" peoples beyond Rome's frontiers. Many of these tribes were assimilated into the empire in the late fourth and early fifth centuries, further heightening the clash between Arianism and what became Catholicism.

Opponents of Arianism gradually gained the upper hand. In 380 C.E., at a time when the Roman Empire was split into Western and Eastern halves, the emperors Gratian, Valentinian II (ruling in the west), and Theodosius (ruling in the east) issued a joint edict designed to stamp out Arianism.

The document cannot be called subtle. It states,

> We desire all people, whom the benign influence of our clemency rules, to turn to the religion which tradition from Peter to the present day declares to have been delivered to the Romans by blessed Peter the Apostle. . . . [T]his faith is that we should believe, in accordance with apostolic discipline and Gospel teaching, that there is one Godhead, Father, Son and Holy Spirit, in an equal Majesty and a holy Trinity. We order those who follow this doctrine to receive the title of Catholic Christians, but others we judge to be mad and raving and worthy of incurring the disgrace of heretical teaching, nor are their assemblies to

> receive the name of churches. They are to be punished not only by Divine retribution but also by our own measures, which we have decided in accordance with Divine inspiration.[4]

Not only were Christians divided, but pagans remained on the scene. Many historians believe that most rural residents of Europe continued to practice some pagan rituals even after they had supposedly converted to Christianity. Paganism's last official gasp occurred twenty-four years after the death of Constantine the Great, when one of his nephews, Julian II, came to the throne. Greatly enamored of the ancient Greeks, Julian, whom history knows as "the Apostate," attempted to restore paganism as the empire's official religion. He dismissed Christians from high office and ordered them removed from the teaching academies. Julian's efforts, however, were simply too little too late. After reigning less than two years, Julian was killed during a rear-guard action while leading his forces in a battle against the Persians in 363 C.E. His successor, the short-lived Jovian, immediately restored the privileges of Christianity. They were never to be taken away again.

Throughout the fourth century, Christianity continued to grow and win converts among the Roman population. Paganism's power and influence waned, and the old gods fell. During the reign of the emperor Theodosius I (379–395), the reeling pagan forces received a blow from which they never recovered. Theodosius officially established Christianity as the Roman Empire's state religion and began instituting steps to shut down pagan worship. Pagan rituals such as animal sacrifice were banned, and pagan temples were closed. Although individual pagans survived until well after the collapse of the Roman Empire in the west, paganism as a religious and political force was crushed, and the ancient faith gradually passed into the pages of history.

By the time of Theodosius, the Roman Empire was divided into two spheres—eastern and western, each with its own emperor. In 476, the Western Empire, which had been under constant siege by various Germanic "barbarian" tribes north of the Rhine River for many decades, finally collapsed. By this time, however, even most of the "barbarians" had adopted Christianity and had become more or less Romanized. A Germanic king, Odoacer, deposed the last western emperor, a youth named Romulus Augustulus. The crown of Romulus Augustulus passed to Zeno, the emperor reigning in the east, but this was a mere formality. Zeno could do nothing at that time to recover the west and in fact didn't even try.

The Eastern Empire, with its capital at the grand city Constantine the Great founded, Constantinople (modern-day Istanbul, Turkey), survived and metamorphosed into what historians call the Byzantine Empire (which was officially Christian). But the Western Empire was no more. Gradually, Western Europe broke up into a series of Germanic kingdoms. Thus, 476 C.E. marks the year when most historians stop talking about the Roman Empire and begin talking about the Middle Ages.

Christianity was not consolidated during this period. In fact, there were many schisms and competing sects. As has been noted, during his reign, Constantine intervened on more than one occasion to resolve theological problems, expressing his hope to create one universal, "catholic" church (the term coming from the Greek word *katholikos*, meaning universal or general). In 325, he called bishops together at Nicaea, a city located in what is today Turkey, to hammer out the essentials of the Christian faith. The council emerged with a list of tenets known as the Nicene Creed. Bishops who refused to submit to this document were labeled heretics and expelled from Christendom.

During its long years of growth, Christianity had always had bishops in Rome and other cities, even when the empire was officially pagan and hostile to the new faith. Some of these bishops became martyrs, having been executed during periods of persecution. In the post-Constantine period, the bishop of Rome was considered the most important spiritual leader of the church and from that office emerged the institution of the papacy. (Even today the pope is known officially as the Bishop of Rome.) The rudiments of what we know today as the Roman Catholic Church were in place.

The pope in Rome did not always wield absolute control over the church. After the collapse of the Western Empire, Rome fell into a long dark age and became something of a backwater. Although the pope remained in Rome, there were periods after the fall of the Western Empire when spiritual leaders in Constantinople actually had more power.

Imperial forces of the Byzantine Empire did succeed in briefly reestablishing control in Rome during the sixth century, but eventually formal government in central Italy began to break down. Besieged by competing forces, Rome was subject to repeated sacks and sieges by outside forces that wanted to control the city. It physically deteriorated and became a dim memory of the glorious metropolis it had been for so many centuries. At first, church leaders relied on various governments in the region for protection and patronage, but gradually the papacy took on the trappings of a government itself, with the pope as head of state.

The church would come to play a dominant role in Europe during the Middle Ages. The life of the common citizen in Western Europe during this period was dominated by his or her relationship to the land. The vast majority of people were peasants, farmers who worked the fields daily from sunup until sundown. In this way, they carved out a meager living.

By the 700s, much of Western Europe was fragmented and consisted of various fiefdoms ruled by often aggressive lords who were frequently at war with their neighbors. The thirst for expansion was great.

A huge chasm separated the peasants from the wealthy; there was no middle class. The Roman Catholic Church was a powerful force that often held absolute power over the affairs of the government.

This religious monopoly gave the Catholic Church great influence, and popes such as Leo III frequently intervened in governmental affairs. For instance, the church during this era claimed that it had the right to crown and depose kings, pointing to an incident in 751 when a pope crowned Pepin the Short "king by the grace of God."

The relationship between church and state cut both ways, and the dependency was often mutual. Kings needed the endorsement and prestige of the church to hold office. The church, militarily weak at its headquarters in Rome, needed the armies of the state for its defense. Since the popes believed they had the authority to install kings, they did not hesitate to call on them for assistance. If, for example, a region of Europe were facing invasion by an outside army, the pope might demand that the king send troops to defend the region.

Despite the fierce competition between rulers, some leaders did attempt to unify Europe. Charlemagne, who ruled the Frankish kingdom of what is today France and Austria from 768–814, was an example. The deeply religious king pushed the boundaries of his empire southeast into what is today Italy, as well as north and southwest.

Charlemagne eventually controlled much of Western Europe. On Christmas Day in the year 800, Pope Leo III proclaimed him "Emperor of the Romans," referring to the glory that had once been the Roman Empire.

To the south of Charlemagne's empire, Muslim armies ruled, and to the north, fierce Vikings, who were mostly pagan, dominated. In Western Europe, there was no other religious force except Catholicism. The Protestant Reformation was still hundreds of years away, and, while there were certainly people testing the boundaries of the church, no formalized religious opposition existed.

Charlemagne was an aggressive proponent of Christianity. He often forced people in the areas he conquered to accept baptism or be killed. After Charlemagne's death in 814, the great empire he had created splintered and chaos ensued as Muslim raiders from the south and Viking warriors from the north swept across Europe.

The Influence of the Roman Catholic Church

Against this backdrop of frequent confusion, the Roman Catholic Church was the one stable force everyone could rely on to remain the same. By the 1100s, the church had formalized its hierarchical structure, from parish priest to pope. (The same structure remains intact today.) The church by this time had also fully developed its seven sacraments. These rituals, most of which occurred at points where a peasant's life underwent change—marriage, childbirth, death—meant that the church touched nearly everyone's life at one time or another. The church was seen as universal, unchanging, and infallible—a truly catholic movement.

Because of the church's overwhelming presence and formalized rituals, it in many ways took on the functions of local government to the peasants who were close to the land, and perhaps geographically far away from the king's seat of power. For instance, the church ran charities and provided various social services. Church officials even collected taxes and maintained a court system that had the power to levy fines.

Popes were well aware of the great power of their church. Most issued decrees stating flatly that all governments had a duty to submit to the church and its teachings. The church's power was enhanced because of its extreme wealth in the form of land holdings. For example, the church controlled a region called the Papal States, located in what is today Italy. This region existed for hundreds of years as a separate state before being incorporated into Italy.

Because the political power of Catholicism was so great, it was inevitable that the popes would come into conflict with civil rulers. Indeed, there was a constant struggle for power between the church and the state spanning hundreds of years in the Middle Ages. Some kings sought to place curbs on the church's reach in the hopes of gaining more power for themselves. The church naturally resisted these efforts.

Popes versus Kings

For instance, King Henry II of England tried to limit church power in the mid-1100s. Henry had a keen interest in the law and established a traveling court system to deal with legal matters throughout the country. (His reforms led to the jury system still used in the United States today.)

But Henry II made one mistake. He sought to transfer some court functions from the Roman Catholic Church to the state. Henry believed, for instance, that some clergy members who were accused of misconduct should be tried in secular courts, probably reasoning that church leaders were more likely to get an unbiased hearing there.

Thomas Becket, the archbishop of Canterbury, strongly opposed the proposal. The disagreement made the two men bitter enemies. Word of the feud spread, and one day four of Henry's knights decided to take matters into their own hands. They entered Becket's cathedral and murdered him. The knights might have thought they were doing Henry's bidding, but their action had negative fallout. Henry, facing the threat of excommunication by the pope, had to abandon his court reform.

Church-state conflict also ravaged Germany and parts of Italy, with the conflict lasting hundreds of years. In the mid-900s, Pope John XII proclaimed King Otto I of this region "Emperor of the Romans" in appreciation for Otto's providing some military assistance that John had sought. Otto, sensing that John XII was a weak church leader, used the relationship to his advantage. When John died, Otto proclaimed one of his own assistants pope. A pattern was thus set, and for the next four decades German kings chose the popes.

The papacy during this period was often in a state of confusion, and the close tie between church and state only made matters worse. Henry III, a leader who came after Otto I, regarded the church as a tool of the state. At one point, three men each claimed to be pope, giving Henry III an opportunity to intervene. The king solved the dispute by ordering all three men dismissed and installing his own candidate as pope. Henry continued selecting popes for several years.

After Henry III's death the situation reversed, and the church gained the upper hand. Henry's son, Henry IV, was a weak ruler who assumed the throne after this father died in 1056. At this time the intelligent, crafty Pope Gregory VII was in office, and he quickly seized the opportunity to restore the church's lost power. Henry IV resisted these efforts, and his dispute with Gregory VII escalated to such a degree that the pope in 1076 excommunicated the king as well as ordered him from the throne. In 1077,

Henry IV was forced to travel to Italy to beg the pope for forgiveness and readmission into the church. When Henry arrived at the pope's winter castle at Canossa in the Italian Alps, Gregory kept him waiting in the cold rain and snow for three days before granting him an audience. The pope agreed to suspend Henry's excommunication, but the two remained in conflict. In 1080, Gregory VII excommunicated Henry again and took the additional step of naming Duke Rudolf of Suabia to Henry's throne.

Despite Gregory VII's triumph, the clashes between church and state persisted in Germany after both men were dead. Key to the dispute was the issue of who had the power to appoint bishops—kings or popes. Finally, in 1122, leaders of church and state met in the German city of Worms in an attempt to resolve the matter. (Henry IV's successor, Henry V, represented what was called the Holy Roman Empire—Germany, Italy, and Burgundy; the pope at the time was Calixtus II.) The resulting Concordat of Worms gave church leaders the right to appoint bishops but allowed kings control over certain secular duties of the clergy. The Concordat, while a well-intentioned effort, did little in reality to ease the struggle between church and state during this period. Leaders from both institutions continued to meddle in the affairs of the other.

Emperor Frederic I Barbarossa attempted to curb papal power in the 1150s and 1160s. In 1177, Frederic went so far as to have rival popes anointed, but eventually he gave up and asked Pope Alexander III for absolution. There was no clear successor to the crown after Frederic's death, and for many years after that no man could hope to rule the region without papal sanction.

This period marked something of a turning point—with the advantage going to the church. As two scholars wrote in a 1967 study, "Taking the theory of the superiority of the spiritual over the temporal power as their starting point, [church] thinkers were no longer content with its occasional application to the monarchs embodying a separate temporal power, but they began to shape the doctrine that the Church and the Pope, her supreme representative, actually possessed and could exercise full power both over the Church and the State."[5]

In 1198 another very powerful pope, Innocent III, came to power. Innocent insisted that the church should have control over all kings, whom he regarded as simply servants of the church. Innocent achieved great success by using two powerful weapons of the papacy—excommunication of political leaders who disagreed with him and interdiction, a practice whereby a pope excommunicated an entire country or region.

Interdiction was Innocent's greatest tool. Denying an entire nation the services of the church greatly increased the pressure on the country's leader. Peasants saw the church as the only path to Heaven, and interdiction condemned everyone to the fires of eternal Hell. People clamored for a speedy return to the church.

At one point Innocent III placed all of England under interdict and forced King John Lackland to agree to pay him a yearly fee and essentially to serve as a papal vassal before lifting the decree. Innocent also used his powers to depose leaders in Italy and Germany and put his own supporters on those thrones. Innocent, who died in 1216, was perhaps the most powerful pope the world has ever known.

Later popes had mixed success in dealing with the state. In 1294 Boniface VIII took issue with a plan by French King Philip IV to tax the clergy. The two were unable to resolve the matter, and Philip ordered Boniface imprisoned. The king went so far as to send a type of commando brigade to capture the pope. Boniface was quickly released but died soon thereafter. As a result, the power and influence of the papacy decreased.[6]

In 1378, the Catholic Church suffered a serious schism that was brought about by secular officials. During the period immediately preceding the schism, French kings controlled the papacy. Philip IV had even moved the papacy's headquarters from Rome to Avignon, a city in southern France.

People in Rome demanded an Italian pope, but French leaders balked at this request. Eventually, two men—one French and one Italian—claimed to be pope. For the next forty years popes reigned in both Rome and Avignon, and secular rulers sided with the pope of their choosing, usually for political, not spiritual, reasons. In 1414 a church council began working on a plan to heal the schism, leading to a single pope in office in Rome three years later.

Church over State and State over Church

So it went, a back-and-forth struggle between church and state that sometimes resulted in church over state but just as often state over church. In any case, neither institution was truly free, and neither was untainted by corruption.

Against this backdrop occurred events such as the sporadic Christian Crusades of the 1100s and 1200s, whereby Christians attempted to wrest control of Middle Eastern Holy Lands from the Muslims. The Crusades were often instigated by popes and led by kings ostensibly in the name of Christianity, but the real goal of these forays was secular—to achieve better trade routes and commercial arrangements for business. None was highly successful.

The situation remained much like this—a see-saw type battle for power between church and state—throughout the Middle Ages. Since the Roman Catholic Church had no competition, its power continued to solidify. Periodic church councils were held to determine questions of doctrine and faith. Those who strayed from church dogma were often dealt with harshly, especially during the first Inquisition of the 1200s. Many were accused of heresy against the church and burned at the stake.

Early Rumblings of Dissent

Despite the severe penalties that could be levied for heresy, some bold thinkers dared to disagree with church doctrine. Even though the Catholic Church's power seemed all-pervasive, dissenters gradually grew in number. In time, the voice of the dissenters became too loud and powerful for the church to ignore or squelch.

In the year 1170 a merchant named Peter Waldo of Lyons, France, decided to read the Bible for himself. Inspired by the scriptures, he gave all he owned to the poor and urged others to do the same. Waldo's followers became known as the Poor Men of Lyons. One might think that church officials would applaud their good works, but in fact the pope saw the Poor Men as a threat because they dared to preach to the people in language the common man could understand. (Most people at this time were illiterate, and the church used Latin as its official language.)

Waldo was ordered to submit to church discipline but refused. He was excommunicated, and his followers fled to remote valleys in the Alps. A church that bears Waldo's name, the Waldensians, still exists today.[7]

Critics began publishing broadsides that took the Catholic Church to task. In 1324 two priests, Marsilisu of Padua and John of Jandun wrote a book called *Defender of the Peace* that claimed that popes should hold only spiritual, not civil, power. An English priest named John Wycliffe adopted these ideas and began preaching that persons could be saved by appealing to God directly, without the aid of priests. This was in direct conflict with church teachings.

Although other critics clamored for reform, little was done. The church simply persecuted those who disagreed with it or excommunicated them. Or, worse, it subjected them to the horrors of the Inquisition, which was established by Pope Innocent III in 1233. Writer Morris Bishop argues that the Inquisition actually achieved much of what it intended—the suppression of heresy—but at a cost. He observed, "Ideas can be stamped out by the elimination of everyone who holds the ideas. However, this is a very costly process. The Inquisition succeeded in those areas where it operated, but it also did the church immense harm."[8]

What type of harm? Bishop writes that by the later Middle Ages, many people were disillusioned with the Catholic Church and mocked it openly. In some parts of France, he writes, people held mock masses where they led garishly dressed donkeys to the altar. Part of this anger was due to crushing taxes the church and state, working in tandem, imposed on the people to pay for military operations. As a result, writes Bishop, "a sullen anticlericalism spread, aggravated by the failure of the crusades, by an angry conviction that the church had gulled the people, that God had left his soldiers in the lurch."[9]

The seeds for change had been sowed. This disaffection with the church would continue to gather steam. Eventually, it would not be so easily extinguished.

The Protestant Reformation

What is known today as the Protestant Reformation began in the 1500s when church critics began to increase in numbers and solidify their arguments against the Roman Catholic Church. Their dissatisfaction with Catholicism was multifaceted, and Reformation leaders joined the call for reform for different reasons. In general, though, many felt that the Catholic Church had become obsessed with wealth and power and had thus strayed from its role as God's church on Earth. Reformers sought to bring the faith back to the people and re-emphasize personal salvation and piety.

An example of the church's emphasis on money, many reformers said, was the practice of selling indulgences, or pardons from sin. The sale of indulgences had originally been limited only to those who engaged in extremely pious acts, but by the 1500s popes had taken to selling them simply to raise money.

The Reformation sparked first in Germany with the ideas of Martin

Luther, a Catholic monk. Luther studied the Bible and came to the conclusion that the Catholic Church's heavy emphasis on ceremony was misguided. All that mattered, Luther argued, was that sinners sincerely seek forgiveness. God would take care of the rest.

Luther was incensed when in 1517 a Dominican friar arrived in Wittenberg, where Luther resided, to sell indulgences. The friar had been ordered by Pope Leo X to raise money for the rebuilding of St. Peter's Church in Rome. As the story goes, the friar told the poor that for every coin they dropped into his box, a soul would depart Purgatory and fly into Heaven.

Later that year, on October 31, Luther executed a bold plan of action: At the door of the Catholic church in Wittenberg he posted the Ninety-Five Theses, a document that strongly attacked the sale of indulgences. Luther did not intend his action to amount to a formal break with the Church and did not at this early stage think of himself as a reformer, but obviously his actions had severe consequences. Church leaders could not let such a brazen challenge go unanswered. They began to attack Luther and the reforms he suggested. The battle was under way.

Luther had the good fortune to live during a time when mass communication was becoming possible. The printing press had been invented, and, while illiteracy was still common, an educated, influential class of merchants and artisans did exist. Luther spread his ideas through a series of pamphlets that summarized his thinking. He continued to argue strongly that people did not need priests or other intermediaries to communicate with God. Catholic Church leaders were infuriated. In 1520, Pope Leo X excommunicated Luther. Luther responded by burning the decree in public.

A special church council was convened to condemn Luther and ban the sale of his writings. Luther's life was in danger, but because Germany lacked a strong central government he was able to flee to the Saxony region, where he sought protection from its ruler. While there, Luther continued to promote his ideas and write pamphlets.

Luther worked feverishly to translate the Bible into German. Until this time, most common people had never actually read the Bible since most peasants could not read in their own language, let alone the Latin of the Catholic Church. Luther's translation meant that Germans who could read would have access to the Bible for the first time.

The religion that became known as Lutheranism began to spread. Eventually, Luther officially formed a new church, which he believed was in keeping with biblical edicts concerning religion.

Leaders in some parts of Germany began to accept Lutheranism and even establish it as a state religion. Others saw the new faith as a threat. One leader, Charles V, attempted to crush Lutheranism through military action but failed. The 1555 Peace of Augsburg that ended the conflict guaranteed each German ruler the right to choose a state religion.

While Luther's ideas and the chain of events he set into motion are crucial to world history, it is important to keep in mind that Luther, as important as he is to the development of religious liberty hundreds of years later across the sea in North America, did have faults. For instance, Luther did not believe in religious liberty, as we understand the term today. Although he sought the freedom to interpret the Bible in a way that differed from the view of the Catholic Church, Luther then assumed that his interpretation was the only correct one and persecuted those who disagreed. He was convinced that those who took issue with his views were inspired by Satan and called the pope the Antichrist. Luther was also a virulent anti-Semite who wanted to exterminate the Jews. He had hoped that Jews would join him in criticizing the Catholic Church. When they did not, he called for setting fire to synagogues and forcing the Jews out of Germany.

Like so many early dissenters from established churches, Luther seemed to find it easier to endorse freedom of conscience in theory than in practice. Despite these faults, however, the actions that Luther took were a crucial bridge to events that were to unfold later. In that respect, he is a key figure in the development of true religious liberty—even though he never supported that concept himself.

The Reformation in England

Luther's success spurred other reformers. Many new Christian denominations took shape and began to grow. Although Luther's ideas did spread to England, they had little impact there. The Reformation in England was sparked by a wholly different chain of events. King Henry VIII, who had a reputation as a strong defender of the Roman Catholic Church, brought about change for largely personal reasons. Seeking a male heir to his throne, Henry VIII wanted to divorce his wife, Catherine of Aragon, and marry Anne Boleyn, an attendant to the queen.

Pope Clement VII refused to grant Henry an annulment of his marriage to Catherine, mostly for political reasons. Clement feared the power of Catherine's nephew, Charles V of Spain, whose forces had attacked and sacked Rome in 1527.

Enraged, Henry VIII disestablished Catholicism in England and set up his own church, the Anglican Church, or the Church of England. (It is known in the United States today as the Episcopal Church.) The archbishop of Canterbury became the highest religious authority in the land, and Henry VIII quickly received his divorce. In fact, he married five more times.

Not satisfied with disestablishing the Roman Catholic Church, Henry set out to make England a purely Anglican nation. He launched a reign of terror against Catholics that soon spread to Lutherans and Anabaptists (the precursors of today's Baptists). One of Henry VIII's favorite tactics for disposing of heretics was death by fire. Two pyres were set side by side; a Catholic was burned on one, an Anabaptist or a Lutheran on the other. It was a startling change for a king who had in 1521 been proclaimed "defender of the faith" by Pope Leo X.

After Henry's death confusion reigned in religious matters for England's citizens. His successor, Edward VI, retained Anglicanism and persecuted Catholics, but following his reign Queen Mary re-established Catholicism for five years, in turn persecuting Protestants. Mary's reign was marked by such great religious persecution that history knows her as "Bloody Mary." Finally, under Elizabeth I, England returned to Anglicanism, which remains the country's state church today.

Calvin's Geneva

In what is today Switzerland, Reformation leader John Calvin founded a Protestant church based on a rigid code of beliefs he spelled out in a 1536 work titled *The Institutes of the Christian Religion*. That same year, a French theologian in Geneva, then a town of about 15,000, persuaded the city fathers to appoint Calvin as the official teacher of religion. Calvin accepted and quickly began imposing his brand of orthodoxy on everyone.

Calvin had forced the town council to swear an oath pledging to uphold his form of Christianity. In 1538 he tried to impose the oath on the entire city. Angry residents forced him from power. But five years later Geneva was so strife with religious tension and violence that the town council decided only Calvin could impose order. They invited him back.

Calvin's second regime was quite severe. He banned celebrating Christmas and Easter and the ringing of church bells. A reign of terror soon followed. Calvin and his supporters raided private homes, inspected books, and interrogated servants, eager to stamp out heresy. Laws prohibiting dancing and gambling were strictly enforced, and violations brought swift punishment. Calvin's enforcers closed down the theaters and tried to rid the city of its taverns.

During the first five years of his rule, thirteen citizens were hanged, ten were decapitated, and thirty-five were burned at the stake. Seventy-six people were driven from their homes; large numbers of people fled the city. Official records of the city from this period tell of a man who smiled during a baptism and got three days' imprisonment. Another man, on a hot summer day, fell asleep during a sermon and was sent to prison. Another ended up behind bars for refusing to name his son Abraham. Calvin, it seems, had assumed a God-given right to name newborn children in town.

Calvin believed in predestination—the idea that God has already chosen who gets into Heaven and who doesn't. One resident of Geneva who publicly disagreed with this doctrine was flogged at the crossways of the city and then expelled. A book printer who had dared to criticize Calvin had his tongue perforated with a red-hot iron and was driven from town. Another critic was tortured on the rack and then executed merely for calling Calvin a hypocrite.

Perhaps the most unfortunate of all was Miguel Servetus, who wrote a lengthy tome attacking Calvin and even sent him personal letters, thoughtfully pointing out where Calvin had gotten it wrong. For some reason, Servetus decided to pass through Geneva and attended a church service where Calvin preached. He was arrested and thrown into a filthy prison where he was left, half-starved and frozen, for months before being burned at the stake on October 27, 1553. Calvin ordered all copies of Servetus's book destroyed.

Two years later a faction of citizens attempted a revolt. They were put down. Nine years later, in 1654, Calvin fell ill and died. He had preached theocracy until his dying day and never expressed regret for the system he established in Geneva.

Despite the heavy-handed flavor of Calvin's ideas, his thinking spread to other countries, notably France, where the presence of Calvinists among the heavily Catholic population resulted in bloody conflict. In 1572, for instance, Catholics fell upon the Huguenots and slaughtered thousands on St. Bartholomew's Day.

Calvin's religious ideas also caught on and spread to Scotland and the

Netherlands. Some in England eventually embraced the thinking of Calvin as well, where the faith went by the name of Puritanism. This strand of Calvinism was eventually exported to North America in the 1660s.

New Religions Take Hold

Although leaders of the Catholic Church launched attempts to reverse the effects of the Reformation by initiating a series of internal changes, their actions simply came too late. The Church called councils to clarify Catholic doctrine and took active steps to stamp out what was considered heresy within the Church, but to no avail—Protestant religions continued to spread.

The Catholic Church certainly remained an important influence in Europe and later in many other parts of the world, but it now had to accept a future of sharing that influence with a variety of Protestant denominations.

The Reformation gave rise to a variety of new Christian denominations. Some died out quickly but others survived and exist until this day. They include Baptists, Quakers, Lutherans, Congregationalists, and Presbyterians. And the Reformation had a direct impact on events that were to unfold in the United States 250 years after Martin Luther took his hammer to Wittenberg.

Notes

1. Anatole G. Mazour and John M. Peoples, *World History: People and Nations* (Orlando: Harcourt Brace Jovanovich, 1990), p. 62.
2. Michael Grant, *The Roman Emperors: A Biographical Guide to the Rulers of Imperial Rome, 31 B.C.–A.D. 476* (New York: Scribner's Sons, 1988), pp. 73–74.
3. Ibid., p. 221.
4. Sidney Z. Ehler and John B. Morrall, *Church and State through the Centuries* (New York: Biblo and Tannen, 1967), p. 8.
5. Ibid, p. 51.
6. Mazour and Peoples, *World History*, p. 269.
7. Morris Bishop, *The Middle Ages* (Boston: Houghton Mifflin Company, 1987), p. 172.
8. Ibid., p. 173.
9. Ibid., p. 174.

3

Made in America: The Evolution of Church-State Separation in the United States

Americans can be fuzzy on their history. Most schoolchildren know that Columbus "discovered" the new world and that some years later colonists from Europe began to settle in North America. After that, the details get hazy for a lot of folks.

Further complicating matters, the settlement of America by Europeans is shrouded in a lot of pseudopatriotic rhetoric designed to perpetuate national mythology more than convey accurate information. Thus, even today many youngsters are taught that the first settlers in New England came to America for religious freedom.

That is only half of the story. The Pilgrims and Puritans came for religious freedom all right—but only for themselves. They had absolutely no interest in promoting freedom of religion for anyone else. Once on these shores, they set up harsh theocracies where every aspect of religious life was regulated and a state-imposed orthodoxy was strictly enforced.

Pilgrims and Puritans

In reviewing this period, it is helpful to keep in mind the distinction between Pilgrims and Puritans. Both groups dissented from the Church of England and came to America, but each had different ideas about the type of religious state they would establish.

Pilgrims founded Plymouth Bay Colony in 1620. They were separatists who broke completely with the Church of England. They believed that the church was so corrupt and had strayed so far from the true faith that the only way to set things right was to start all over again from scratch.

Puritans established Massachusetts Bay Colony in 1630. They never broke entirely with the Church of England, hoping instead to purify the church (hence their name) and return it to what they considered to be the right course.

Of the two, Pilgrims were slightly more open-minded about religious toleration. Unfortunately, their colony struggled from day one to eke out even a meager survival and was eventually absorbed by the nearby Puritan colony.

The Puritans had no use for religious liberty, as we understand the term today. By their thinking you either agreed with them on religious matters or left town. Church and state were melded into one. By law, only members of the Puritan church, which ultimately became the Congregationalists, could vote or serve in the state assembly. The Puritans were Calvinists. Heavily influenced by John Calvin, the Reformation leader, Puritans expected the civil leaders of government to enforce religious dictates. They argued that if government did not curb sin, society would fall apart. In many ways, today's Religious Right activists are their spiritual descendants.

In Massachusetts, the colony's General Court levied a tax on all citizens to support religion and the clergy. Those who didn't pay went straight to jail, no questions asked. Even ministers were kept under close control. Since ministers were paid by the government, any who rebelled were quickly cut off and replaced.

Fortunately, the Puritan theocracy of Massachusetts was not duplicated in other colonies. Remember, not everyone who settled in the colonies did so for religious reasons. Some were entrepreneurs who came seeking new business opportunities. Others, such as craftsmen and artisans, were lured over by the colonists in need of their special skills. Still others came simply to escape legal difficulties back home and make a fresh start in a new land. Thus, it's not accurate to suggest that most of the first European settlers came to America for reasons that had anything to do with religion; relatively few of them did.

Naturally, not everyone who came to America had Puritan leanings. Baptists, Quakers, Deists, even a small number of Catholics and Jews eventually arrived on these shores. Some tried to settle in Massachusetts, but finding themselves unwelcome and weary of fighting the powers that be, opted to move elsewhere. Others did stay behind to fight.

Roger Williams's Rhode Island Colony

One settler who was not about to roll over or voluntarily depart was the iconoclastic preacher Roger Williams. Williams began making trouble for the religious authorities in Massachusetts almost as soon as he arrived in Boston.

Williams was an unusual character for the times. A devout Christian, he was absolutely convinced that his views on religion were correct and that any rational being would in time come around and agree with him once the facts were laid bare. But Williams insisted with equal force that the state should have no business in enforcing orthodoxy. A person's understanding of religion and truth, Williams insisted, must come from within. He argued for complete freedom of conscience, a concept he called "soul liberty."

Wrote Williams, "I must profess, while Heaven and Earth lasts, that no one Tenet that either London, England, or the World doth harbor, is so heretical, blasphemous, seditious, and dangerous to the corporal, to the spiritual, to the present, to the Eternal Good of Men, as the bloody Tenet . . . of persecution for cause of Conscience."[1]

Because Williams absolutely railed against the church-state union of Massachusetts, he soon came to the attention of the state's ecclesiastical and civil authorities. When the General Court decided that every member of the colony should take a loyalty oath to the governor ending in the phrase, "So help me, God," Williams went on the warpath.

"A magistrate ought not to tender an oath to an unregenerate man," wrote Williams, because it would cause the oath taker "to take the name of God in vain."[2]

By 1635 the Puritan leaders had had enough of Williams. The General Court found him guilty of "disseminating new and dangerous opinions" and banished him from the colony. Williams was ordered to return to England.

Accompanied by a small band of dedicated followers, Williams ignored the decree and fled south to what is today Rhode Island, where he founded the city of Providence. He announced that all who chose to live there would enjoy full religious and political freedom. Williams's proclamation proved the sincerity of his beliefs, as he soon had to suffer many religious views he personally found distasteful. For example, Williams detested Quakers and often blasted them in his writings. Yet in Rhode Island Quakers worshipped unmolested, at least during the years of Williams's oversight.

It was Williams who coined the phrase that may have been the grandfather to Thomas Jefferson's famous "wall of separation" between church and state metaphor (although there is no evidence that Jefferson knew of it). In his 1644 treatise, *The Bloudy Tenet of Persecution, for cause of Conscience*, Williams warned against opening "a gap in the hedge, or wall of separation, between the garden of the church and the wilderness of the world." A decent distance between church and state, he maintained, would keep the purity of the church intact and safe from the corrupting influence of government.

It should be pointed out, however, that Williams's Rhode Island was no paradise where multiple religious groups lived in harmony. In fact, the colony got off to a raucous start. The citizens argued among themselves frequently, despite Williams's pleas that they put aside their differences and work together for the good of the new community. Eventually, the squabbling did die down, and Rhode Island prospered, despite its rocky start.

Another early dissenter of the Puritan church-state union in Massachusetts was Anne Hutchinson, a renegade would-be religious reformer who dared to hold unauthorized religious meetings in her home. Hutchinson was expelled from the colony by Gov. John Winthrop in 1638 and fled to Rhode Island. She settled there for a while before moving on to New York, where she died at the hands of the Indians. When told of her death, Winthrop remarked, "God's hand is the more apparently seen therein, to pick out this woeful woman to make her, and those belonging to her, an unheard of heavy example of [the Indians'] cruelty."[3]

Hutchinson's brother-in-law, John Wheelwright, who also preached opinions deemed heretical by the state, met with a less unpleasant fate. Tried and found guilty by the General Court, he was banished from the colony and refused the right of an appeal.

Church and State in Other Colonies

Experiences in other colonies varied, but none matched the level of religious freedom found in Rhode Island. In many states, citizens were taxed to support the Protestant denomination of their choosing, a practice known as "multiple establishment." In other states, a single church was established.

There were sporadic attempts at increasing religious liberty in some colonies. Pennsylvania, for example, was founded by William Penn, a Quaker who embraced religious toleration. Penn and the other Quakers had been cruelly persecuted throughout the colonies, and every colony (save Rhode Island) had laws banning their worship. In Massachusetts, a band of Quakers who had been exiled from Boston dared to return and were promptly hanged.

Under Penn's Great Law of 1682, all persons who believed in one God and agreed to live peacefully in the colony were welcomed. Unfortunately, in practice toleration was extended primarily to Protestants, and Sunday religious observances were required by law. Still, the Pennsylvania laws were a step forward, and some groups found the atmosphere there liberating. Roman Catholics, for example, enjoyed more freedom in Penn's colony than they had anywhere else, and by the time of the Revolution, Pennsylvania was the only colony where Catholics could hold services without fear of molestation.

The Calvert family, which settled Maryland, were converts to Catholicism who founded the colony as a haven for members of that often-persecuted group. The colony's Act of Toleration of 1649 extended religious liberty to all Christians. But the colony never had a Catholic majority, and in time the act was repealed when Protestants came to power in Maryland and established the Church of England. (Maryland was also subject to periodic raids by neighboring Protestants in Virginia who feared their Catholic neighbors.)

In short, religious liberty, as we understand the concept today, existed nowhere in colonial America outside of Williams's Rhode Island. Citizens were usually taxed to support religion. Strict Sunday laws were rigidly enforced. Blasphemy was a capital offense. Laws required men to believe certain tenets of Christianity before they could hold public office. Some colonies were clearly theocracies; others came very close to that.

Undoubtedly the harshest colony remained Massachusetts, where the dangers of church-state union were vividly illustrated in an outbreak of witch trials in 1692. As the hysteria spread, nineteen accused "witches"—all but one of whom were women—near Salem were executed by civil authorities working in conjunction with church leaders. Eighteen were hanged and one was crushed to death with stones. The incident, which appalled leaders in some of the other colonies, went a long way to demonstrate the dangers of a church state.

The Beginnings of Separation

Eventually, even the harshness of Massachusetts's church-state union began to fade. Why did things change? To answer that question, it is necessary to look with greater detail at the experience of one key state, Virginia, and two of its most famous sons—Thomas Jefferson and James Madison.

Virginia, like many of the original colonies, was founded primarily for economic reasons. But there was a religious component, too. Captain John Smith, founder of the colony, declared it the duty of all Virginians to "preach, baptise into the Christian religion and by the propagation of the Gospel to recover out of the arms of the devil, a number of poor and miserable souls wrapt up unto death in almost invincible ignorance."[4] (He was referring to Native Americans.)

The Anglican Church was established as Virginia's state church, and a series of religiously inspired laws was quickly laid down. Blasphemy was punishable by death. Those who spoke "impiously" of the Trinity or the Christian faith could be executed. The punishment for nonattendance at church services was a monetary fine for the first offense, whipping for subsequent offenses. Those who cursed could have a "bodkin," a type of small, sharp dagger, thrust through their tongues.

These harsh rules, published in 1612, were later softened. Nonattendance at church, for example, was made punishable by monetary fines alone. Still, this was no period of true liberalization. Quakers and Catholics were flatly barred from the colony, and parents could be fined for failing to have their children baptized. Denial of the Trinity could lead to a three-year jail sentence.

In addition, all Virginia residents were forced to support Anglicanism through taxation, whether they believed in the tenets of the church or not. Every taxpayer was required to turn over a bushel of corn and ten pounds of tobacco to support the church. In 1632, the legislature upped the mandatory contribution, requiring all taxpayers to also contribute their twentieth calf, goat, and pig.[5]

Laws like this, common in many Southern states where Anglicanism was the established religion, angered many colonists and helped spur revolutionary fervor. By the mid-1700s, Anglicanism was a minority religion in the southern states, yet all residents were still forced to pay taxes to support Anglican ministers. Gradually, feelings of discontent over this system began to grow.

(It is important to note here that state-supported religion did little to encourage piety in colonial America. Historian Robert R. Handy estimates that by 1800 only 10 percent of the population were church members and cites the "overwhelming indifference to religion." Two other scholars, Roger Finke and Rodney Stark, put the number of "religious adherents" in 1776 a little higher at 17 percent. In any case, church membership did not begin to take off in America until after the adoption of the First Amendment, which gave the country true religious freedom through the separation of church and state. Today U.S. church membership stands at nearly 50 percent, and the vast majority of Americans—church members or not—say religion is important to them.)

A general spirit of intolerance toward other religions fueled this fire. In states like Virginia other religions were permitted to exist but were restricted in many ways, especially in their evangelical activity.

Baptists had an especially tough time in Virginia. During the period of 1768 to 1774, known as the "Great Persecution," they were frequently imprisoned or publicly whipped. In the town of Fredericksburg, several Baptist ministers were thrown in jail for refusing to pay a licensing fee imposed on "dissident" clergy.

James Madison

Here is where James Madison enters the story. In 1774 the young Madison witnessed a shocking sight: Five or six men in the adjoining county had been imprisoned for publishing religious views at odds with the state's orthodoxy. Madison was incensed. In a letter to his friend William Bradford Jr., who lived in Philadelphia, he called the men "well meaning" and spoke on their behalf.

"That diabolical, hell-conceived principle of persecution rages among some and to their eternal infamy the clergy can furnish their quota of imps for such business," Madison wrote. "This vexes me the worst of anything whatever. . . . I have neither patience to hear, talk, or think of anything relative to this matter; for I have squabbled and scolded, abused and ridiculed, so long about it to so little purpose, that I am without common patience. So I leave you to pity me and pray for liberty of conscience to revive among us."[6]

Naturally Madison was not the only man in the colonies who understood the importance of religious liberty. As the colonies grew, the idea germinated among others in the population. What the movement needed were leaders to take the cause forth. Men like Madison and Jefferson later played that role.

Looking back on the situation today, Madison seems an odd choice to fill the role of great advocate of religious liberty. As a young man he was frail and frequently of poor health. Small in stature, he was once described by a contemporary as a "withered little applejohn." Even Madison himself did not expect to live long. (As it turned out, he lived into his mid-eighties.)

Madison and other forward thinkers of his time had been influenced by the writings of various European philosophers, notably John Locke. Locke, an early advocate of religious freedom, argued that government should exist only to protect the inalienable rights of the people. Church and state, Locke argued, served distinctly different functions in society and should be separate. Churches, he maintained, are voluntary associations that must be supported without coercion from the state. Locke's *Letter on Toleration* laid down these ideas in a powerful argument.

It should be noted that Locke's views, while far-sighted for the time, do fall short of our understanding of toleration today. He would not have extended toleration to Roman Catholics and nonbelievers, and, although Locke argued that no one church should be established by law, he seemed to see little harm in government favoring Christianity generally.

Madison and Jefferson were clearly influenced by Locke's ideas and to some extent perfected them. As church-state scholar Leo Pfeffer observes, "The logical extension of [Locke's] ideas was, however, effected by Jefferson, Madison and the others responsible for the American experiment."[7]

Though keenly interested in new ideas such as those presented by Locke, young Madison was unsure of what to do with his life. Like many young men of his day, he studied theology, taking a degree at the College of New Jersey, today known as Princeton University. Madison studied there until 1772, when he returned to his Virginia home in Orange County.

In 1776 Madison was elected to the Virginia Convention, a sort of shadow government operating outside of British authority. Madison was only twenty-five at the time and on the verge of assuming a great role in American history.

As a Convention member, Madison worked with fellow Virginian George Mason in writing a declaration of rights and body of laws that would guide Virginia once independence was declared. Mason shared Madison's interest in religious liberty and drafted language that would guarantee religious toleration. Madison, suspicious that the concept of mere toleration did not go far enough, suggested substitute language guaranteeing that "all men are equally entitled to the full and free exercise of religion," which was in time adopted. Madison also sought to add language disestablishing the Anglican Church in Virginia, but the Convention rejected it.

The Virginia Convention declared independence and adjourned in July. Shortly thereafter Madison was elected to the newly created House of Delegates. In October he returned to Williamsburg, the colonial capital, for the body's first session.

Madison was assigned to the Committee on Religion, and began working with a new ally, Thomas Jefferson, on another attempt to end church establishment in Virginia. Madison may have been influenced by an appeal from Presbyterians in Prince Edward County. Members of that religious group petitioned the House of Delegates to deliver them from "a long night of Ecclesiastical bondage" and asked that "without delay, all Church establishments . . . be pulled down, and every tax upon conscience and private judgment be abolished" so that Virginia might become an "asylum for free inquiry, knowledge, and the virtuous of every denomination."[8]

Madison worked with Jefferson in an effort to comply with the Presbyterians' request by proposing legislation disestablishing the Anglican Church in Virginia. The move turned out to be premature, and it was blocked by powerful legislators, such as Edmund Pendleton, who favored retaining church establishment. Despite the failure, Madison and Jefferson had advanced the idea of church-state separation and laid the groundwork for future success.

During the waning years of the Revolution, Madison was chosen to be a delegate to the Continental Congress, a body charged with formulating policy for the soon-to-be independent United States. With a peace treaty signed with Great Britain, Madison returned home to Orange County in 1784 and again won a seat in the Virginia House of Delegates.

The Henry Bill

Almost immediately Madison became involved in a battle over separation of church and state. Patrick Henry, the patriot best known for uttering the phrase, "Give me liberty or give me death," introduced a bill that would have levied a general assessment on all state citizens to support ministers of Christian religions.

Henry's "Bill Establishing a Provision for Teachers of the Christian Religion" is quite severe by today's standards. It required all persons "to pay a moderate tax or contribution annually for the support of the Christian religion, or of some Christian church, denomination or communion of Christians, or for some form of Christian worship."[9]

Although it sounds oppressive to today's ears, Henry's bill was actually more tolerant than previous colonial establishment provisions. Under it, Christians in Virginia would have at least had the freedom to choose which church to support instead of being required to back one denomination. But Madison, ever the forward thinker, still found the measure full of shortcomings.

The assessments bill, Madison argued, was "obnoxious on account of its dishonorable principle and dangerous tendency."[10]

Henry sincerely believed that his proposal would safeguard the morality of the population. The bill was nothing new; versions of it had come up before in the Virginia legislature. Every time opposition from religious minorities was swift and angry, with Baptists leading the charge.

In some respects, politics of the colonial period was not so different than today, and Madison was able to use procedural moves to delay consideration of the bill until late in 1785—almost a year after the measure was introduced. In the interim period, a bill establishing the Episcopal Church in Virginia was introduced in the House of Delegates.

The establishment bill was a result of fallout from the Revolution. In the post-Revolutionary period, it hardly seemed appropriate to continue the establishment of the Church of England in the newly born United States. Some legislators, seeking to clarify the status of the church, backed the establishment bill.

Madison abhorred the idea of established churches, of course, but even he threw his weight behind the measure and voted for establishment. Madison saw no way he could successfully fight both that measure and Henry's general assessment bill. Since Madison considered the Henry bill much more dangerous to religious freedom, he decided to concentrate his energies on defeating it.

Madison's move illustrated his shrewd political maneuvering. An established church, Madison realized, was no longer what the people of Virginia wanted. If the establishment bill should pass, he figured, it would not last long. Madison was correct. Two years after its passage, the bill establishing the Episcopal Church in Virginia was repealed.

Madison used the eleven-month period before consideration of the Henry general assessment bill wisely. At Mason's urging, he penned what is today regarded as one of the classics of religious freedom—the "Memorial and Remonstrance against Religious Assessments" (see Appendix 3).

The "Memorial and Remonstrance" is a list of fifteen reasons why Henry's bill should be rejected, and, by extension, why religion does not need the support of government. The document was circulated widely throughout Virginia in the interim period and had a powerful influence on many who read it. Opposition to the Henry measure poured in from counties around the state, and thousands of opposition letters flooded the lawmakers' chambers.

Asserting "it is proper to take alarm at the first experiment on our liberties," the "Memorial and Remonstrance" observed in part, "Who does not see that the same authority which can establish Christianity, in exclusion of all other Religions, may establish with the same ease any particular sect of Christians, in exclusion of all other Sects? That the same authority which can force a citizen to contribute three pence only of his property for the support of any one establishment, may force him to conform to any other establishment in all cases whatsoever?"[11]

Elsewhere the "Memorial and Remonstrance" asserts, "If Religion be not within the cognizance of Civil Government how can its legal establishment be necessary to Civil Government? What influence in fact have ecclesiastical establishments had on Civil Society? In some instances they have been seen to erect a spiritual tyranny on the ruins of the Civil authority; in many instances they have been seen upholding the thrones of political tyranny; in no instance have they been seen the guardians of the liberties of the people."[12]

Madison's ploy worked. In the interim election, many supporters of the assessment bill lost their seats. When the Virginia legislature reconvened in the fall of 1785, the mood of the new body was clearly running against the Henry bill. No doubt many lawmakers were influenced by a stack of letters and petitions denouncing the bill that had poured into the legislature from all over Virginia. Henry himself had been elected governor of Virginia (partly with Madison's help), where he could no longer speak on its behalf from the floor of the legislature. This sealed the measure's fate. It was soundly defeated.

Thomas Jefferson's Religious Freedom Bill

Madison decided to press his victory to its limits by resurrecting Thomas Jefferson's 1779 "Bill for Establishing Religious Freedom." Jefferson's measure, which declared that "no man shall be compelled to frequent or support any religious worship, place, or ministry whatsoever," got nowhere when originally introduced. On the heels of the defeat of the Henry general assessment bill, Madison believed the time was right to push it through.

At the time, Jefferson was in Paris representing the interests of the U.S. government in France. He kept in close communication with Madison and followed the developments concerning his religious freedom bill.

Jefferson's bill was passed by a 60–27 vote in January 1786. Calling it "sinful and tyrannical to compel a man to furnish contributions for the propagation of opinions which he disbelieves and abhors," the measure takes a strong stand against state-supported religion and guarantees religious free exercise.

Reads the bill, "Be it therefore enacted by the General Assembly of Virginia that no man shall be compelled to frequent or support any religious worship, place or ministry whatsoever, nor shall be enforced, restrained, molested or burdened in his body or goods, nor shall otherwise suffer on account of his religious opinions or beliefs, but that all men shall be free to profess, and by argument to maintain, their opinions in matters of religion, and that the same shall in no wise diminish, enlarge or affect their civil capacities."[13]

Jefferson insisted that his bill was designed to protect *all* religious practitioners. He took great pride in noting that efforts to amend the measure by limiting its protections to Christians only were rejected. This was an important step forward. Prior to Jefferson's bill, many lawmakers believed that religious freedom should be extended to Christians only or, in an even more limited view, to only Protestant Christians.

Jefferson had a much broader perspective. In his autobiography, Jefferson noted that the effort to amend the bill so that it would apply to Christians only "was rejected by a great majority, in proof that they meant to comprehend, within the mantle of its protection, the Jew and the Gentile, the Christian and Mahometan, the Hindoo, the infidel of every denomination."[14]

Thanks to the efforts of Jefferson and Madison, Virginia, in the space of a few years, went from state-established religion to a system that offered complete religious freedom to Christians, Jews, Muslims, believers, and nonbelievers alike. This is a remarkable accomplishment.

Pastors for Separation

Jefferson and Madison confined themselves primarily to the world of politics. As they labored in the legislature, some religious leaders were spreading the gospel of church-state separation to their flocks, and, by extension, to the general population.

Chief among them was Baptist minister John Leland. Leland, a Massachusetts native, had settled in Virginia during the time of the great struggle for religious liberty there. Like Madison, Leland was dismayed to see dissenting preachers in jail for their religious views.

Leland's writings echo some of the comments made by Jefferson. Leland, defending freedom of conscience, wrote, "Government should protect every man in thinking, and speaking freely, and that one does not abuse another . . . all should be equally free, Jews Turks, Pagans and Christians."

On another occasion Leland wrote in opposition to the idea that holders of public office should have to believe certain things about religion before they could even run. (Such "religious tests" were common in many colonies.) Wrote Leland, "If a man merits the confidence of his neighbors in Virginia—let him worship one God, twenty Gods, or no God—be he Jew, Turk, Pagan, or Infidel, he is eligible to any office in the state."

This statement is interesting, as it parallels language Jefferson used. Jefferson once observed in a letter that it did him no disservice if his neighbor believed in "twenty gods or no god—it neither picks my pocket nor breaks my leg."[15] As we have seen, Jefferson also spoke of the need to extend religious liberty not just to the various sects of Christians but also to "the Jew and the Gentile, the Christian and Mahometan, the Hindoo, the infidel of every denomination." Leland and Jefferson were acquainted. On January 1, 1802, the day Jefferson wrote his famous letter to the Danbury (Connecticut) Baptist Association lauding the "wall of separation between church and state" (see below), Leland arrived at the White House with a "mammoth cheese"—a gift from Baptists in Massachusetts, where Leland was then residing.

Leland never hesitated to speak out on this issue. In 1791 he penned a tract titled "Rights of Conscience and therefore Religious Opinions not cognizable by law" which states in part, "Government has no more to do with the religious opinions of men than it has with the principles of mathematics."[16]

Unlike Jefferson, who was a rationalist and something of a religious skeptic, Leland's support for church-state separation was anchored in his theological views. In 1790 he wrote, "The notion of a Christian commonwealth should be exploded forever. . . . [I]f all the souls in a government were saints of God, should they be formed into a society by law, that society could be not a Gospel Church, but a creature of the state."

(Clergy in other states also played a pivotal role in the struggle to establish the separation of church and state in America. In Massachusetts, Pastor Isaac Backus, a Baptist minister, went so far as to refuse to pay a church tax and was arrested. In 1774 he wrote a document blasting the tax, which asserted in part, "[R]eligion is a concern between God and the soul with which no human authority can intermeddle."[17])

The Bill of Rights

Madison's next achievement concerned the Bill of Rights. Many Americans may be surprised to learn that the Bill of Rights—the first ten amendments to the Constitution—was actually a kind of constitutional afterthought. The Constitution was originally written without one. Indeed, many framers saw no need for a Bill of Rights. Madison himself was originally in this camp.

Certainly Madison did not oppose a Bill of Rights because he feared the concept of civil liberties. His view, not uncommon in his day, was that by listing the rights of citizens in the Constitution, the government was implying that *only* those rights were to be granted to the American people. Madison thus feared that the enumeration of rights would serve as a natural limitation on freedom. (This problem was taken care of by the Ninth Amendment, which deals with unenumerated rights and essentially states that just because certain rights are listed in the Constitution, no one should assume that the American people do not retain other rights as well.)

This is not to imply, however, that religious freedom was not discussed at the original Constitutional Convention of 1787. Indeed, Charles Pinckney, a young South Carolina delegate, proposed language stating that "the Legislature of the United States shall pass no law on the subject of religion."[18]

Although Convention delegates did not adopt this language, they did accept another of Pinckney's proposals forbidding religious tests for federal office. The prohibition is found in Article Six and reads, "[N]o religious test shall ever be required as a qualification to any office or public trust under the United States."

Luther Martin, a Maryland delegate, later reported that this proposal was adopted "by a great majority of the Convention and without much debate." Martin noted, however, that "there were some members so unfashionable as to think that a belief in the existence of a Deity, and of a state of future rewards and punishments would be some security for the good conduct of our rulers, and that, in a Christian country, it would be at least decent to hold out some distinction between the professors of Christianity and downright infidelity or paganism."[19] Martin's report is strong evidence that a "Christian nation" faction had its say during the convention—and that its views were consciously rejected.

The Constitution fashioned in 1787, largely by Madison, is a secular document. There is no mention of God, Jesus Christ, or a Supreme Being anywhere in the document. As we have seen, a minority faction of delegates pressed for some type of recognition of Christianity in the Constitution, but their views were rejected.

Contrary to common belief, convention delegates did not even lead off their deliberations with prayer. Although Benjamin Franklin made such a suggestion a month into the proceedings, the Convention adjourned rather than vote on his proposal and did not take it up again after reconvening.

Franklin made an eloquent plea on behalf of prayer. It is frequently cited by Religious Right activists today. Some go on to assert that the delegates were so moved that they dropped to their knees in prayer. Former

U.S. senator Jesse Helms (R-N.C.) used to tell this story frequently on the floor of the Senate when arguing in favor of school prayer. The account he told was highly detailed—and utterly false.

Unfortunately for Helms, the story about Franklin's plea for prayer told by today's Religious Right activists is largely fiction. Franklin did make an impassioned appeal for prayer, but the Convention did not act on his suggestion. The record here is clear. The delegates did not pray as a body. Some later admitted they feared that if word got out that the Convention had turned to appealing for divine intervention, the people might assume things were going badly.

As leading Franklin biographer Carl Van Doren writes, "Though the proposal may have seemed strange from the freethinking Franklin, it was sincere. . . . While it was received with respect, no action was taken on it. 'The Convention,' Franklin noted on his manuscript, 'except for three or four persons, thought prayers unnecessary.'"[20]

The omission of God in the Constitution was not intended as a slight. Although the action angered some religious leaders, Madison insisted that the move was for the best. He worried about what such references to a deity could lead to, insisting that the Constitution had created not even "a shadow of right in the general government to intermeddle with religion."[21]

(Incidentally, the omission of God in the Constitution has served to vex today's Religious Right activists, who insist that the United States was founded as a "Christian nation." Since Madison's statement and the omission serve as a great embarrassment to them, some have taken to asserting that the document recognizes Jesus Christ at the end, where the date contains the *pro forma* phrase "in the year of our Lord"!)

Despite the Convention's work, it soon became apparent that some states—notably North Carolina and Rhode Island—would not ratify a Constitution lacking a Bill of Rights. Accordingly, debate began on a series of amendments in 1789. By the time work began, Madison had changed his mind, maintaining that he now favored an amendment to guarantee "all essential rights, particularly the rights of Conscience in the fullest latitude, the freedom of the press, trial by jury, security against general warrants, etc."

Jefferson too advocated a Bill of Rights. Writing to Madison from France he insisted "[A] bill of rights is what the people are entitled to against every government on earth . . ." and asserted that freedom of religion be among those rights.

The First Amendment Takes Shape

Madison was charged with the assignment of drafting what eventually became the First Amendment. His first effort is quite different from what was eventually settled on, but contains much of the spirit of the religious freedom guarantee we know today. It reads, "The civil rights of none shall be abridged on account of religious belief, nor shall any national religion be established, nor shall the full and equal rights of conscience in any manner or on any pretext be infringed."[22]

Much has been made of Madison's use of the word "national" in this version by today's opponents of church-state separation, who argue that all Madison intended to do was prevent the government from establishing a national church—not provide for church-state separation.

This weak argument has been thoroughly demolished by respected constitutional scholar Leonard W. Levy in his excellent book *The Establishment Clause: Religion and the First Amendment.* Levy points out that at the time the First Amendment was drafted, it was intended to apply only to the federal government. The word "national" was added, he writes, in order to make it clear to the states that the prohibition was limited to Congress. And, as Levy points out, the word was quickly removed during debate over the language of the amendment. Madison himself added that he believed the people feared that one religious denomination might assume prominence in the United States or perhaps two powerful groups would join together to establish a religion to which they would compel others to conform. He saw adding the word "national" as one way of making it clear that the amendment would specifically prevent this from happening.[23]

An eleven-member House committee, which included Madison, began working on the language and soon rewrote it to read, "No religion shall be established by law, nor shall the equal rights of conscience be infringed." A second committee-approved proposal read, "No state shall infringe the equal rights of conscience."[24]

The proposals were then referred to the full House of Representatives. For a time the House favored a version reading, "Congress shall make no laws touching religion, or infringing the rights of conscience." But the House ultimately adopted a version put forth by Fisher Ames of Massachusetts. It read, "Congress shall make no law establishing religion, or to prevent the free exercise thereof, or to infringe the rights of conscience."[25]

The amendment then moved to the Senate. The Senate considered and rejected three alternative versions, which are listed below:

- "Congress shall make no law establishing one religious sect or society in preference to others."
- "Congress shall not make any law infringing the rights of conscience, or establishing any religious sect or society."
- "Congress shall make no law establishing any particular denomination of religion in preference to another."[26]

The fact that these versions were defeated clearly indicates that today's opponents of church-state separation are wrong in stating that all the First Amendment was intended to do was ban the establishment of a national church. Were that the case, versions one or three above would have sufficed. Obviously, the Senate had something more far-reaching in mind.

After a short recess the Senate took up the matter of the religion clauses again. The record of these deliberations is sketchy, but we do know that the Senate eventually emerged with the following language: "Congress shall make no law establishing articles of faith or a mode of worship, or prohibiting the free exercise of religion."[27]

House members, however, refused to accept the Senate's version of the religion clauses. A joint conference committee was appointed to resolve the matter. Madison played a key role in these negotiations, and on September 24 the final wording of the religion clauses was announced: "Congress shall make no law respecting an establishment of religion, or prohibiting the free exercise thereof."

As Levy points out, the Constitution grants the government limited powers. The First Amendment was carefully drafted to tell the government what it may *not* do in matters of religion. Today's opponents of church-state separation, who assert that the amendment somehow grants government the right to give nonpreferential aid to religion, stand on crumbling ground. The legislative history of the religion clauses proves exactly the opposite. The First Amendment is a command to government to keep its hands off religion—neither aiding nor hindering it—to the fullest extent possible.

State legislatures began approving the Bill of Rights, some rather quickly, others dragging out the process. By the end of 1791, the Bill of Rights had been ratified by a majority of the states and was an official part of the Constitution of the new country.

Jefferson and the "Wall of Separation"

Ten years later a group of Baptists in Danbury, Connecticut, wrote to President Thomas Jefferson to express their thoughts on religious liberty. Because this letter and Jefferson's reply are so important to church-state history, it's important to look at both in some detail.

Before looking at the Danbury letter, it's necessary to take some time to demolish a common Religious Right argument about it: that Jefferson was not qualified to comment on the First Amendment since he was in France at the time it was drafted.

Obviously, Jefferson was a lot closer to the drafting of the First Amendment than any modern-day commentator. Jefferson and Madison corresponded regularly about religious freedom issues, and even though the mail was much slower then, the volume of letters generated on both sides is impressive. Madison, who was in many ways Jefferson's protégé, took Jefferson's views to the Constitutional Convention and the sessions that resulted in the drafting of the Bill of Rights.

In addition, Jefferson wrote the Virginia Statute for Religious Freedom, which many scholars agree was an inspiration for the First Amendment. Jefferson, a figure of towering intellect and strong personality, could influence a debate without even being in the room. It was Jefferson's ideas, not his physical presence, which influenced the Convention.

Jefferson, therefore, was well qualified to comment on the First Amendment—and that's just what he did on January 1, 1802, writing in response to a letter he had received that previous October from the Danbury Baptist Association.

Why did the Baptists write to Jefferson? On one level, they simply wanted to congratulate him on his election to the presidency. But, not surprisingly, they had another motive. The Baptists knew Jefferson was now in a position of power, and they wanted something from him: They wanted religious freedom.

Remember, at this period in history, even though the Bill of Rights had been in effect for ten years, it did not apply to the states. Thus, many states still had officially established religions. Connecticut was one of these states.

Baptists in Connecticut had been unhappy with their lot for a long time. Originally a type of mild Congregationalist theocracy, Connecticut had moved toward a different system of state-supported religion by the middle of the eighteenth century. Instead of a single established church,

Connecticut allowed communities to vote on which church they wanted to support with tax funds. At first glance, it sounds like a system like this would result in tax support flowing to multiple sects. But in practice, it meant subsidies mainly for the Congregationalists, who wielded political control in most towns.

In 1784 state legislators passed a "Toleration Act" designed to allow members of dissenting faiths to be exempted from the majority-imposed church taxes—but only after they had pleaded their case before a local magistrate and proved their membership in another denomination. Many members of minority religions were simply not willing to do that and were infuriated that they were even asked to do it.

This new system may have looked like liberalization to Connecticut's leaders, but to members of often-persecuted minority faiths it was an outrageous violation of freedom of conscience. Further inflaming Baptist anger, a powerful combination of government officials and church leaders essentially ignored the Toleration Act, working in tandem to make it next to impossible for adherents of dissenting faiths to opt out.

Everything about the system riled Baptists. Even if they could successfully win an exemption from local church taxes, Baptists were offended at the very idea of having to appeal to a government official for this type of relief.

Jefferson's election to the presidency in 1800 gave Connecticut dissenters a glimmer of hope. Baptists in other states had worked with Enlightenment thinkers like Jefferson in an unusual alliance to champion religious liberty. Undoubtedly, Danbury's Baptists knew of Jefferson's leading role in the struggle to end state-established religion in Virginia. Surely, they must have felt, the president would turn a sympathetic ear to the persecuted believers of Connecticut.

On October 7, 1801, three members of the Danbury Baptist Association—Nehemiah Dodge, Ephraim Robbins, and Stephen S. Nelson—wrote to Jefferson to express their hope that his expansive view of religious freedom would sweep the nation. Observed the Baptists, "Sir, we are sensible that the President of the United States is not the national legislator and also sensible that the national government cannot destroy the Laws of each State; but our hopes are strong that the sentiments of our beloved President, which have had such a genial affect already, like the radiant beams of the Sun, will shine and prevail through all these States and all the world till Hierarchy and Tyranny be destroyed from the Earth."

In his New Year's Day reply, Jefferson agreed with the sentiments expressed and went on to speak of the First Amendment's impact. He wrote, "Believing with you that religion is a matter which lies solely between man and his God, that he owes account to none other for his faith or his worship, that the legitimate powers of government reach actions only, and not opinions, I contemplate with sovereign reverence that act of the whole American people which declared that their legislature should 'make no law respecting an establishment of religion, or prohibiting the free exercise thereof,' thus building a wall of separation between Church & State."

Continued Jefferson, "Adhering to this expression of the supreme will of the nation in behalf of the rights of conscience, I shall see with sincere satisfaction the progress of those sentiments which tend to restore to man all his natural rights, convinced he has no natural right in opposition to his social duties." (See the full text of the Danbury Baptists' letter to Jefferson and his reply in Appendix 2.)

Despite Jefferson's unorthodox religious views, New England Baptists looked to him as a champion and hoped his perspective on church-state relations would spread throughout the fledgling nation. Jefferson and the Baptists of New England had a common foe: the reigning Federalist political establishment in that part of the country, which was often supported by Congregationalist preachers who favored close ties between their religion and the government. These clergy had worked hard to try to defeat Jefferson in 1800. One Federalist newspaper said the question boiled down to this: Would the nation choose "GOD—AND A RELIGIOUS PRESIDENT; Or impiously declare for JEFFERSON—AND NO GOD." Rumors circulated throughout New England that Jefferson, if elected, would quickly order all Bibles rounded up and burned.

Jefferson had suffered mightily at the hands of the New England clergy, but he refrained from taking a shot at them in the Danbury letter. Instead, he chose to use the missive as a vehicle to outline a broader principle—religious liberty undergirded by the separation of church and state. Jefferson believed only this system could protect freedom of conscience for all, and he told the Baptists as much.

The Danbury letter had the desired effect and has become perhaps the leading original source for understanding Jefferson's view of the Constitution's religious liberty provisions. The rhetoric has also rung down through the ages. It was cited by the Supreme Court as early as 1879. Writing in *Reynolds* v. *United States*, Chief Justice Morrison R. Waite observed, "Coming as this does from an acknowledged leader of the advocates of the measure, it may be accepted almost as an authoritative declaration of the scope and effect of the amendment thus secured."[28]

Jefferson took the time to craft a careful reply to the Danbury Baptists. Contrary to the assertions of some in the Religious Right, Jefferson did not simply dash off a quick response. He did exactly the opposite. Historical evidence shows that Jefferson saw the reply as an opportunity to make a major pronouncement of his views on religious liberty. In fact, Jefferson first proposed using the letter as a vehicle for explaining why as president he refused to issue proclamations calling for days of prayer and fasting.

Jefferson made his intent clear in a memo to Levi Lincoln, his attorney general. Attaching the Baptist letter, Jefferson wrote, "Averse to receive addresses, yet unable to prevent them, I have generally endeavored to turn them to some account, by making them the occasion, by way of answer, of sowing useful truths and principles among the people, which might germinate and become rooted among their political tenets. The Baptist address, now enclosed, admits of a condemnation of the alliance between Church and State, under the authority of the Constitution. It furnishes an occasion, too, which I have long wished to find, of saying why I do not proclaim fastings and thanksgivings as my predecessors did."

Continued Jefferson, "The address, to be sure, does not point at this, and its introduction is awkward. But I foresee no opportunity of doing it more pertinently. . . . Will you be so good as to examine the answer, and suggest any alterations which might prevent an ill effect, or promote a good one among the people?"[29]

Robert O'Neil, a Jefferson scholar at the University of Virginia, told *Church & State* magazine in 2002 that Jefferson's "wall" metaphor is "one of the most quotable and early presidential sound bites." The phrase, O'Neil added, "is not casual. . . . The Danbury letter does not read like a note that was simply tossed off. It reads like a serious statement. If it had been merely a routine response, it would have had much less of the eloquence that you find in that phrase."[30]

Jefferson's plan to use his reply to the Danbury letter as a vehicle for making a major public policy announcement was not unusual. Political leaders of the founding period frequently used personal letters to disseminate their views. In an era where there was no television, radio, or Internet, at a time when there was no such thing as a press conference, politicians had to rely on newspapers, pamphlets, and informal channels to spread information. Most politicians of Jefferson's era did not expect personal letters to remain private. Indeed, many later ended up in print in newspapers (most of which were highly partisan).

Lincoln, probably aware that Jefferson's reply to the Baptists would not likely remain private for long, advised caution. He recommended that Jefferson remove the material about days of prayer and fasting, believing it would hurt Jefferson politically in New England—where many of the clergy were already very anti-Jefferson. (Jefferson also shared his draft with Gideon Granger, the postmaster general. Granger told Jefferson he liked it as written and made no substantial changes.)

Jefferson agreed to make Lincoln's changes and removed the material about days of fasting and prayer—but with clear reluctance. Retrieving the original draft reply from the attorney general, Jefferson bracketed the passage about prayer days and jotted in the margin, "This paragraph was omitted on the suggestion that it might give uneasiness to some of our republican friends in the eastern states where the proclamations of thanksgiving, etc. by the Executive is . . . respected."

The ease with which Jefferson acquiesced to this suggestion indicates that he was not interested in using the letter to attack the Federalists or make any sort of partisan political statement (as some critics of church-state separation have asserted). Rather, Jefferson saw the letter from the Baptists as an opportunity to make his views clear on separation of church and state—and he took it.

Other false claims about the Danbury letter are easy to debunk. Religious Right propagandist David Barton claimed in his self-published 1989 book, *The Myth of Separation*, that later in the letter Jefferson wrote that the wall of separation was meant to be "one-directional," protecting the church from the state but not the other way around. Barton also alleged that Jefferson added that "Christian principles" should always guide government.

These assertions appear nowhere in the letter, and Barton corrected the errors in later editions of his book—although he continues to dismiss the letter as unimportant and distort its contents and meaning in other ways. But the "one-directional wall" myth has gained much currency among the Religious Right activists and still appears with great regularity in their publications and on their Web sites.

Jefferson and "Christian" Government

The assertion that Jefferson favored "Christian principles" in government is especially galling. Jefferson clearly believed no such thing. But rather than go to a public library and check their facts, the Christian Coalition and other Religious Right groups have simply continued to spread this distortion. They are either abysmally ignorant or engaging in an outright deception.

In fact, Jefferson's views on Christianity's relationship to government are clear and can be easily uncovered with a little bit of research. In an 1824 letter to John Cartwright, Jefferson expressed anger at judges who had based rulings on their belief that Christianity is part of the common law. Cartwright had written a book critical of these judges, and Jefferson was glad to see it.

Observed Jefferson, "The proof of the contrary, which you have adduced, is controvertible; to wit, that the common law existed while the Anglo-Saxons were yet pagans, at a time when they had never yet heard the name of Christ pronounced, or knew that such a character had ever existed."

Jefferson challenged "the best-read lawyer to produce another script of authority for this judicial forgery" and concluded, "What a conspiracy this, between Church and State!"[31]

Unfortunately for the Religious Right, even a cursory glance at Jefferson's record unmasks their deceptions. As president, Jefferson put his wall of separation theory into practice. For example, he refused to issue proclamations calling for days of prayer and fasting, holding that they violate the First Amendment. As we have seen, Jefferson considered explaining his opinion on the matter of proclamations in his letter to the Danbury Baptists. He did not include that material, but later, as he was preparing to leave public office, Jefferson explained his stand on religious proclamations in an 1808 letter to Samuel Miller.

"I do not believe," Jefferson wrote, "it is for the interest of religion to invite the civil magistrate to direct its exercises, its discipline or its doctrines; nor of the religious societies, that the general government should be invested with the power of effecting any uniformity of time or matter among them. Fasting and prayer are religious exercises; the enjoining them an act of discipline. Every religious society has a right to determine for itself the times for these exercises and the objects proper for them, according to their own particular tenets; and this right can never be safer than in their own hands, where the Constitution has deposited it. . . . Everyone must act according to the dictates of his own reason, and mine tells me that civil powers alone have been given to the President of the United States, and no authority to direct the religious exercises of his constituents."[32]

A Few Inconsistencies

As strict a separationist as Jefferson was, however, he did backslide occasionally. For example, Jefferson approved treaties with Indian tribes that underwrote religious education for them, approving expenses to "propagate the Gospel among the Heathen." Again, Religious Right activists have tried to make the most of this and have claimed that Jefferson must not have favored strict separation since he took this action.

The Religious Right overlooks two points, however. One, the early U.S. government considered Indian tribes foreign nations, and it is likely that Jefferson believed the First Amendment had no weight in the government's dealing with them. Secondly, Jefferson believed that religion would "civilize" Native Americans and improve relations between the tribes and settlers who were pushing westward. Finally, in many places, Christian missionaries had already established amicable relationships with the Indians and were providing various humanitarian services. Instead of duplicating these efforts, the cash-strapped early government employed the religious agencies to accomplish their secular goals. Like politicians today, Jefferson was sometimes willing to set aside a vital constitutional principle for the interests of national security.

The latter explanation may even be too hard on Jefferson. Keep in mind that the Bill of Rights was a radical idea. It would have been a miracle if it were applied without a hitch. And indeed it was not always smoothly applied. There were plenty of bumps along the way. For example, the same Congress that approved the ten amendments also shortly thereafter passed the Sedition Act, legislation that flew directly in the face of the First Amendment's free speech and free press clauses by punishing anyone who made "false, scandalous, or malicious" statements about the government.

Religious Right groups make other false claims about Jefferson. They often assert, for example, that as president of the Washington, D.C., school board Jefferson approved the use of the Bible in class, saying, "I have always said, always will say, that the studious perusal of the sacred volume will make us better citizens."

In fact, this quotation, like so many others circulated by the Religious

Right, is false. Jefferson never said it. The man who spread it around so much—David Barton again—has conceded he lacks an original source for it and has advised his own readers to stop using it. (It still pops up in letters to the editor all over the country.)

It is true that near the end of Jefferson's first term as president, plans were made for the establishment of public schools in the capital city. These plans say nothing about Bible instruction, but do mention the teaching of "reading, writing, grammar, arithmetic" and occasionally "geography and Latin."[33]

Jefferson did serve as president of this local school board, but it was largely a ceremonial post. Jefferson was much too busy as president of the country to tend to this chore. The board continued its work without him, and in 1812, *three years after Jefferson left the White House*, board members voted to adopt a curriculum put forth by British educator Joseph Landcaster, which incorporated the Bible in the classroom. Jefferson was not the president of the school board—or even a member—when this action was taken.

What did Jefferson really think about using the Bible in public schools? He was wary of it. Better to teach youngsters history, Jefferson opined in his *Notes on Virginia*, "Instead, therefore, of putting the Bible and Testament into the hands of the children at an age when their judgments are not sufficiently matured for religious inquiries, their memories may here be stored with the most useful facts from the Grecian, Roman, European and American history."[34] Scholar Leonard Levy has written, "In matters of education, however, Jefferson was a complete secularist, never deviating in any significant degree."[35]

Madison under Attack

Religious Right advocates and accommodationists have made similar attempts to discredit Madison's credentials as a separationist. But once again their arguments persuade only the uninformed. For example, accommodationists like to point out that early in his career Madison approved of the concept of congressional chaplains paid for with public funds. What they omit is Madison's later thinking, in which he reversed his position and came out solidly in opposition to state-paid chaplains, writing, "The establishment of the chaplainship to Congress is a palpable violation of equal rights, as well as of Constitutional principles."[36]

Likewise, Religious Right activists point to an early piece of legislation Madison introduced in the Virginia legislature that would have punished sabbath breakers. The history surrounding this bill is fuzzy at best, and it's quite possible Madison might have sponsored it for political reasons (just as he voted for the Anglican Church establishment bill). Or Madison might simply have wanted to give the government some mechanism for punishing those who disrupted church services (a problem in some colonies). Madison may also have introduced it as part of a package of legislation providing a penal code for Virginia in the wake of the Revolution, intending to update it and remove the antiquated portions later. If this were the case, the law would still reflect pre-Revolution measures protecting the Church of England. Lastly, the bill could have been a youthful mistake taken before Madison's thinking on religious freedom jelled.

Whatever the case, this incident is a minor blotch on Madison's otherwise impeccable credentials as a separationist. It is dwarfed by his numerous expressions of support for church-state separation and has been taken out of proportion by the Religious Right; despite their wild allegations, it cannot be used to blacken Madison's achievements in pioneering the concept of religious liberty.

Lastly, antiseparationists point out that Madison during his presidency issued proclamations calling for days of prayer and fasting. Again they tell only half of the story. Later in life Madison concluded that his actions had been unconstitutional. He justified his actions by pointing out that he served during a time of war (the War of 1812) and said he was always cautious to make the proclamations "absolutely indiscriminate and merely recommendatory."[37]

Like Jefferson, Madison's credentials as a separationist are well established in his personal writings. In fact, Madison was stricter on separation than any other president, including Jefferson.

In an 1819 letter to Robert Walsh, Madison wrote, "The civil government, though bereft of everything like an associated hierarchy, possesses the requisite stability and performs its functions with complete success whilst the number, the industry and the morality of the priesthood, and the devotion of the people have been manifestly increased *by the total separation of the church from the state*"[38] (emphasis mine). Madison here was referring to the experience in Virginia, reflecting back during a period of his life when he was no longer active in government. Virginia's experience, he believed, was a model for the nation.

Also, in an undated essay called the "Detached Memoranda" that historians believe was written in the early 1800s, Madison wrote, "Strongly guarded . . . is the separation between Religion and Government in the Constitution of the United States."[39]

In 1833 Madison responded to a letter sent to him by Jasper Adams, president of the College of Charleston. Adams had written a pamphlet titled "The Relations of Christianity to Civil Government in the United States," which attempted to prove that the United States was founded as a Christian nation. He asked Madison for some comments about the piece.

Madison gently but firmly rejected Adams's ideas, pointing out that the question to be settled centers on whether Christianity is best served by government support or voluntary contributions. Madison made it clear that he believed the latter, writing, "In the Papal system, government and religion are in a manner consolidated, and that is found to be the worst of government."

Madison continued, "In most of the governments of the old world, the legal establishment of a particular religion and without or with very little toleration of others makes a part of the political and civil organization and there are few of the most enlightened judges who will maintain that the system has been favorable to either religion or to government. The tendency to a usurpation on one side or the other, or to a corrupting coalition or alliance between them, will be best guarded against by an entire abstinence of the government from interference in any way whatever, beyond the necessity of preserving public order, and protecting each sect against trespass on its legal rights by others."

The American experience, Madison concluded, would be the "decisive test."[40]

Adams sent his pamphlet to other influential figures of the day, including Supreme Court Justice Joseph Story, who enthusiastically endorsed its ideas and said the United States should align itself with Christianity. Religious Right activists claim that Madison must have endorsed the Christian nation concept himself, since he had appointed Story to the High Court. Again they either don't know or won't tell the whole story. The truth is, Madison appointed Story to the Supreme Court with clear reluctance and offered him the position only after four others had turned it down. (The Supreme Court at that time was considered a low prestige, hardship post that required frequent traveling.) Tragically, Story is regarded as a hero by today's Religious Right while Madison and Jefferson are ignored, defamed, or lied about.

(Story's church-state views were quite extreme, even by the standards of today's Religious Right. He defended Massachusetts's harsh system of church establishment all of his life and advocated strict enforcement of blasphemy laws and religious tests for public office—in clear violation of the Constitution.)

As president, Madison had opportunities to put his separationist philosophy into action. In 1811 he vetoed two bills he believed would violate church-state separation. The first was an act incorporating the Episcopal Church in the District of Columbia that gave the church the authority to care for the poor. The second was a proposed land grant to a Baptist church in Mississippi. Had Madison believed that all the First Amendment was intended to do was bar setting up a state church, he would have approved these bills. Instead, he vetoed both, and in his veto messages to Congress explicitly stated that he was rejecting the bills because they ran afoul of the First Amendment. Some Madison scholars have argued that the crux of his thinking on church-state separation can be found in those veto messages.

It's important to note that the Episcopal incorporation bill did not award government funds to the church in order to care for the poor. It merely charged the church with this task and granted an official incorporation. To Madison, even this went too far. In his veto message, he wrote that the church could care for the needy without an official commission from government.

In his veto message to Congress, Madison wrote that he was rejecting the measure in part because it "exceeds the rightful authority to which governments are limited by the essential distinction between civil and religious functions, and violates in particular the article of the Constitution of the United States which declares that 'Congress shall make no law respecting a religious establishment.'"[41]

Madison was so strict a separationist that in 1790 he expressed concern that a census he had proposed could lead to church-state entanglement if it attempted to count the number of ministers in the country. Madison proposed leaving a count of the professional classes out of the census, saying, "As to those who are employed in teaching and inculcating the duties of religion, there may be some indelicacy in singling them out, as the general government is proscribed from interfering, in any manner whatever, in matters respecting religion; and it may be thought to do this, in ascertaining who and who are not ministers of the gospel."[42]

According to Madison biographer Ralph Ketcham, one of the reasons Madison opposed the creation of a national bank is that he feared it would be granted the power to incorporate religious denominations, leading to church-state entanglement.[43]

Finally, evidence proves that Madison, like Jefferson, was confident that separation of church and state would protect both the institutions of government and religion. Late in his life Madison wrote a Lutheran minister about this matter, declaring, "A due distinction . . . between what is due to Caesar and what is due to God, best promotes the discharge of *both* obligations. . . . A mutual independence is found most friendly to practical religion, to social harmony, and to political prosperity."[44]

Again, these examples do not sound like the views of a man who believed that the First Amendment was intended only to bar a Church of the United States.

Madison's life-long advocacy of church-state separation is largely forgotten today except by scholars who have studied his political career. Unfortunately, Madison's achievements and service to the nation in this area tend to be overshadowed by his less-than-successful presidency. Madison served two terms as Jefferson's successor, but most scholars agree that he was a far better legislator and builder of the government than he was a president.

Madison's first term was dominated by tensions with Great Britain, which culminated in the War of 1812. The American army, poorly organized, poorly outfitted, and poorly led, was no match for British troops, and New England states flirted openly with secession or rejoining the British Empire. A low point came in August 1813 when British warships sailed up Chesapeake Bay and landed troops in Maryland which marched on Washington, D.C. Madison and other legislators had to flee the capital, and many federal buildings, including the White House, were burned.

Garry Wills, a history professor at Northwestern University, provides an overview of Madison's presidency in his book *James Madison*. Wills is critical of Madison's presidency but writes favorably of Madison's earlier work on behalf of church-state separation.

"Madison's views on religious freedom are the inspiration for all that was best in his later political thought," observes Wills.

> This was the first subject to which he devoted his prodigious capacity for research and reflection. . . . Some modern critics of Madison's separation of church and state think it is a "secularist" position, one that somehow downgrades or disables religion. On the contrary, he observed the greater sincerity of religious practice under conditions of freedom. This became a touchstone for him of the blessings of freedom in gen-

> eral. It was a religious insight before it was a political one. And his view has been vindicated in the history of the United States. Under our system, which separates church and state, religion has flourished more than in any modern industrialized society.[45]

Inventing History

Opponents of church-state separation, unable to find support for their views in the historical record, have simply invented a new "history" by selectively culling material from the writings, speeches, and actions of certain framers. One of their favorite tricks is to point to the many speeches several framers made discussing the importance of religion to good government. These comments certainly do exist, but they say more about the framers' views on religion than they do church-state separation. Many of the framers were quite devout and believed religion was necessary for government to function, but that did not preclude them in any way from being advocates of church-state separation.

Other framers had a more skeptical view of traditional religion. Jefferson, for example, cannot be termed an orthodox Christian. Although he frequently spoke highly of the morals of Jesus Christ as recorded in the Bible's New Testament, Jefferson did not accept the divinity of Jesus and went so far as to rewrite the New Testament, removing all references to miracles and claims by Jesus to be the Son of God. Called *The Life and Morals of Jesus Christ*, or informally the "Jefferson Bible," the tome remains in print today.

Jefferson was also firmly convinced that allowing religious leaders to entangle themselves with government would prove an obstacle to human progress and liberty. In an August 14, 1800, letter to Jeremiah Moor he observed, "The clergy, by getting themselves established by law and ingrafted into the machine of government, have been a very formidable engine against the civil and religious rights of man."[46]

In 1818, after Connecticut finally disestablished its state church (Congregationalism), Jefferson rejoiced. In a letter to John Adams he said he was glad "that this den of priesthood is at length broken up, and that a protestant popedom is no longer to disgrace American history and character."[47]

In an October 31, 1819, letter to William Short, Jefferson went so far as to list everything about orthodox Christianity that he disbelieved. These included, "The immaculate conception of Jesus, his deification, the creation of the world by him, his miraculous powers, his resurrection and visible ascension, his corporeal presence in the Eucharist, the Trinity; original sin, atonement, regeneration, election, orders of the Hierarchy, etc."[48] Jefferson once advised his own nephew to question even the existence of God, telling him that the deity would respect open inquiry more than slavish devotion based on "blindfolded fear." (If Jefferson were alive today, the Religious Right would tear him apart for daring to express views like this.)

To be sure, Jefferson was no atheist. He specifically denied that in his writings. And Jefferson never took the view that all religion was detrimental to human progress. But he was firmly convinced that unions of religion and government held people back and condemned them all of his life.

Some Religious Right groups have attempted to make Madison into an evangelical Christian too. Unlike Jefferson, who frequently corresponded with friends about religion and outlined his personal beliefs in letters, Madison was reluctant to talk about his personal religious views. Nominally an Episcopalian, Madison is regarded by some as a Deist. Madison biographer Ralph Ketcham believes that Madison was never an ardent believer.

A few years ago, Religious Right groups began circulating a quote by Madison lauding the Ten Commandments, asserting that Madison believed that American government is somehow based on this ancient legal and moral code.

The quotation in question has Madison saying that the United States has "staked the whole future of American civilization, not upon the power of government, far from it. We have staked the future of all of our political institutions upon the capacity of each and all of us to govern ourselves . . . according to the Ten Commandments of God."

Once again, "Christian nation" propagandist David Barton was largely responsible for spreading this quotation far and wide. In 1998, Barton admitted that he had not been able to find an original source for the quote and urged people to stop using it.

Researchers at the University of Virginia, where Madison's papers are kept, searched diligently for the quote. They came up empty-handed and concluded that Madison never said it. Although now considered bogus, the quotation still appears in Religious Right publications, attributed to Madison. This is what passes for "research" in the world of the Religious Right.

A few Religious Right leaders have tried over the years to retroactively baptize Jefferson and Madison, but it just doesn't work. Their own words show how silly such efforts are. Unable to claim Jefferson and Madison, many in the Religious Right fall back on Patrick Henry, who often made comments about the necessity of Christianity for good government. Henry was clearly an advocate of church-state union, but, as the Virginia experience proves, his views failed to carry the day. When the Religious Right quotes Henry, they are quoting the losing side as well as endorsing the views of a man who pushed incessantly for church taxes. Henry's comments, while interesting historically, tell us little about the church-state view that eventually prevailed.

In other cases, antiseparationists have simply downplayed the role of some framers. Religious Right activists who aren't trying to adopt Jefferson as one of their own attempt instead to write him off entirely. Other Religious Right groups simply minimize the important contributions of great Americans and point enthusiastically to language endorsing Christianity found in the Mayflower Compact, as if the theocratic state that document inspired is a good model for today's society. Tragically, their well-orchestrated campaign of misinformation has had results. Today millions of Americans believe that Jefferson's wall of separation is a myth and that all the framers sought to do was bar forever a Church of the United States.

I opened this chapter by pointing out that Americans have always been weak on their history. Even those who ought to know better sometimes fall into this trap. In his 1985 dissent to a Supreme Court ruling on school prayer, William H. Rehnquist, now chief justice of the United States, regurgitated the entire Religious Right's pseudohistorical line, discounted Jefferson, and said the government could aid religion as long as no one denomination was preferred over others.

Although this view has been soundly shown to be erroneous by numerous scholars since then, Rehnquist is sticking with it. He has concluded that he knows more about religious liberty than Jefferson and Madison and flatly stated: "The 'wall of separation between church and state' is a metaphor based on bad history, a metaphor that has proved useless as a guide to judging. It should be frankly and explicitly abandoned."[49]

Deep in the heart of the Virginia countryside, Jefferson and Madison must be spinning like tops in their graves.

Notes

1. Edwin S. Gaustad, *Liberty of Conscience: Roger Williams in America* (Grand Rapids, Mich.: Eerdmans, 1991), p. 85.

2. Edmund S. Morgan, *Roger Williams: The Church and the State* (New York: Harcourt, Brace and World, 1967), pp. 31–32.

3. Leo Pfeffer, *Church, State and Freedom* (Boston: Beacon Press, 1953), p. 67.

4. Ibid., p. 68.

5. Allan Nevins and Henry Steele Commager, *A Pocket History of the United States* (New York: Simon & Schuster, 1981), p. 19.

6. Ralph Ketcham, *James Madison: A Biography* (Charlottesville: University Press of Virginia, 1971), p. 57.

7. Pfeffer, *Church, State and Freedom*, p. 91.

8. Ibid., p. 75.

9. Ibid., p. 98.

10. Ketcham, *James Madison*, p. 162.

11. William T. Hutchinson and William M. E. Rachal, *The Papers of James Madison* (Chicago: University of Chicago Press, 1962), pp. 298–304.

12. Ibid.

13. Ibid.

14. Pfeffer, *Church, State and Freedom*, p. 102.

15. Saul K. Padover, *Thomas Jefferson on Democracy* (New York: Mentor Books, 1958), p. 109.

16. Pfeffer, *Church, State and Freedom*, p. 89.

17. Ibid.

18. Ibid., p. 110.

19. Ibid., p. 111.

20. Carl Van Doren, *Benjamin Franklin* (New York: The Viking Press, 1938), p. 748.

21. Pfeffer, *Church, State and Freedom*, p. 110.

22. John M. Swomley, *Religious Liberty and the Secular State* (Amherst, N.Y.: Prometheus Books, 1987), p. 45.

23. Leonard W. Levy, *The Establishment Clause: Religion and the First Amendment* (New York: MacMillan, 1986), pp. 97–100.

24. Swomley, *Religious Liberty*, p. 47.

25. Ibid., p. 46.

26. Ibid., p. 49.

27. Ibid., pp. 48–49.

28. *Reynolds* v. *United States*, 98 U.S. 145 (1879).

29. Charles C. Haynes, *Religion in American History: What to Teach and How* (Alexandria, Va.: Association for Supervision and Curriculum Develop-

ment, 1990), p. 51.

30. Rob Boston, "Priority Mail," *Church & State*, January 2002.

31. Pfeffer, *Church, State and Freedom*, p. 214.

32. Padover, *Thomas Jefferson*, pp. 115–16.

33. Jim Allison, "Thomas Jefferson Supported Bible Reading in School?" Separation of Church and State Homepage (http://members.tripod.com/~candst/index.html).

34. Quoted in Leonard Levy, *Jefferson and Civil Liberties: The Darker Side* (New York: Quadrangle, 1973), pp. 8–15

35. Ibid., p. 9.

36. Robert S. Alley, *James Madison on Religious Liberty* (Buffalo, N.Y.: Prometheus Books, 1985), p. 92.

37. Merrill D. Peterson and Robert C. Vaughan, *The Virginia Statute for Religious Freedom* (New York: Cambridge University Press, 1988), pp. 302–306.

38. Alley, *James, Madison*, pp. 80–81.

39. Ibid., pp. 89–94.

40. Ibid., pp. 86–87.

41. Norman Cousins, *In God We Trust: The Religious Beliefs and Ideas of the American Founding Fathers* (New York: Harper & Brothers, 1958), p. 317.

42. Bernard Schwartz, *The New Right and the Constitution: Turning Back The Legal Clock* (Boston: Northeastern University Press, 1990), p. 32.

43. Ketcham, *James, Madison*, p. 165.

44. Ibid., p. 167.

45. Garry Wills, *James Madison* (New York: Henry Holt and Company), p. 18.

46. Cousins, *In God We Trust*, p. 130.

47. Edwin S. Gaustad, *Faith of Our Fathers: Religion and the New Nation* (San Francisco: Harper & Row, 1987), p. 49.

48. Cousins, *In God We Trust*, pp. 148–49.

49. *Wallace* v. *Jaffree*, 105 S.Ct. 2479 (1985).

4

The *De Facto* Protestant Establishment: Church-State Relations in Late Nineteenth-Century America

As the last chapter indicated, Religious Right activists have worked feverishly to try to discredit Thomas Jefferson, James Madison, and other leading figures who helped pioneer church-state separation in the United States.

Unable to blacken the characters of these great Americans, the anti-separationists have zeroed in on minor inconsistencies in the records of the men in an effort to show that they did not intend to instill separation of church and state.

It just doesn't work. Looked at in whole, the records of Jefferson and Madison prove beyond a doubt that both were ardent separationists who knew full well the extent of the new political order they helped create. Of course, as we have seen, this does not mean at all that the men were opposed to religious freedom. Jefferson and Madison wrote about the need for freedom of conscience and saw separation of church and state as the best way to ensure that concept.

Jefferson and Madison were quite capable of recognizing the importance of religion to society and also supporting church-state separation. Supporting separation and acknowledging religion's role in life are not mutually exclusive, despite the Religious Right's attempt to claim otherwise.

(Oddly enough, Jefferson was attacked frequently in his day by conservative religious elements who disagreed with his stand for full religious liberty for all. They often branded him an infidel. Today, Religious Right leaders like Tim LaHaye continue this attack by calling Jefferson an atheist, despite his Deistic beliefs and frequent praise for the moral teachings of Jesus.)

Searching for "Christian America"

When they are not working to discredit Jefferson and Madison, the Religious Right is waxing nostalgically for a return to the days when the United States was a "Christian nation."

Although Religious Right activists often assert that a Christian nation was the original intent of the framers, as the review in the last chapter clearly shows, this simply is not true. Had a Christian republic been the framers' desire, they were certainly capable of stating that forthrightly in the Constitution. That they did not do so, and in fact rejected calls to do so, is a devastating blow to the Religious Right.

Many Religious Right boosters are also unaware that officials of the early U.S. government at least once explicitly denied that the United States was founded on Christian principles. Article 11 of the Treaty of Tripoli, a peace agreement signed between the United States and the Muslim region of North Africa in 1797 after negotiations that took place primarily under the administration of George Washington, bluntly states, "As the Government of the United States is not, in any sense, founded on the Christian religion; as it has in itself no character of enmity against the law, religion or tranquility of Musselmen [Muslims]; and as the states never have entered into any war or act of hostility against any Mohometan nation, it is declared by the parties that no pretext arising from religious opinion shall ever produce an interruption of harmony existing between the two countries."[1]

Historian Morton Borden points out that Joel Barlow, a government official who served as counsel to Algiers, translated the Arabic version of the treaty into English. Barlow, a big advocate of secular government, apparently added the language found in Article 11 on his own.

Religious Right activists today argue that since Barlow took the action unilaterally, the statement found in Article 11 does not accurately reflect the sentiments of the U.S. government. Again, that is a distortion of the truth. The true story behind the treaty leads to the opposite conclusion.

The treaty as amended by Barlow was forwarded to high government officials for approval in 1797. Timothy Pickering, the secretary of state, endorsed it and President John Adams concurred, sending the document on to the Senate. The Senate in turn approved the treaty without one word of objection. During this multilayered review process, Article 11 never raised an eyebrow. Obviously, the various government officials who examined the treaty saw the wording of Article 11 as noncontroversial and believed that it accurately reflected the tenets of the new U.S. government. Had they believed differently or been convinced that the United States was founded on Christian principles, they never would have approved the document as written by Barlow.

Barlow biographer James Woodress notes that neither Washington, nor Pickering, nor the Senate found the passage objectionable. Writes Woodress, "Its meaning was clear: because the United States had not adopted Christianity as a state religion and therefore held no official enmity for Islam, no pretext arising from religious differences should ever produce disharmony between the two states."[2]

The United States had sound reasons for making this type of assurance with Tripoli. At the time, North African pirates were terrorizing U.S. shipping on the high seas. Sailors, crew members, and passengers captured by Tripoli's pirates could look forward to being paraded through the streets of Tunis with signs around their necks identifying them as "Christian dogs." Some were later sold into slavery or held for ransom.[3] Muslims in the region had a centuries-long conflict with the Christian states of Europe and assumed that the U.S. government, being a spawn of Great Britain, would also officially espouse Christianity.

Unable to find support for the "Christian nation" concept in post–Revolutionary War America, the Religious Right looks to a different period of history as their model for a Christian republic. They are speaking primarily of a period that occurred some years after the adoption of the Bill of Rights, a period that began around the time of the Civil War and which lasted into the early part of the twentieth century.

The Religious Right looks so fondly on this period because the country at this time was dominated by white male Protestants. These times were not so great for others—especially racial minorities, Roman Catholics, Jews, other religious minorities, and women—but that is of little concern to those who harbor dreams of theocracy.

The Northwest Ordinance

Before examining this period in a little more detail, it is important to look at one more accomplishment from the eighteenth century—the Northwest Ordinance. It is necessary to discuss the ordinance in some detail because it is often cited by antiseparationists as proof that the framers did not mean to separate religion and government. The case they make is superficial at best, but, due to the myth's persistence it must be debunked here.

Thomas Jefferson wrote the Northwest Ordinance in the 1780s to help outline the United States' long-range policy for settling the "west" (then basically anything west of the Appalachian Mountains). The U.S. government had acquired new territories after the Revolution, and settlers were penetrating these rugged lands to create new communities. Some type of policy was needed to guide these pioneers in the hope that new states would eventually be added to the growing union.

Jefferson's first draft of the ordinance was secular and contained no references to religion. In 1785 Jefferson's draft fell into the hands of a congressional committee for revision. The committee agreed that education would be important to every township settled under the ordinance, and accordingly they mandated that the central section of each township be reserved for the support of education.

A proposal was then made that a section of each township north of the area reserved for educational purposes be earmarked for religion. Several members of the committee, notably Charles Pinckney of South Carolina, were nervous over this suggestion. Pinckney recommended amending it to say the land would be used for the "support of religion and charitable uses."

But some members of the committee were unwilling to go along with that. A suggestion was made that the land be reserved simply for "charitable purposes." This too could not gain support of the majority, and a stalemate ensued.

As is often the case in politics, a compromise was struck. Article III of the ordinance was drafted to read, "Religion, Morality and knowledge being necessary to good government and the happiness of mankind, schools and the means of education shall be forever encouraged."

Had the committee wanted to endorse state support for religion, church-state scholar Edwin Gaustad points out, the Article would have ended, "schools *and churches* shall forever be encouraged." But there was no way legislators, ever mindful of separation of church and state, were going to go that far. Thus, the watered-down language that the Religious Right sees as devastating to separation of church and state actually underscores the concept, once the full history behind it is explained.

Religious Right propagandists such as Gary DeMar and David Barton are loath to discuss the complete history behind the Northwest Ordinance because it deflates their arguments. Reading DeMar's 2002 book, *America's Heritage*, one would think that the Northwest Ordinance is as important as the Constitution.[4] DeMar's confusion is perhaps understandable, since he refuses to tell his readers the whole story behind the ordinance.

The truth is, the content of the ordinance was heavily influenced by a group of New England land speculators called the Ohio Company Associates, and the famous sentence found in Article III was chiefly a result of that group's political machinations.

Researcher Jim Allison of the Separation of Church and State Homepage explains the whole story on his Web site. A summary, based on Allison's work, follows.

Composed primarily of Revolutionary War veterans, the Ohio Company Associates were led by Manasseh Cutler, who served as the chief agent. Cutler, a former army chaplain, was known as a "wheeler-dealer" from New England.

Congress was eager to ensure that Cutler and his group would buy and develop large tracts of land in the Ohio territory. Accordingly, they practically gave the land away to the Ohio Company Associates—allowing the group to have more than a million acres of land at a very low price. The company also picked up an option on another five million acres.

Being New Englanders, members of the Ohio Company were suspicious of the church-state relationship that was unfolding in the new nation. (They were also paranoid that "popery" was going to gain a foothold in the country and drive out Protestantism.) States in New England, it must be remembered, clung to their established churches long after most other states had discarded them. New Englanders were much more likely to oppose separation of church and state than people living in other regions of the country. Some years later, when Jefferson became president, some New England clergy reacted with near panic.

In any case, Cutler and his associates saw an opportunity to give the New England view of church-state relations a boost by establishing closer ties between religion and government in the new Ohio territory. Accordingly, they pressed for some type of recognition of religion in the Northwest Ordinance. The ordinance was drafted before the Constitution was written, under the old Articles of Confederation, and this gave Cutler the political leverage he needed. Using his influence, Cutler pressured lawmakers in the New England states to refuse to approve the ordinance unless it contained some recognition of religion.

Congress, eager to get the Ohio project moving, acquiesced. Two days before the ordinance was approved, the following sentence was added to Article III: "Institutions for the promotion of religion and morality, schools and the means of education shall forever be encouraged." In the final version, this was changed to the language that was finally approved: "Religion, morality, and knowledge being necessary to good government and the happiness of mankind, schools and the means of education shall forever be encouraged."

Thus, as Allison notes, "[T]he Ohio Company Associates were unable to get everything they wanted. While they were successful in getting Congress to agree that religion and morality were necessary to good government, the language of the ordinance did not explicitly authorize support for religious institutions or religious instruction in the schools." In fact, Allison points out, an effort to add direct government support for religion to the ordinance was rejected by Congress.

Allison concludes, "[T]he first sentence of Article III would likely never have been written at all in the absence of the influence of the Ohio Company Associates. Further, the language of the Ordinance was watered down to obscure any direct support for religion. There is nothing in the history of the Ordinance, in other words, to suggest that the first sentence of Article III was either a well thought out policy, or a deliberate attempt by Congress to aid religion."

The ordinance, Allison points out, was rewritten by that last Continental Congress, meeting in New York, before the First Amendment was drafted in Philadelphia. Thus, the final version was not the handiwork of the framers of the Constitution. Some scholars, Allison notes, have questioned whether the Northwest Ordinance was ever constitutional. Indeed, in 1851 the Supreme Court declared in *Strader* v. *Graham* that the Northwest Ordinance was no longer in force, ruling that several of its sections were unconstitutional.

As the debate over the Northwest Ordinance shows, the need to keep church and state separate was still very much alive in the fledgling U.S. government. It didn't take long, however, for the importance of that principle to fade in the eyes of governmental leaders. As the 1800s progressed, the nation began to slowly drift from the principles laid down by Jefferson and Madison.

Nineteenth-Century Generic Protestantism

Despite the Constitution's pronouncement that church and state should be separate, the political and social reality of American life by the mid-nineteenth century is that the two institutions often worked hand-in-hand.

The United States of this period was an overwhelmingly Protestant country. More often than not, its laws in the nineteenth century reflected general Protestant religious doctrine. It should also be noted that most laws were local in origin and as such reflected regional religious attitudes and biases. Blasphemy was a crime in most parts of the country, Sunday laws were strictly enforced and public education reflected an overtly Protestant flavor.

Just as today, political leaders of the day talked a good line about American religious freedoms and the great measure of liberty offered to the country's citizens. But the unpleasant truth is that nineteenth-century America was a mild form of Protestant theocracy. In this period, Protestantism was America's *de facto* established religion.

This statement can even be qualified by adding "mainstream" before Protestant. The large Protestant groups—Methodists, Baptists, Presbyterians, Episcopalians, Congregationalists, and the like—held power and influenced government. Small Protestant groups that sprang up during the nineteenth century—Mormons, Seventh-day Adventists, and Christian Scientists—were branded as undesirable and written out of the power base. In many cases, they had to fight for their religious freedoms. Other non-Protestant minorities, such as Jews and Catholics, were tolerated only to the extent that they did not rock the boat. When members of these groups finally did begin to assert for their rights, violence often ensued, as the burning of a Boston convent in 1834 and Philadelphia's "Bible War" so sadly attest. (See chapter 5 for full discussion.)

The *de facto* Protestant establishment was made possible because most Americans were Protestant and because the federal courts rarely involved themselves in church-state matters. Therefore, there was little to stop lawmakers from passing and enforcing laws that had religious veneers. At this time, the First Amendment and the Bill of Rights were not seen as binding on the states. Although the Fourteenth Amendment was passed following the Civil War, it was not interpreted as applying the Bill of Rights to the states until well into the twentieth century.

To be more precise, it should be noted that this period of *de facto* establishment did not begin until the time of the Civil War. That bloody and emotionally wrenching conflict may have been the impetus for closer ties between church and state. Some ministers in the North were convinced that God had put the nation at war with itself as a form of punishment for excluding Him from the Constitution. They began pressing for legal changes to bring religion and government closer together.

In the early part of the nineteenth century, a general understanding remained that government should not promote religion. To be sure, this sentiment was more common among political leaders than the people. In 1825, Congress passed legislation requiring post offices to handle mail on Sundays. Many people protested, arguing that Sunday mail handling violated the Christian Sabbath.

Congress debated the matter on and off for a few years before deciding in 1829 to retain Sunday mailing handling. A Senate committee that dealt with post offices had examined the issue. Sen. Richard M. Johnson of Kentucky, reporting for the committee, made it clear that government had no business favoring Sunday as a state-mandated day of rest.

"It is not the legitimate province of the Legislature to determine what religion is true, or what is false," Johnson observed. "Our Government is a civil and not a religious institution. Our constitution recognizes in every person the right to choose his own religion, and to enjoy it freely, without molestation. Whatever may be the religious sentiments of citizens, and however variant, they are alike entitled to protection from the Government, so long as they do not invade the rights of others. . . . They [Sunday mail handling opponents] appear, in many instances, to lay it down as an axiom, that the practice is a violation of the law of God. Should Congress, in their legislative capacity, adopt the sentiment, it would establish the principle that the Legislature is a proper tribunal to determine what are the laws of God. It would involve a legislative decision in a religious controversy, and on a point in which good citizens may honestly differ in opinion, without disturbing the peace of society, or endangering its liberties. If this principle is introduced, it will be impossible to define its bounds. Among all the religious persecutions with which almost every page of modern history is stained, no victim ever suffered but for violation of what Government denominated the law of God. To prevent a similar train of evils in this country, the constitution has wisely withheld from our Government the power of defining the divine law."[5]

State Court Rulings

But within a few decades, sentiments like that were becoming less common among political leaders. What happened? Aside from the Civil War, it is important to remember that at this time in history, many church-state disputes were seen as state problems. Most church-state matters, then, were left chiefly to state legislators, and disputes, if they occurred at all, were resolved by state courts. Judges at this level were often appointed under political patronage systems or to fulfill campaign debts. In many cases, upholding the law was not their prime interest. Some seemed to make many of their decisions based on public opinion, not constitutional commands. As a result, several court decisions emerged from the states that today are seen as at odds with religious freedom and separation of church and state. The country began to stray from the Jeffersonian/Madisonian construct.

Religious Right activists often try to use these court rulings to "prove" that America is a "Christian nation." They do not point out that these rulings were aberrations that emerged during a period of intolerance and religious persecution. This era is something to be ashamed of; it is hardly an appropriate model to look toward for today's church-state relationship.

To be certain, many state courts in the nineteenth century did refer to the United States as a "Christian nation" or implied that Christianity should receive some type of special protection from the state. James Kent, a New York Supreme Court justice, declared in an 1811 blasphemy case, "[T]he people of this state, in common with the people of this country, profess the general principles of Christianity as the rule of their faith and practice; and to scandalize the author of these doctrines is not only in a religious point of view, extremely impious, but even in respect to the obligations due to society, is a gross violation of decency and good order."[6] (Kent later partially retracted these views.)

In 1822 the Pennsylvania Supreme Court, in another blasphemy case, wrote, "Christianity, general Christianity, is and always has been a part of the common law . . . not Christianity founded on any particular religious tenet; not Christianity with an established church, and tithes, and spiritual courts, but Christianity with liberty of conscience to all men."[7]

The fact that these statements occurred in the context of blasphemy trials indicates how quickly the church-state separation principle had deteriorated. Early American leaders were wary of blasphemy statutes. John Adams, our nation's second president, told Thomas Jefferson, "I think such laws a great embarrassment, great obstructions to the improvement of the human mind. . . . I wish they were repealed."[8]

Jefferson echoed those sentiments and insisted that the government refrain from setting itself up as a guardian of religious orthodoxy. As was noted in the last chapter, he once observed, "It does me no injury for my neighbor to say there are 20 gods or no god. It neither picks my pocket nor breaks my leg."[9]

Nevertheless, prosecutions for blasphemy were a serious problem in nineteenth-century America. In 1836 thc Massachusetts Supreme Court upheld the conviction of Abner Kneeland, a freethinker who had been found guilty of publishing articles that questioned the biblical account of Jesus' life. Kneeland served sixty days in jail. By law, he could have received a public whipping or been sent to the pillory.

Likewise, the New York and Pennsylvania cases mentioned earlier both resulted in convictions.

The *Holy Trinity* Case

The U.S. Supreme Court even fell victim to this "Christian nation" mentality from time to time. Religious Right activists frequently cite 1892's *Holy Trinity Church* v. *United States* decision as proof that the High Court considered the United States a "Christian nation." But as usual, they don't tell the whole story.

In the ruling, Justice David Brewer flatly declared "this is a Christian nation." To this day, historians debate what Brewer meant by the term. It is unclear whether he meant to say the country's laws should reflect Christianity or was simply acknowledging the fact that most Americans are Christians.

Most people who cite the *Holy Trinity* case do not know what is was really about. Attorney and researcher Susan Batte of the Separation of Church and State Homepage explains the facts behind the case in some detail on that Web site. I am indebted to her for this synopsis.

Holy Trinity was an immigration case. It concerned an act passed by Congress that was designed to limit legal immigration and place restrictions on the ability of American firms to hire laborers from overseas. Holy Trinity Church in New York, which had contracted with a minister in England to be its pastor, was accused of violating the law.

As Batte writes,

> At issue in the case was whether or not the church's action violated the Act which prohibited "any person, company, partnership, or corporation . . . to assist or encourage the importation or migration of any alien . . . under contract or agreement . . . to perform labor or service of any kind in the United States." The *holding* of *Holy Trinity* was based on an interpretation of the purpose of the Act. The Court concluded that the purpose of the Act was to prohibit the importation of foreign unskilled persons to perform manual labor and manual services. A Christian minister, the Court reasoned, is a "toiler of the brain," not a manual laborer; Holy Trinity Church, therefore, was found not to have violated the Act when it secured a contract for the holy man's employment.[10]

Batte then discusses the Court's rationale and how it reached the decision that only manual laborers were covered by the act. It is at this point in the decision that Brewer's dicta begins. He writes that "beyond all these matters no purpose of action against religion can be imputed to any legislation, state or national, because this is a religious people." Brewer then gives a summary of America's religious history and concludes, "These, and many other matters which might be noticed, add a volume of unofficial declarations to the mass of organic utterances that this is a Christian nation."

Batte goes on to write,

> Whether or not America was a Christian Nation was not even at issue in *Holy Trinity*. The actual dispute or controversy the Court had to decide had nothing at all to do with religion. The parties in *Holy Trinity* did not question whether the Immigration Act's purpose was "for or against religion" generally or specifically. So when Brewer begins his religious history lesson with, "no purpose of action against religion can be imputed to any legislation, state or national, because this is a religious people," he refers to no particular statute, no particular actor. He has moved outside the actual facts of this case and the statute at issue to address the vague application of general principles to law in general. His statements, therefore, create no rule of law, and provide no useful precedent for future legal disputes.

(Batte also analyzed another case sometimes cited by "Christian nation" advocates. In a 1931 decision, *U.S.* v. *Macintosh*, an ordained Baptist minister was denied naturalization because he was unwilling to take an oath swearing that he would bear arms in defense of the country unless he believed the war necessitating the defense to be morally justified. In the opinion, Justice George Sutherland wrote, "We are a Christian people, according to one another the equal right of religious freedom, and acknowledging with reverence the duty of obedience to the will of God." As Batte points out, this statement is again dicta. In any case, the central finding of *Macintosh* was overturned fifteen years later.)

Brewer may have believed that the United States was officially Christian, but even he failed to use the *Holy Trinity* case as precedent when given an opportunity. Five years after the *Trinity* ruling, a dispute arose concerning legalized prostitution in New Orleans. A Methodist church challenged a city ordinance allowing prostitution in one area of the city. The church argued that prostitution should be illegal everywhere in New Orleans, arguing that the activity was inconsistent with Christianity "which the Supreme Court of the United States says is the foundation of our government."

Writing for a unanimous court, Brewer completely ignored the church's argument and upheld the New Orleans policy.[11] Brewer's bypass in this case suggests that he did not mean to imply in *Holy Trinity* that the United States should enforce the dictates of Christianity by law. Had that been Brewer's intention, he surely would have upheld the Methodists' claim.

What did Brewer really believe? It is hard to say. In 1905 he published a short book titled *The United States a Christian Nation*. What Brewer has to say in this book is very interesting, and needless to say, rarely quoted by the Religious Right since it seems to be at odds with their view.

"But in what sense can [the United States] be called a Christian nation?" asked Brewer in the book. "Not in the sense that Christianity is the established religion or the people are compelled in any manner to support it. On the contrary, the Constitution specifically provides that 'Congress shall make no law respecting an establishment of religion or prohibiting the free exercise thereof.' Neither is it Christian in the sense that all its citizens are either in fact or in name Christians. On the contrary, all religions have free scope within its borders. Numbers of our people profess other religions, and many reject all."

Continued Brewer, "Nor is it Christian in the sense that a profession of Christianity is a condition of holding office or otherwise engaging in public service, or essential to recognition either politically or socially. In fact, the government as a legal organization is independent of all religions."[12]

The passage strongly suggests that Brewer simply meant that the United States is "Christian" in the sense that many of its people belong to

Christian denominations and many of the country's customs and traditions have roots in Christianity. Brewer expounds on this theme for the rest of his ninety-eight-page book, predicting that Christianity will one day unify the American masses and make the United States a leader in world affairs.

Whatever Brewer's views about the United States as a Christian nation, it is important to realize that the concept has never been embraced by the Supreme Court. The *Holy Trinity* ruling, for example, is something of a legal anomaly that has been cited favorably only once by the Supreme Court since it was handed down. Brewer is an obscure Supreme Court justice who has never been considered one of the giants of the Court. *Holy Trinity* is a largely forgotten ruling that has no bearing on the type of church-state relationship the framers intended for this nation. *Holy Trinity* and an entire string of bizarre nineteenth-century High Court rulings—that upheld segregation of the races, that decreed that women could be barred from practicing law, and that struck down laws designed to end the national scandal of child labor—cannot seriously be considered today as appropriate guidelines for American society. They are products of their time and reflect cultural biases of the era, not solid constitutional law. Most have been relegated to forgotten volumes of legal history—where they belong.

"Christian Nation" Amendments

Not satisfied with the *de facto* establishment of Christianity in the U.S. government, precursors to today's Religious Right organizations pushed incessantly during the nineteenth century for a constitutional amendment that would add some type of endorsement of Christianity to the Constitution.

The movement was spearheaded by the National Reform Association, a coalition formed in 1863 by representatives from eleven Protestant denominations. One of the group's stated goals was "to secure such an amendment to the Constitution of the United States as will declare the nation's allegiance to Jesus Christ and its acceptance of the moral laws of the Christian religion, and so indicate that this is a Christian nation."

In 1864 the group petitioned Congress to amend the preamble of the Constitution to read, "We, the people of the United States, humbly acknowledging Almighty God as the source of all authority and power in civil government, the Lord Jesus Christ as the Ruler among the nations,

His revealed will as the supreme law of the land, in order to constitute a Christian government, and in order to form a more perfect union, establish justice, insure domestic tranquility, provide for the common defense, promote the general welfare, and secure the inalienable rights and blessings of life, liberty, and the pursuit of happiness to ourselves, our posterity and all the people, do ordain and establish this Constitution of the United States of America."[13]

The amendment languished in Congress for years, occasionally being reintroduced. Finally in 1874 the House Judiciary Committee voted against its adoption. The committee said it took the action "in full realization of the dangers which the union between church and state had imposed upon so many nations of the Old World, with great unanimity that it was inexpedient to put anything into the Constitution or frame of government which might be construed to be a reference to any religious creed or doctrine."[14] The Christian nation amendment was introduced in Congress again in 1882, but this time it died in committee.

(Another "Christian America" amendment resurfaced nearly one hundred years later, when similar proposals were introduced in Congress in 1961, 1963, and 1965. The proposed addition to the Constitution would have had the United States "devoutly" recognize "the authority and law of Jesus Christ, savior and ruler of nations, through whom are bestowed the blessings of almighty God." One of the measure's sponsors was Illinois congressman John Anderson, who ran for president as an independent in 1980. During the '80 campaign, Anderson dismissed the effort as a foolish move from a young congressman, saying, "It was a dumb thing to do, and I should not have introduced it.")[15]

Alongside the activities of the National Reform Association, religiously conservative ministers attacked the Constitution from the pulpit, usually because it lacked reference to God. In 1845 the Rev. D. X. Junkin wrote, "It (the Constitution) is negatively atheistical, for no God is appealed to at all. In framing many of our public formularies, greater care seems to have been taken to adapt them to the prejudices of the INFIDEL FEW, than to the consciences of the Christian millions."[16]

Junkin's words merely echoed previous attacks on the Constitution that had been delivered from pulpits all over the country since the ratification of the document. In 1793 the Rev. John M. Mason of New York called the lack of references to God in the Constitution "an omission which no pretext whatever can palliate." Much like today's Religious Right extremists, Mason was certain divine retribution would soon rain down upon the country and said God's vengeance would "overturn from its foundations the fabric we have been rearing, and crush us to atoms in the wreck."[17]

In 1811 the Rev. Samuel Austin told his congregation that the Constitution "is entirely disconnected from Christianity." Austin said this "one capital defect" would lead "inevitably to its destruction."[18]

These early attacks on the Constitution underscore how conservative religious forces have varied their rhetoric against the First Amendment over the years. In the nineteenth century, fundamentalist clerics acknowledged the secular nature of the Constitution and called for amending it to include references to God or Christianity. Most Religious Right activists today have abandoned this strategy and in the face of all available evidence insist that the Constitution was somehow written to afford special protection to Christianity.

(The most extreme elements of the Religious Right are more honest, however. Christian Reconstructionist Gary North [see chapter 9] has brazenly called the Constitution a "Secular Humanist" document and called for scrapping it outright in favor of a new governing document based explicitly on the Bible—or at least his interpretation of the Bible.)[19]

Censorship of the Arts

Christian amendment or not, many states continued passing and enforcing laws implicitly based on Protestant Christian principles. The arts were often targets of severe state regulation, and a type of religiously based censorship was widely imposed.

A good case study of the result of the *de facto* Protestant establishment on the arts in nineteenth-century America is found in Alan Nielsen's interesting book *The Great Victorian Sacrilege*. The volume tells the story of Salmi Morse, an eccentric Jewish entrepreneur who attempted to stage a theatrical version of the passion of Jesus Christ in the late 1800s in San Francisco and New York.

Outraged preachers and newspaper editors flamed public opinion against the play, arguing that it was sinful to depict the life of Christ on the stage. (Many ministers of that day frequently preached against all forms of theater.) In San Francisco, the city Board of Supervisors passed a hastily written ordinance to ban performances of the play.

Morse's attempt to fight the ordinance in court was unsuccessful. As

Nielsen relates, Judge Robert F. Morrison, upholding the ban on the play, ruled in effect that Morse's play offended Christianity, and that since Christianity required protection from the government, nothing could stop the state from squelching the performance.

Wrote Morrison, "The Board of Supervisors has seen fit to prohibit the exhibition in question because such exhibition is, in their opinion, against good morals, because it is calculated to bring religion, which is the foundation of all morality, into ridicule and contempt, and because the sacred mysteries of the passion and death of the Redeemer upon the cross are too solemn and sacred to be made the subject of a theatrical exhibition."[20]

The story was much the same in "enlightened" New York City. A young crusading newspaper editor, Harrison Grey Fiske, made a name for himself by repeatedly attacking the play and egging on the city's conservative religious establishment. Spurred by the hysteria, the city Board of Aldermen held a special session to discuss Morse's play. Although one alderman recommended caution, saying a law banning the play would "introduce a religious element into the Board, which all of us should deprecate," the board overwhelmingly favored action.[21]

Just the threat of legal action scared off the play's backers, and the performance was canceled. Three years later, when Morse finally succeeded in briefly staging the passion in New York City, a state senator hurriedly prepared "An Act to prevent any attempt to personate or represent Jesus Christ, the Saviour of Mankind, in any exhibition, show, play, dramatic or other theatrical performance." As the bill speeded toward passage in the New York legislature, municipal officials in New York City used procedural moves to shut the play down. Morse's passion play was finished in New York.

Compare the controversy over Morse's passion with the 1988 flap over the movie *The Last Temptation of Christ*. The Universal Studios film, which attempted to depict the human side of Jesus, was denounced by fundamentalists and labeled "blasphemous" from coast to coast. Boycotts against Universal were launched, but all legal efforts to stop the film from being showed failed outright.

In Escambia County, Florida, the county commissioners voted 4 to 1 to ban the film after a theater owner in Pensacola announced plans to show it. Almost immediately legal action was filed, and a federal judge declared the ordinance unconstitutional.

Another group of outraged fundamentalists filed a lawsuit in federal court arguing that the movie somehow infringed on their right to freely practice their religion. No federal court took the case seriously. The suit was rejected all the way up the federal court system and ultimately by the Supreme Court as well.

Unlike 1892, in 1988 there was a general understanding that the state should have no say in matters of religious orthodoxy. It simply is not the role of the government to determine what view of Jesus is correct and to censor any views that don't fit in the state's picture. It is difficult to imagine a more dangerous role for the government to take on.

Sunday-Closing Laws

Aside from blasphemy, a second issue that underscores the *de facto* Protestant establishment of the nineteenth century is the proliferation of mandatory Sunday closing laws, also known as "blue laws." These laws, which restricted commercial and sometimes leisure activity on Sundays, were always religiously motivated. The thinking of the Protestant majority was that Sunday, which most Protestants honor as the Sabbath, was in need of special protection by the state.

The laws were particularly vexing for Jews and Seventh-day Adventists, two groups that worship on Saturdays. For Jewish shopkeepers, the laws served as an economic penalty. Devout Jews felt compelled to close their shops on Saturday. On Sunday, a day when they might have made up business lost on Saturday, they were forbidden to open under state laws. (In some states, Seventh-day Adventists spent time in jail because they were caught working on Sundays.)

Eventually, this situation became the basis for a lawsuit challenging blue laws at the Supreme Court, a case that will be looked at more closely in chapter 8.

Cultural Factors

The *de facto* Protestant establishment was made possible in part because there was little organized opposition to it. America in the first half of the nineteenth century was much more religiously homogenous than it is today. Protestant denominations held sway throughout the country.

That began to change after the Civil War, as immigration increased from Ireland, Poland, and other countries with large Roman Catholic populations. Eventually, the nation's Catholic population grew to the extent that members of that faith could exercise political muscle. This led to a significant degree of Protestant-Catholic tension. (Some of this was played out over the role of religion in public schools. See chapter 5 for more information.)

Catholics grew politically powerful in some regions—notably New England and Mid-Atlantic states such as Pennsylvania and Maryland. As Catholics grew in number and became a political force, some Protestants and their clergy responded by trying to reassert the traditional Protestant character of the nation. They were not above using the legislative and legal systems to assert Protestant authority.

Many Protestants viewed Catholics with great suspicion—and the church's leaders in Rome may have given them some reason to. During much of this period, the Catholic Church was led by very conservative popes who did not help matters by issuing official decrees that alarmed U.S. Protestants.

In 1864, for example, Pope Pius IX issued the "Syllabus of Errors," a document that specifically repudiated the concepts of religious freedom and separation of church and state. The Syllabus was issued in reaction to calls that the Church liberalize some of its views, a drive championed by some European Catholics.

In the Syllabus, Pius listed various doctrinal, social, and government doctrines that were in conflict with Catholic theology. These included secular government, the idea that the Church should stay out of political affairs, secular public education, and the idea that governments should strive to protect religious liberty for all.

Section 55 of the Syllabus blatantly condemns the idea that "The Church should be separated from the State and the State from the Church."

In the nineteenth century, pope repeatedly attacked the idea that governments should protect religious liberty for all. To do so, these popes argued, was "heresy." It gave "error" and "false religions" equal weight with Catholicism. Pope Pius VII (1800–1823) termed such a policy "a disastrous and ever-to-be deplored heresy." Pope Gregory XVI (1831–1646) called the state's failure to stamp out "heresy" (other religions) "insanity," and Pius IX (1846–1878) called it "a monstrous error . . . most pernicious to the Catholic Church and to the salvation of souls."[22] (The church did not back away from these harsh views until well into the twentieth century.)

Many Protestants interpreted these types of statements as an attack on the values and features of American life. The United States was not a Catholic nation at the time, yet the Syllabus seemed to say that governments had a duty to submit to Rome. Inevitably, some Protestants responded to this pronouncement by insisting that the government take steps to protect Protestantism.

Returning to Separation

The *de facto* Protestant establishment was a throwback, but it did not last. Eventually, an attitude reflecting the proper relationship between church and state, which was pioneered in the post-Revolutionary period and lay neglected for nearly one hundred years, re-emerged. Following the Civil War, courts became increasingly reluctant to look for religious justification to uphold laws. Steven K. Green, former legal director for Americans United for Separation of Church and State who has researched the Christian nation concept extensively, reports that after 1860 courts began turning to secular justifications to uphold blasphemy statutes or school Bible reading laws. In other cases, judges rejected the laws outright.

By the mid-twentieth century, church-state cases became more common at the Supreme Court, especially after the High Court ruled in 1940 that the Fourteenth Amendment binds the Bill of Rights on the states. Eventually a line of decisions was spawned that laid down the church-state relationship still with us today.

Many of the High Court's rulings have focused on two controversial issues, both related to education—religion in public schools and public aid to sectarian schools—as well as issues over free exercise. Of course, the Supreme Court has examined many other church-state issues such as religious symbols on public property, mandatory Sunday closing laws, and taxation of churches.

The next section of the book will look at some of these controversies in depth.

Notes

1. Morton Borden, *Jews, Turks and Infidels* (Chapel Hill: University of North Carolina Press, 1984), pp. 76–79.

2. James Woodress, *A Yankee's Odyssey: The Life of Joel Barlow* (Philadelphia: J. B. Lippincott Company, 1958), p. 179.

3. A. B. C. Whipple, *To the Shores of Tripoli: The Birth of the U.S. Navy and Marines* (New York: William Morrow and Company, 1991), p. 26.

4. Gary DeMar, *America's Heritage* (Fort Lauderdale, Fla.: Coral Ridge Ministries, 2002), pp. 66–67.

5. Anson Stokes, *Church and State in the Unites States, Volume II* (New York: Harper & Brothers), pp. 15–16.

6. *People* v. *Ruggles*, 8 Johns. (N.Y.) 290 (1811).

7. *Updegraph* v. *Commonwealth*, 11 Serg. & Rawle, Pa. (1822).

8. Joseph L. Conn, "Blasphemy Laws in America: 'A Great Embarrassment,'" *Church & State* (April 1989): 9.

9. Saul K. Padover, *Thomas Jefferson on Democracy* (New York: Mentor, 1946), p. 109.

10. Susan Batte, "Is the United States a Christian Nation?" Separation of Church and State Homepage (http://members.tripod.com/~candst/index.html).

11. *L'Hote* v. *New Orleans*, 177 U.S. 587.

12. David J. Brewer, *The United States a Christian Nation* (Philadelphia: The John C. Winston Company, 1905), p. 12.

13. Leo Pfeffer, *Church, State, and Freedom* (Boston: Beacon Press, 1953), p. 209.

14. Ibid., p. 210.

15. "The Candidates, the Platforms, and Church-State Issues," *Church & State* (September 1980): 6–10.

16. Borden, *Jews, Turks and Infidels*, p. 60.

17. Ibid., p. 59.

18. Ibid.

19. Gary North, *Tools of Dominion* (Tyler, Tex.: Institute for Christian Economics, 1990), pp. 1190–1216.

20. Alan Nielsen, *The Great Victorian Sacrilege: Preachers, Politics and the Passion, 1879–1884* (Jefferson, N.C.: McFarland & Co., 1991), p. 114.

21. Ibid., p. 159.

22. Michael Davies, *The Second Vatican Council and Religious Liberty* (Long Prairie, Minn.: The Neumann Press, 1992), p. 62.

5

Religion in Public Schools: The Issue That Won't Go Away

Few issues in American life are as dogged by misinformation and muddled thinking than the role of religion in public education. If public opinion polls are any indication, this is one issue where confusion reigns in the minds of most of the American people. Plenty of disinformation circulates, and much of it is put forth deliberately by those who know better but have political or personal reasons for concealing the truth. This chapter will set the record straight and give a true accounting of the long controversy over religion in public schools.

Children *Can* Pray in School

One thing needs to be stated up front: Absolutely *nothing* in the Constitution, the laws of the United States, or any state, city, or municipality anywhere prohibits children from praying in public schools. The Constitution, in fact, explicitly *protects* the rights of children to pray in schools in a nondisruptive, noncoercive fashion. As long as these guidelines are followed, no student can lawfully be denied the right to say a prayer in school.

So why all the confusion? The problem stems from two widely misunderstood Supreme Court rulings of the 1960s—decisions in which the High Court ordered school officials and other government bureaucrats to stop writing prayers for children or forcing them to participate in Bible reading and other religious exercises in public schools. True, the Court ruled 6–1 in 1962 and 8–1 in 1963 to get the government out of the prayer and Bible reading business, but never once did the justices say that students can't pray on their own or read the Bible during free time if they choose. Today, many youngsters undoubtedly do so, but when it comes to an issue as emotional as school prayer, it seems no one ever thinks to ask the students what actually goes on in American public schools. Rather, too many people just take the old myth "Kids can't pray in school" and use it in efforts to raise money, win converts, or collect votes.

I will return to the school prayer decisions shortly, but before that it is necessary to briefly review the rise of American public education and the role religion has played in it. Examining this history is important because it shows the interfaith disharmony that has often developed over religion in public schools. Americans would do well to look at this past before adopting any proposal to reintroduce sectarian worship into our schools.

The Origins of Public Education

First, it is crucial to remember that the concept of free, universal, public education as we know it today is a relatively recent idea. While public education existed in some parts of colonial America, many parents did not take advantage of it. Early American society was heavily agrarian, and children often worked the fields alongside parents and other family members. Every available hand was needed to help out. If the children were educated at all, they either received schooling during the winter months or perhaps received some instruction at home.

The New England colonies made the strongest effort to establish public elementary schools, and several states in this region passed laws mandating schooling for children—usually just boys. Public education was scarcer in the middle colonies such as Pennsylvania and Maryland and virtually nonexistent in the South outside of the cities. (Ironically, however, one of the first "public" schools was established in Charleston, South Carolina, in 1720. Under the school's bylaws, the headmaster was required to be a member of the Church of England, and the staff had to teach religion according to the church's precepts.)

The gap between the rich and the poor was extremely wide during these years. Most people were poor or led modest lives tied to the land. But at the top was a small corps of wealthier landowners, merchants, and leaders. Naturally, the wealthy of colonial society provided for their children's education, often through private tutors. When sons got old enough for college, they were often shipped off to Europe to study or sent to one of the few colleges that were operating in America by this time. But this aristocracy was a minority, and, since there was no middle class to speak of in early America, most people fell into the great collective of the working masses. For these people, formal education was not considered necessary.

Although Massachusetts had created public schools as early as 1635, in most of the colonies education of the masses was not a priority. Following the Revolution, some enlightened leaders began proposing a system of free, universal education.

Thomas Jefferson, again thinking ahead of his time, proposed a bill in 1779 before the Virginia legislature that would have established a series of elementary schools to teach the basics—reading, writing, and arithmetic. Ever mindful of church-state separation, Jefferson even suggested that "no religious reading, instruction, or exercise shall be prescribed or practiced, inconsistent with the tenets of any religious sect or denomination."[1] Jefferson did not see public schools as the proper agent to form children's religious views.

Jefferson's bill did not pass, but he had set into motion a concept that would later come to fruition. Some years later, Virginia lawmakers took the main features of his idea and blended them into a public education plan.

As years passed, the idea of public education supported through taxation evolved in the United States and came to be accepted. The schools, however, were in no way religiously neutral. Schools tended to reflect a generic Protestant flavor, the dominant religion of the nation at the time. Lessons in otherwise secular subjects were often tied to the Bible. For instance, children might learn to read by using Bible stories.

Obviously, such a system could not long survive. As the population of the post-Revolutionary United States expanded, sections of the country became less and less religiously homogenous. Soon members of what had been minority religious groups began clamoring for their rights of representation in the schools, too. Sectarianism's days in the public school system were numbered.

Enter Horace Mann

In his book *Church, State and Freedom*, church-state scholar Leo Pfeffer recounts Horace Mann's struggle against sectarianism in public schools. Mann, a Massachusetts Unitarian who served in the state senate, helped engineer a new state law stating that no textbooks could be used in public schools that "are calculated to favor any religious sect or creed."

As secretary of the first Massachusetts Board of Education, Mann enforced the law vigorously. Religious leaders and many educators opposed to his reforms denounced Mann as an atheist, but Mann stuck to his plan. All efforts to have him removed from the post failed, and Mann remained in the slot until 1848, when he resigned to enter Congress.

Mann was not opposed to general programs of religious instruction in public schools; he simply opposed sectarianism. He did not oppose using the Bible in schools, for example, and he argued that it could be viewed as a nonsectarian work. Ironically, Mann today is attacked by some Religious Right advocates even though he favored using the Bible in public schools!

Although Mann was not a separationist as we understand the term today, he blazed an important trail by insisting that sectarianism in public schools was inappropriate. Clearly there remained problems with his approach. Many of today's religious leaders, for example, would dispute Mann's claim that the Bible is a nonsectarian work or that it can be used in a nonsectarian manner. Still, in spite of his faults, Mann was a forward-looking thinker who helped lay the groundwork that led to the development of a modern system of public education that is religiously neutral and open to all students.

Protestant-Catholic Strife over Schools

When Mann and other educators of the nineteenth century talked about the Bible or religion in public schools they almost always meant the Protestant version of the Scriptures. Roman Catholics were still a rarity in the country at this time. Catholics did not start arriving on American shores in significant numbers until the late 1830s and 1840s and with the great waves of immigration in the post–Civil War era and early twentieth century.

The small numbers of Catholics who did choose to live in America could find life difficult. Guaranteed the right to worship by the Constitution, they no longer had to worry about their priests being shackled and thrown into prison or their churches being raided by agents of the state. However, many overt forms of prejudice still existed, especially in employment. But the one area where Catholics encountered the greatest frustration was in the public school system.

The *de facto* Protestant establishment was not kind to Roman Catholics. Bible reading and prayers were common in some schools, but they were not Catholic prayers, and the version of the Bible read was the King James, not the Catholic Douay.

The situation was exacerbated, as the last chapter indicated, by ultraconservative popes in Rome who frequently issued official pronouncements attacking separation of church and state and the very idea that government had a duty to protect freedom of worship for everyone. Church leaders at this time believed that governments had a God-given right to suppress "heresy" and "error"—that is, non-Catholic religions. This attitude only furthered the divide between Catholics and Protestants in America.

To understand why Roman Catholics were so upset over religion in the public schools of the nineteenth century, it is necessary to know a little about the theological divide between Catholics and Protestants. In nineteenth-century public schools, the Bible was generally read by a teacher or administrator "without comment." This was seen as one way of getting around Mann's bar on sectarianism, but it overlooks the fact that reading Scriptures without comment is in itself a Protestant practice.

Generally speaking, many Protestants believe they are free to interpret the Bible as their individual consciences dictate. Catholics do not believe this to the same degree as Protestants do and recognize the authority of priests and other religious leaders in assisting church members in interpreting the Bible. Thus, reading the Bible "without comment" forced Catholic children in public schools to participate in a fundamentally Protestant practice.

Also keep in mind that the Lord's Prayer, seen as "nonsectarian" and agreeable to most Protestant groups of the time, is not the same as the similar Catholic prayer known as the "Our Father." Yet it was the former that was recited in public schools every day, and needless to say never uttered was a wholly Catholic prayer such as the "Hail Mary."

Catholic children were not simply required to sit through religious exercises alien to them; they were often forced to take an active role in them. Great insensitivity reigned in some parts of the country as the Protestant majority laid down the rules for religious exercises in public schools.

In those public schools where daily prayer and Bible reading were common, teachers and administrators brooked no dissent when it came to participation in daily religious exercises. In 1859, an eleven-year-old Catholic boy in Boston named Tom Wall was ordered by his teacher to read the Ten Commandments from the King James version of the Bible. Knowing that the Douay version lists the commandments in different order, the boy refused and was beaten until he relented. The teacher was taken to court, but a judge dismissed all charges.[2]

As the number of Catholics grew, slowly but steadily, priests and bishops came to believe that they could no longer keep silent about what they rightly perceived as a great violation of religious freedom. In 1840 a council of Roman Catholic bishops met in Baltimore and issued a statement urging Catholic parents to resist Protestant prayers and the practice of reading the Bible "without comment" in public schools.

Catholic Protests Escalate

Some Catholics living in the country's quickly growing urban areas decided to push for their rights. In New York City, where Catholic parents had been protesting mandatory religious practices for years, the superintendent of schools responded to Catholic concerns and ruled that prayer could not be required as part of the school day and that Catholic pupils had the right to opt out of school exercises when the Protestant King James Bible was used.

Things quickly got ugly. Even though the Catholic parents were not requesting that the religious practices be terminated—merely that their children not be required to sit through them—violence erupted. The local bishop posted armed guards in front of Catholic churches to ward off attacks by vandals and other troublemakers.

During a similar flap over religious exercises in Philadelphia's public schools in 1844, an even more violent riot broke out in that city that lasted three days. Violence erupted after the city's Board of Education voted to allow Catholic children to be excused from mandatory religious exercises or use their own version of the Bible. (Again, all the Catholics were asking for was that their beliefs be respected, not that the Protestant practices be stopped entirely.) Catholic churches and the homes of Catholic parents were burned; thirteen people were killed.[3]

In later years violence on a smaller scale broke out in other areas. In 1854 in Ellsworth, Maine, an outraged mob tarred and feathered a missionary priest, John Bapst, after he urged a parishioner to go to court and fight a school board regulation requiring children to read the King James Bible.[4]

Abuses such as these led to the creation of the Catholic school system in America. Fed up with the overt Protestant flavor of the public schools and desiring a system that would inculcate their own values, American Catholics created one.

Early conflicts over religion in public schools led to court battles in several states. In many cases, the actions were filed by disgruntled Catholic parents—sometimes backed by Jews—who desired a secular educational system.

(In light of this history, it is remarkable that today some conservative Catholics have joined the movement for a school prayer amendment. How easily some forget their own history!)

Early Court Rulings

In Cincinnati, Ohio, Catholic parents in 1869 challenged the common practice of Bible reading in public schools and urged the Board of Education to pass a resolution ending the religious activity. After heated debate, the measure passed 22–15. The action was promptly challenged in court by a group supporting state-sponsored prayer.

A local court agreed with the prayer boosters and asserted that the board had no authority to exclude the religious practices from school, going as far as to call Christianity a requirement of good government.

On appeal, the Ohio Supreme Court overturned the ruling and said the school board had the right to exclude the Bible if it wanted to. The court did not rule that prayers and Bible reading in public schools were unconstitutional—such rulings would come later—only that the public schools were not required to hold daily religious exercises.

In eloquent language the court observed, "United with government, religion never rises above the merest superstition; united with religion, government never rises above the merest despotism; and all history shows us that the more widely and completely they are separated, the better it is for both."[5]

Eventually state courts in some areas of the country began to rule that the practices of mandatory vocal prayer and Bible reading "without comment" were unconstitutional in public schools.

One of the earliest rulings was in Illinois, where in 1910 the state supreme court struck down a variety of religious exercises in public schools, including required prayer, Bible reading, and daily hymn singing that students were required to take part in. The case had been brought by a group of Catholic parents.

In a major step forward, the Illinois high court found the practices unconstitutional even though objecting students could in theory be excused. The court, ruling that the purpose of public schools is secular education, not the inculcation of religious doctrine, wrote, "The exclusion of a pupil from this part of the school exercises in which the rest of the school joins, separates him from his fellows, puts him in a class by himself, deprives him of his equality with the other pupils, subjects him to a religious stigma and places him at a disadvantage in the school, which was never contemplated. All this is because of his religious belief."[6]

Supreme courts in other states struck down similar practices during this period. Many were in the West and Midwest, where several state constitutions contain especially strong church-state separation provisions and require public schools to remain free from sectarian control. The Wisconsin Supreme Court declared required devotional practices unconstitutional in 1890. Nebraska followed suit in 1903. But several state courts—notably Iowa, Massachusetts, and Kentucky—examined the practices and found them constitutional. In the bulk of the states, however, the matter never came up in court.

Despite these early court actions, many Americans today continue to believe that state-sponsored prayer and Bible reading occurred all over the country until the Supreme Court rulings of 1962 and 1963. History proves this simply was not the case.

How Common Was Religion in Schools?

In 1960, Americans United for Separation of Church and State undertook a survey of Bible reading in public schools. (Keep in mind that this was two years before the first prayer case reached the U.S. Supreme Court.) The findings are quite illuminating. Only five states had laws on the books requiring daily Bible reading. Twenty-five states had laws allowing "optional" Bible reading. Courts in eleven states had declared the practice unconstitutional. The remaining states had no laws on the books one way or the other.[7] The practice, it seems, was not as common as is today believed, and one could argue that the trend was running in favor of a court-mandated phase-out, state by state.

Other evidence indicates that school-sponsored prayer and Bible reading simply weren't as common in public schools as the Religious Right today claims.

Boardman W. Kathan, a United Church of Christ minister, has researched this area extensively. In 1989 he reported his findings in the journal *Religious Education*. Kathan found that as public schools evolved in the post-Revolutionary period, there was a general attitude of indifference toward religion among the general public. While the Bible was often used in schools as a reader and speller, formal daily prayers and devotional readings were held sporadically, often only when a local clergyman visited the school.

Shortly before the Civil War, a great interest in educational reform arose in the United States. Alongside that came the Second Great Awakening, which created a renewed interest in religion among Americans. During the Awakening, which was a Protestant phenomenon, some people began to argue that public schools should inculcate Protestant values. As a result, formal rituals of prayer and Bible reading developed in some schools.

However, it was not until the twentieth century that such practices began to find their way into state law. Kathan reports that prior to 1900, only Massachusetts had a law on the books dealing with prayer and Bible reading in public schools. Between 1910 and 1930, seventeen states and the District of Columbia passed similar laws.[8] The movement to get these ordinances on the books was spearheaded by a powerful lobby of conservative church groups, led by the National Reform Association.

These laws were quickly challenged in court. Many of the early school prayer cases took place in state courts because church-state cases were a rarity in the federal courts prior to the 1940s. The Supreme Court had not yet ruled that the Fourteenth Amendment applies the Bill of Rights to the states. Hence, in matters of religious freedom the U.S. Supreme Court was quick to defer to lower state courts.

The Supreme Court Gets Involved

By the 1960s that had changed. A number of other factors in American society had also changed. For one thing, religious minorities were growing in numbers and becoming more confident of their rights in society. The burgeoning black civil rights movement undoubtedly inspired religious minorities, who came to believe that they too should enjoy the full fruits of American liberty—including religious freedom.

Jews, atheists, Catholics, minority Protestants, and others who felt disenfranchised because of the religious flavor of the public schools began looking to the federal courts for relief. In doing so, they initiated a series of landmark court rulings that increased religious freedom for all Americans but that remain controversial and poorly understood until this day.

The first school prayer case was decided by the U.S. Supreme Court in 1962. The Religious Right would have Americans believe that the justices suddenly decided the time was right to begin an assault on religion in public schools. However, the High Court had heard disputes over religion in public schools prior to 1962. These disputes were probably the result of greater access to the federal courts that Americans received after the High Court announced its incorporation doctrine in 1940.

In 1948, the Supreme Court struck down voluntary religious instruction programs run by outside groups on site at public schools. In *McCollum* v. *Board of Education*, the Court ruled that public schools had no business helping religious groups evangelize youngsters.

Wrote Justice Hugo Black, "Here not only are the State's tax-supported public school buildings used for the dissemination of religious doctrines. The State also affords sectarian groups an invaluable aid in that it helps provide pupils for their religious classes through the use of the State's compulsory public school machinery. This is not separation of Church and State."[9]

Four years later, in *Zorach* v. *Clauson*, the Court upheld such plans during the school day as long as they occur off school property. These classes, known as "released-time" programs, still take place in some public school districts.

The famous 1962 case, *Engel* v. *Vitale*, was something different: a direct challenge in the nation's highest court to a school-sponsored program of prayer. The facts of the case were not in dispute. The prayer was clearly state supported. Indeed, the challenge revolved around a prayer written by school bureaucrats. The New York Board of Regents composed what they believed was a "nonsectarian" prayer and urged local school district officials to tell teachers to lead students in the prayer at the start of each day. The Regents believed the prayer would ward off the evils of juvenile delinquency and Communism.

About 10 percent of the school districts in New York elected to use the prayer, one of them being the Herricks School District of New Hyde Park on Long Island.

A group of New Hyde Park parents quickly challenged the prayer practice. Although the parents lost at the first court level, when the dispute reached the Supreme Court the decision wasn't even close. The justices struck down the official state prayer by a 6–1 vote. (One justice did not participate, and there was a vacancy on the Court.)

The Court majority ruled that the prayer program had the effect of unconstitutionally involving the government in religious matters. Observed the justices, "It is no part of the business of government to compose official prayers for any group of the American people to recite as a part of a religious program carried on by government."[10]

Reaction was swift. Some members of Congress, ever eager to exploit complex, emotion-laden issues for personal gain, denounced the decision. Sen. Robert C. Byrd, a West Virginia Democrat, remarked, "Can it be that we, too, are ready to embrace the foul concept of atheism? Somebody is tampering with America's soul. I leave it to you who that somebody is."[11]

Byrd's comment was the first of many attempting to link application of church-state separation by the courts to Soviet hostility toward religion. Since then, the argument has been repeated time and time again by those who oppose the separation principle. Some have gone as far as to suggest that the Soviets invented church-state separation. Statements like this unveil an abysmal ignorance of U.S. history. Jefferson coined the wall metaphor in 1802, a full *115* years before the Communist state arose in Russia in 1917.

Far from being an expression of Communism, the Court's ruling in *Engel* increased religious freedom in America. For the first time parents had complete control over what prayers their children would say and what religious texts they would be exposed to. It is difficult to understand how anyone could oppose a court ruling that allows parents to decide what religious exercises their own children take part in.

In a press statement issued shortly after the ruling, Americans United for Separation of Church and State pointed out that the *Engel* decision increased religious freedom. "The Court's decision is a blow to the totalitarian concept of government," observed the statement. "There are those among us who want government to take over everything. Now this thinking invades the most intimate and personal realm known to man—that of religious experience."

Continued the statement, "Public school children in New York State have been, in effect, required by law to pray and have been regimented in their prayers. To establish such a religious exercise upon these citizens is an unconstitutional use of governmental authority. . . . The decisive point of difference between a free government and a Communist or Fascist government is this—that the free government does not try to run everything. Certain matters are deliberately left to the personal conscience and decision of the people themselves. Religion is eminently one of these matters and the Supreme Court has now enabled us to keep it so."[12]

Religious Right propagandist David Barton claims in his books and videotapes that the Supreme Court failed to base the *Engel* decision on history or prior church-state precedents.[13] Barton has apparently not taken the time to actually read the decision he so roundly criticizes. In it, Justice Hugo Black reviews church-state relations in the colonial period in making the case against government involvement in religion. In his concurring opinion, Justice William Douglas cited several previous church-state cases.

Madalyn Murray O'Hair

At this point, the reader might be wondering, "What about Madalyn Murray O'Hair? Wasn't she involved in all of this?" O'Hair's role in the prayer cases constitutes one of the great myths of American church-state relations.

Briefly, the myth goes something like this: Until 1962, prayers occurred in every public school in America. Madalyn Murray O'Hair, an atheist, filed a lawsuit and had them all removed. Millions of people in fundamentalist churches all over America believe this story. There is only one problem with this scenario: It isn't true.

As history indicates, several states had already removed school-sponsored devotional exercises, some as early as 1890, long before O'Hair arrived on the scene. Secondly, O'Hair's case was only one of three cases heard by the Supreme Court in 1962 and 1963 concerning school prayer.

O'Hair, who in the 1960s was a resident of Maryland, filed her case to block the mandatory recitation of the Lord's Prayer in Baltimore public schools at the start of the school day. At the same time, Pennsylvania resident Ed Schempp was pursuing litigation to stop mandatory devotional Bible reading in Philadelphia-area public schools on behalf of his son, Ellery, a student at Abington Senior High School.

The Schempps won the case at the federal appeals court level, and Pennsylvania lawmakers responded by changing the law to allow students to opt out of the religious exercises with parental permission. The Schempps said the new scheme still unconstitutionally promoted Christianity at state expense and returned to court. The appeals court agreed, but the school district appealed. The Supreme Court agreed to settle the controversy.

The Supreme Court consolidated the Schempps' case with Murray O'Hair's case, *Murray* v. *Curlett*, under the name *Abington Township School District* v. *Schempp*. In an 8–1 ruling released on June 17, 1963, the Court struck down both exercises.

O'Hair, who died in 1995, for many years proclaimed herself as the woman who "got prayer kicked out of schools" and used her notoriety to establish a nationwide atheist network, but her claims were exaggerated. Make no mistake, O'Hair was vilified for bringing the case, and her unpopular stand required considerable personal courage on her part. But the legal effort removing government-sponsored prayers and other religious exercises in public schools involved lots of other people who should not be overlooked. No one person can take the credit.

Like the *Engel* ruling before it, nothing in the *Schempp* decision in any way infringes on the right of students to voluntarily read the Bible or pray during free time. The justices also went out of their way to stress that the decision should not be construed as hostile to religion or to imply that secular programs of education involving the Bible are not legal.

Observed Justice Tom Clark, "[I]t might well be said that one's education is not complete without a study of comparative religion or the history of religion and its relationship to the advancement of civilization. It may certainly be said that the Bible is worthy of study for its literary and historic qualities. Nothing we have said here indicates that such study of the Bible or of religion, when presented objectively as part of a secular program of education, may not be effected consistently with the First Amendment."

Clark also asserted, "The place of religion in our society is an exalted one, achieved through a long tradition of reliance on the home, the church and the inviolable citadel of the individual heart and mind. We have come to recognize through bitter experience that it is not within the power of government to invade that citadel, whether its purpose or effect be to aid or oppose, to advance or retard. In the relationship between man and religion, the State is firmly committed to a position of neutrality."[14]

Congress Speaks Up

Despite language like that, the *Schempp* ruling, like *Engel* before it, sparked a massive outpouring of outrage. Newspaper editorials denounced the ruling, and politicians across the country took up the cause of "restoring" prayer to public schools.

Nowhere was this battle more pitched than in Congress, where numerous measures were introduced to amend the Constitution to allow for state-mandated prayer programs.

About a month after the *Schempp* ruling was handed down, Rep. Frank Becker, a New York Republican, introduced a school prayer amendment. Although at least sixty other similar proposals had been introduced, Becker's was the first to see movement in the House. During the spring of 1964, hearings were held on the Becker amendment. They lasted seven weeks. Despite rabble-rousing from conservative religious leaders and a mail campaign aimed at members of Congress, Becker was unable to obtain the 210 congressional votes he needed to get the amendment out of the House Judiciary Committee.

Members of the Senate also tried to pass a school prayer amendment. Unlike its companion in the House, the measure, sponsored by Sen. Everett Dirkson of Illinois, was able to get out of the Senate Judiciary Committee but failed to garner the two-thirds majority it needed to pass the full Senate. (The measure did receive a simple majority of 49–37.)

The battle over school prayer split the nation's two major political parties. The Republicans were quick to endorse the Becker amendment, and the Republican National Convention went on record supporting a school prayer amendment in the party platform (a position that remains today). The Republicans also tried unsuccessfully to use the issue against the Democrats during the 1964 presidential campaign. This issue still splits the two parties today and usually flares up at least once during presidential elections.

Although school prayer amendments continued to be introduced every year in Congress, the routine quickly became *pro forma*, and most were assigned to languish in congressional subcommittees, never to emerge again. There have, however, been exceptions.

Reagan's "Voluntary Prayers"

In the mid-1980s, the school prayer issue again achieved prominence in Congress and became a matter of public debate. Ronald Reagan, who was elected president in 1980, campaigned on a platform calling for "traditional values" and promised, if elected, to "return" prayer to schools.

Reagan talked incessantly about the need for "voluntary" prayer in schools, but since truly voluntary religious exercises have always been legal in public schools, observers on the church-state scene speculated that Reagan and his supporters must have wanted something more. Sure enough, when the Reagan school prayer amendment was introduced in 1982, a White House briefing paper submitted with it bluntly stated, "[S]tates and communities would be free to select prayers of their own choosing. They could choose prayers that have already been written, or they could compose their own prayers. *If groups of people are to be permitted prayer, someone must have the power to determine the content of such prayers*"[15] (emphasis mine).

There were many parallels between the scene in 1982 and the unsuccessful effort nearly twenty years earlier to pass the Becker and Dirksen amendments. Celebrities holding conservative views but with no background in education, religion, or child psychology were brought in to testify on behalf of the amendment. Politicians again attempted to use school prayer against opponents. But in the end, the outcome was the same. The Senate mustered a simple majority in favor of the amendment by a vote of 55–43, but the vote was eleven short of the required two-thirds majority.

Two years later Reagan and his backers took advantage of another widely misunderstood Supreme Court ruling to fan the flames of hysteria and again promote a school prayer amendment. The High Court ruled 5–4 that year in the case *Wallace* v. *Jaffree* that an Alabama law mandating that public schools set aside a moment of silence for prayer was unconstitutional. The High Court ruled that states have no business designating prayer time for anyone. Once again, a decision that actually increased religious freedom was poorly reported in the media and widely denounced by politicians and antiseparationist religious leaders.

Since the unsuccessful attempts of the mid-1980s, efforts to pass a school prayer amendment have continued, but few amendments are taken seriously. In January 1992, North Carolina senator Jesse Helms, a Republican and frequent ally of the Religious Right, attempted to attach a "sense of the Senate" resolution favoring school prayer to an education bill. The Helms gambit was defeated by a 55–38 vote.

The House of Representatives voted on a school prayer amendment in 1998. Following the Republican takeover of Congress in 1994, House Speaker Newt Gingrich began promising a vote on school prayer. Gingrich asked Rep. Ernest Istook (R-Okla.) to oversee the project. Istook in turn asked several Religious Right groups for help.

Religious Right attorneys argued among themselves for a few years and then finally emerged with a monstrosity that Istook called the "Religious Freedom Amendment." Istook's amendment did more than promote official prayer in public schools. It also required the government to give financial support to religious schools and permitted government to display religious symbols and endorse religion in other ways. Critics said it was designed to remove church-state separation from the First Amendment.

The Istook amendment received a vote in the House of Representatives on June 4, 1998. It received a simple majority but fell far short of the two-thirds needed to pass a constitutional amendment. The vote was 224–203, sixty-four votes shy of passage.

Related Issues

Outside of prayer, the Supreme Court has issued other rulings dealing with religion in public schools. In 1990, the Court ruled 8–1 that the Equal Access Act, legislation designed to allow voluntary student prayer and Bible clubs to meet at public schools during noninstructional time under certain conditions, was constitutional.[16]

Equal Access religion clubs, formed and run by students, now meet in public secondary schools all over the nation. These clubs, which meet during "noninstructional time" (usually before or after school) are completely voluntary, and no student is required or expected to attend. Equal treatment is the key. If a public school allows a Christian club to meet, it must also permit a Muslim club, a Jewish club, an atheist club, or any other type of club students might choose to start. (Schools are not required to allow clubs that would be disruptive, such as a neo-Nazi club, but other than that they are expected to allow freedom of expression.) Equal Access clubs are a good example of how religion can take place in public schools without anyone's rights being violated.

In 1987, the Court struck down a Louisiana law that required public schools to teach "creation science" alongside evolution. The justices, in a 7–2 ruling, held that creationism is a religious doctrine, not a science.[17]

(The Court had earlier ruled in 1968 that Arkansas lawmakers could not ban the teaching of evolution in public schools.)

The Louisiana case produced some good language from the High Court on how the application of separation of church and state to public education protects family rights. Observed Justice William Brennan, "Families entrust public schools with the education of their children, but condition their trust on the understanding that the classroom will not purposely be used to advance religious views that may conflict with the private beliefs of the student and his or her family."

Despite this clear defeat, the well organized and well funded creationist lobby has not given up. They have repackaged their idea and are again trying to sell it to public schools under the name of "intelligent design." Alongside this tactic, creationists are working feverishly to water down instruction about evolution in schools. Unfortunately, they have managed to frighten and confuse so many educators and administrators that some public schools now avoid the subject of evolution all together, seeking to dodge controversy. Creationists are responsible for the dumbing down of an entire generation of American students and have done great damage to science education in this country.

The Religious Right Gets Excited

By 1992, a series of changes had occurred on the Supreme Court. Several members of the Court's staunchly separationist wing, including Justice Thurgood Marshall and Justice Brennan, perhaps the strongest defender of church-state separation on the High Court since Hugo Black, had retired. They were replaced by justices appointed by Presidents Ronald Reagan and George Bush.

Religious Right groups began predicting that a revolution on church-state issues would occur. The new Reagan/Bush Court, they said, would soon modify or overturn outright the Court's school prayer rulings and other matters of church-state jurisprudence.

Early on it appeared that the antiseparationists were correct. One of the new conservatives, Justice Anthony M. Kennedy, was quick to criticize the High Court's church-state cases. In a 1989 controversy dealing with the display of religious symbols on public property, Kennedy bluntly stated, "Substantial revision of our Establishment Clause doctrine may be in order."[18]

The High Court did not have to wait long for the perfect test case to begin its "substantial revision." A controversy soon bubbled up from the federal courts testing the constitutionality of prayers before public school graduation ceremonies. The dispute was brought by a Providence, Rhode Island, family, the Weismans, who protested the inclusion of prayers during the graduation of daughter Deborah from middle school in 1989.

Although pundits on both sides of the church-state controversy predicted at the very least a chipping away at Jefferson's wall, the resulting decision was quite a surprise. On June 24, 1992, the Court issued a 5–4 ruling striking down the state-backed prayers and upholding separation of church and state. In an ironic twist, the majority opinion was written by Justice Kennedy in language that harkened back to the strict separationism of the 1960s and '70s!

"It is beyond dispute that, at a minimum, the Constitution guarantees that government may not coerce anyone to support or participate in religion or its exercise, or otherwise act in a way which 'establishes a [state] religious faith, or tends to do so,'" wrote Kennedy in the *Lee* v. *Weisman* ruling. "The State's involvement in the school prayers challenged today violates these central principles."

Continued Kennedy, "The First Amendment's Religion Clauses mean that religious beliefs and religious expressions are too precious to be either proscribed or prescribed by the State."[19]

Kennedy was joined by Reagan appointee Sandra Day O'Connor and David J. Souter, a Bush appointee. The three, joined by remaining separationists John Paul Stevens and Harry Blackmun, declared that the school prayer decisions of the 1960s are still good law and said government has no right to coerce anyone to participate in religious exercises. The fact that three Reagan-Bush appointees joined the majority should lay to rest for good the notion that opposing school prayer is strictly a "liberal" position. Support for our nation's commitment to religious freedom cuts across ideological lines. (Although it should be noted that Kennedy is no fan of church-state separation when it comes to funding issues. He has repeatedly voted in favor of government financial support for religious schools.)

Separationists may have breathed a collective sigh of relief, but there was a feeling that they had merely dodged the bullet. The ruling, after all, was 5–4. The school prayer decisions of the 1960s saw only one dissenter. In the wake of the *Weisman* ruling, separationists were acutely aware of how precarious their position at the Supreme Court had become. One new appointee, they realized, could change the balance.

President Bill Clinton, who took office in January 1993, named two justices to the High Court—Ruth Bader Ginsburg and Stephen Breyer—thus putting a halt to the Religious Right's effort to overturn the school prayer decisions. In 2000, the High Court ruled 6–3 that public schools could not sponsor prayers before football games. Like the earlier school prayer rulings, the decision in *Santa Fe Independent School District* v. *Doe* was attacked by the Religious Right.

President George W. Bush, elected in 2000, has vowed to nominate justices who will lower the church-state wall. Thus, the school prayer issue could resurface at the High Court.

What the Polls Really Say

Santa Fe v. *Doe* and *Lee* v. *Weisman*, like the other High Court prayer rulings, were widely misunderstood by the American people and, in some cases, deliberately distorted by those with political agendas. Once again, untrue charges that God had been "expelled from the classroom" were levied. In the *Weisman* case, critics glossed over Kennedy's eloquent language explaining how the ruling protects religious belief and unfairly accused the Court majority of "hostility toward religion."

As we have seen, there are a number of misconceptions in the public mind about the scope and effect of the Supreme Court's school prayer rulings. This is reflected in public opinion polls, which commonly show numbers as high as 80 percent in favor of "school prayer."

Many of these polls have been flawed in the manner in which they phrased the crucial question. Most people, when asked, will say they are in favor of "prayer in schools" because such a phrasing implies a voluntary system of prayer (and because many people persist in believing that even voluntary prayer in schools is illegal). Support drops, however, when respondents are asked if they favor required prayer or state-mandated devotional activities.

In 1989 *Parents* magazine performed a valuable public service by commissioning a public opinion poll that asked the proper question. Respondents were asked to choose from three possible prayer scenarios that could occur in public schools.

In the survey, 68 percent agreed with the statement, "Although no prayer should be said aloud, there should be a minute of silence each day so that students could pray silently, meditate, or do nothing if they prefer." Only *17 percent* agreed with the statement, "A prayer should be said aloud once a day in public schools, and students should be required to participate." (Twelve percent favored the statement, "There should be no prayers or moments of silence in public schools.")[20]

I have tried to find a more recent poll that asks about school prayer in this way or in a similar matter but have not been able to locate one. Most continue asking the question in a vague manner. Even though the *Parents* poll is more than ten years old, I believe its findings would still hold if it were repeated today. Most Americans really don't favor forcing prayer on children in public schools. Most people—nearly 70 percent—simply want time to be available for students to say prayers in public schools. Ironically, more than half of the states already have such a moment of silence. If these moments are neutral—that is, not specifically designed to promote prayer—they are perfectly constitutional. Several have been upheld by the federal courts.

Thus, it seems, a countless amount of time and energy has been spent debating an issue that has already been resolved in most states and could be resolved tomorrow in the others through a simple, neutral moment of silence law.

The fact is, most Americans do not want to go back to 1962 when school bureaucrats wrote prayers and coerced children to recite them. Most Americans want to choose for themselves what prayers their children are exposed to or are asked to say. For all their posturing, school prayer boosters have never once explained why it is desirable to have children participate in religious devotions composed by government officials. The prayer boosters' attempts to portray such policies as protective of freedom of religion stand logic and common sense on their heads.

Make no mistake, prior to 1963, a great deal of religious intolerance and forced participation in religion existed in many American public schools. In Pennsylvania, the Bible reading exercise was *mandatory*. The Religious Right often pines for the days when "voluntary prayer and Bible reading" were permitted in schools. Ironically, that's exactly the situation we have today in schools.

There was nothing "voluntary" about the state-mandated exercises in Pennsylvania and other states. In many cases, students could not be excused even if their parents objected. Seeking to avoid litigation, officials in Pennsylvania agreed to change the law to allow for "voluntary" participation in the religious exercises, but it was simply too little too late. Insensitivity and intolerance still reigned. In fact, Ellery Schempp, the brave sixteen-year-old who sparked the case, got things rolling one day by bringing a Koran to class and offering to read it to his classmates during the morning devotionals. He was promptly sent to the principal's office. Today our public schools are free from such intolerance. We should be proud of this fact and resist vigorously any attempt to drag us back to the days of prayer mandated by the government.

Disinformation from the Religious Right

The issue of school prayer is really a nonissue. It is one of the greatest frauds ever perpetrated on the American people. Millions of Americans continue to believe that a schoolchild cannot, at any point in the day, bow his or her head in prayer. They are wrong.

Why does this massive fraud continue to circulate? The primary reason is the Religious Right. The various groups that make up this conglomeration have never been much concerned with accuracy. They have attempted to turn the American people against public education and church-state separation in general. Making people believe the public schools are hostile to any religious expression is one of their key strategies. Sadly, it has been a very successful one.

A good example of this is the often-repeated story about the tiny first-grader who is seized by the brutish public school principal for daring to say a prayer over her lunch. As the story goes, the child is hauled off to the office and berated with the law on school prayer and told to never do "that" again.

But when asked, Religious Right activists are unable to name where this event happened, when it occurred, or who was involved. Not only that, but the basic details often vary from telling to telling. The child's sex, age, and grade level vary wildly.

Televangelist Pat Robertson told a variant of this tall tale on his *700 Club* on December 4, 1992. This time the incident supposedly took place at a public elementary school in Kingsville, Texas, and involved a five-year-old named Shannon. Local reporters decided to look into the matter and called officials at the school.

The school officials' conclusion? "As far as we know, it did not occur," the school's public information director told the press.[21] The school official, Tony Morales, said administrators had "checked and checked and cannot find out anything. We called the principals at all three of our kindergarten campuses, and they are unaware of any incident resembling what was said by Pat Robertson. They do not even know of a girl named Shannon."

Scott Stanford, editor of the *Kingsville Record*, called Robertson's offices in Virginia Beach, Virginia, in an attempt to track down the source of the story. He was told that Robertson had received the details from the American Center for Law and Justice (ACLJ), Robertson's own legal group. But when Stanford called the ACLJ, a staffer told him, "What was said on the air today was the first I had heard of it." Stanford published his findings, hoping that if the incident did occur those involved would come forward. No one ever did.

Concluded Morales, "We keep getting the runaround from the Robertson people. I called them. The school board president called them. But we still don't know any more than we did."

That's no surprise. By now it is clear that this story is an urban myth invented out of whole cloth by the Religious Right. It may circulate incessantly in Religious Right circles, but it is not true; it never happened. When these stories are examined under the harsh light of scrutiny, it always turns out that certain key factors have been conveniently omitted by the Religious Right.

In 1991, for example, a Virginia-based Religious Right legal group called the Rutherford Institute charged that an eleven-year-old fifth grader in Norman, Oklahoma, had been ordered by school officials to stop reading her Bible on the playground during recess and holding informal Bible studies with other students.

The institute trumpeted the case as a gross violation of religious liberty, and on the surface it appeared they were correct. But the entire story crumbled after a television reporter from ABC News went to Norman to investigate. Correspondent Walter C. Rodgers quickly learned that the child, Monette Rethford, had been disturbing other children with aggressive proselytism in the playground and that she had frightened her fellow schoolmates with vivid stories of hell.[22] (The child had obviously been prodded to do these things by her parents; her father told Rodgers that "satanism, humanism, and atheism" are being taught in public schools.) Concerned parents had simply asked the school to keep the child from disrupting recess, and the school complied. Rutherford filed legal action, but the case was settled out of court.

Many of the cases the Religious Right points to as violations of religious liberty are in fact tensions wrought by hyperaggressive students (usually spurred by adults outside the school) who quickly turn off their classmates with loud, continuous preaching. In tiny Blue River, Oregon, the local public high school in 1991–1992 was torn apart by interfaith tensions when student members of a local Baptist church decided to "save" their fellow classmates. Shouting matches erupted between Baptist students and others who did not believe they needed to be saved. Soon this entire rural community was fighting over the incident, and two school board members were ousted during local elections for failing to take the problems seriously.[23]

Many parents send their children to public schools with the understanding that the children will not be pressured there to change their religion. When religious wars do break out, the confrontations can be ugly, and attempts by school officials to keep the peace are often interpreted as attacks on religion. One false step by a principal or superintendent can lead to disaster.

In Metropolis, Illinois, for example, a 1991 squabble over prayers around the a public school's flagpole quickly got out of hand and resulted in yet another Religious Right attempt to claim a violation of religious freedom. The incident started when a group of adults affiliated with a local church arrived on school grounds to pray with students around the pole. School officials had earlier told the adults that, as a matter of school policy, outsiders are not permitted on school grounds during the day. The principal, alarmed over the collection of outsiders on school grounds, followed the superintendent's orders and called the police. Officers came and promptly removed the adults from the school's property. Pat Robertson later aired reports about this incident on *The 700 Club* but failed to point out that the adults were taken away for trespassing, not because they were praying. No students were arrested. Robertson's "reporters" later stuck a camera in the principal's face and demanded an apology. The principal, seeking to end the ugly incident and heal the community, complied.[24]

In 1998, Religious Right groups made a big fuss over an incident in New York City involving a teacher who was disciplined and later fired for praying with students to comfort them after the death of classmate by drowning. The Religious Right tried to portray the teacher, Mildred Rosario, as a victim of an overzealous application of separation of church and state. As it turned out, Rosario had engaged in Pentecostal practices in class, including laying hands on some of the students in a fifth-grade classroom. The activities had alarmed and even frightened some students, who complained to their parents.

Rosario was fired after she refused to say she would not pray with students in the future. It also came to light that officials with the school system were planning to fire her anyway, due to poor work performance and absenteeism. Rosario, backed by Religious Right legal groups, filed a lawsuit to get her job back. It was rejected by the courts.

The list goes on. In numerous cases, incidents described as great violations of religious liberty in public schools by the Religious Right simply fall apart when someone takes the time to make a few phone calls. Unfortunately, those calls are usually not made or if they are, they are not reported in the media. Thus, the claims of assorted far-right groups go unchallenged and enter the media or Religious Right rumor network as truth.

The tragedy of the school prayer issue is that it has unnecessarily divided the American people along theological lines. Denominations have been forced to take sides, and the debate has often been quite unpleasant. The Southern Baptist Convention, for example, switched positions on school prayer in the early 1980s, flip-flopping from opposition to a school prayer amendment to favoring one. The rift on that issue and numerous others has pitted Baptist against Baptist and wounded the denomination.

Likewise, religious minorities, understandably wary of state-supported religion in schools, have been attacked by unthinking clerics and others who characterize their opposition as some sort of antireligious plot. Jews have taken many unfair hits in the arena of public opinion simply because many Jewish leaders have insisted on the right of Jewish children to attend public schools without being subjected to Christian religious exercises. The Jews' objection arises not from any hostility toward Christianity but rather a perfectly understandable desire to maintain their own religious traditions. Surely Christians would demand the same rights were the situation reversed.

More Religious Right Distortions

A few final words must be said about religion in schools. The charge is often made that since "prayer was taken" out of schools, the quality of American education and American life in general has declined. The school prayer rulings have been blamed for everything from juvenile delinquency to the American military disaster in Vietnam.

When it comes to simplistic thinking, this argument is the granddaddy of them all. Still, despite its obvious flaws, it is sometimes taken seriously by Religious Right activists and others. "Christian nation" propagandist David Barton has written an entire book full of charts and graphs purporting to show America's decline since the 1962 *Engel* ruling.[25] In January 1992, Republican senator Jesse Helms of North Carolina used the charts on the floor of the Senate to argue for school prayer.

Because prayer has not been removed from school, the argument immediately fails. However, giving the argument the benefit of the doubt and going one or two steps further really unmasks how ridiculous it is.

The argument that if two events occur in sequence then the former must have caused the latter is a common fallacy of logic known as *post hoc ergo propter hoc* (Latin for "after this, therefore on account of this"). As a moment's thought will demonstrate, the mere fact that two events occur one after the other does not mean they are related. Such an argument is analogous to stating, "Ever since men went to the moon, the world has been getting warmer." Maybe, but you have to do more than just say it; you have to prove there is some type of connection between the two events, and you have to be able to show what that connection is and how it operates.

In the case of the alleged decline of American society, no link has ever been shown relating to the prayer rulings. In fact, the alleged "slip" was caused by wholly unrelated factors.

Barton and others, for example, are fond of claiming that SAT scores have declined since 1962. Under their reasoning, God is displeased with the prayer ruling and has retaliated by making students dumber. But a quick look at the facts unveils the real reason for SAT slippage: More students take the test today.

In the early 1960s, the SAT was taken almost exclusively by upper-class, well educated youngsters who went on to study at prestigious universities. Today the SAT is taken by just about everyone who wants to go to college. Since many more young people from a much wider variety of socio-economic backgrounds take the test today, it's only natural that the scores would drop. Sadly, the type of slipshod "reasoning" typical of Barton is what passes as scholarship according to the Religious Right.

American society is plagued today by a variety of problems. The public school system has not remained unaffected. These problems are caused by complex socio-economic factors and shifts in the way Americans live and work, not to mention the changing dynamic of the American family. Some may search for a simple cause for these disturbing changes, but it just doesn't exist. To blame all of today's problems—from AIDS to the divorce rate—on a 1962 Supreme Court ruling is simplistic thinking.

Besides, not all indices of quality of life have declined since 1962. Many have escalated. Life expectancy is up, and impressive medical advances have occurred. State-sponsored racial discrimination was common in the 1950s and early '60s. It is not tolerated today. Labor-reducing technologies are commonplace. Are these also a result of the 1962 ruling? Quite a powerful decision!

Opinion polls provide a final fatal blow to Barton's theory. Polls taken since 1962 have shown absolutely no reduction of interest in religion among American teenagers. If the school prayer rulings were as detrimental to religion as Barton and others in the Religious Right claim, it stands to reason that the religiosity of teenagers would have sharply dropped since those rulings were handed down.

In fact, just the opposite is true. Teenagers remain religious, as numerous public opinion polls taken recently have shown. The school prayer rulings have helped religion, not harmed it.

The Secular Humanism Canard

Religious Right activists also constantly charge that public schools promote "Secular Humanism," which the Religious Right defines as a "religion" that fosters atheism. Again, a quick look at the facts exposes this claim as nonsense.

There is no doubt that an organized Humanist community does exist in the United States. However, it is so small that "Humanist" does not even register as a category when pollsters ask Americans to describe their religious or philosophical beliefs. (In fact, 90 percent of all Americans say they are believers.) Given the decentralized nature of public education in America, there is no way that such a minuscule group of people could take over the public schools.

The fact is that polls have shown that the majority of people who teach and work in public schools and sit on school boards reflect the religious trends of America at large. That is, the overwhelming majority are Christians of one variety or another.

In 1986 the *American School Board Journal* published the results of a nationwide survey of school board members. The magazine had hoped to compile a profile of the "typical" school board member. Surveys were mailed to 4,441 school board members, and more than 1,400 responded—an excellent return rate that gave the survey an 95 percent accuracy rate.

What did they find? The typical school board member is a white married male between forty-one and fifty years of age. He has children in school, is a college graduate and works in a professional or managerial role and earns between $40,000 and $49,000 annually. Most significantly, he is a registered Republican who describes his views on education as "conservative."[26]

This is hardly the profile of the Secular Humanist that Religious Right groups would have us believe is running our public school system.

The Humanism myth got started because the Religious Right defines "Secular Humanism" as anything they don't like that goes on in the public schools. The situation was much the same in the 1950s, when the great bogeyman threatening our schools was Communism.

Ironically, lately the Religious Right has realized that the Secular Humanism canard has failed to catch on and has shifted its claim, now alleging that public schools are teaching witchcraft and/or "New Age" philosophies. This charge quickly crumbles too with a quick reality check. Polls have shown that the number of Americans following New Age teachings seriously as a religion is small. Similarly, the number of people of who follow Wicca, the modern name for witchcraft, is also small—it may run above 100,000 according to some polls, but in nation of 270 million people, that's not a significant number. It would stretch the bounds of credulity to assume that large numbers of public school teachers were Wiccans. And even if they were, so what? It does not follow that a Wiccan teacher would be bent on forcing his or her religion on to students. Wiccans, in fact, oppose coercion in matters of religion and do not favor using the mechanism of government to spread their views.

The Secular Humanism/witchcraft/New Age charges are untrue. While there certainly are people who follow these beliefs in the country (and they are not the horned demons the Religious Right would have us believe), most public school teachers, like the rest of the population, belong to mainstream faiths.

Education is one of the most demanding careers a person can pursue. The hours are long, the pay is often low, and the work is hard. Instead of being appreciated for their efforts, public school teachers are too often ridiculed, abused, or blamed for the failings of parents. The Religious Right, instead of applauding our teachers for doing their best under exacting circumstances and working with teachers to improve public schools constructively, repeatedly asserts that teachers are dupes for whatever antireligious idea comes along.

Despite the long history of conflict over religion in public schools in the United States and the especially nasty battles in the nineteenth century, many Religious Right activists continue to look to this period as a model for our schools to follow today. They are either ignorant of the history outlined here or are simply unwilling to extend a measure of toleration to those who do not believe exactly as they do.

In the early 1990s, Religious Right activists made a concerted effort to get elected to public school boards. Many succeeded—and then tried to remake public schools in a fundamentalist image. More often than not, these people were removed by the voters at the first opportunity.

"We want to have it like it was 100 years ago, when God, the Ten Commandments and prayer was the focus of the schools," Don Smith, who was elected to the La Mesa/Spring Valley, California, School Board told the *San Diego Tribune* in 1990.[27]

In Vista, California, school board member Deidre Holliday told the *Wall Street Journal* in 1992 that public school teachers should tell students about Christ and lead them in religious exercises. (The voters apparently disagreed. They voted for a recall election and removed Holliday and her Religious Right cronies from the board.)

Remarked Holliday, "It would be wonderful to see the scripture read in schools so that children learn the truth. This is our heritage. Anyone who comes into this country is welcome, but we shouldn't be diluted by others' beliefs."[28]

The Religious Right is correct about one thing: Many who work in public education are suspicious of their agenda as it relates to the schools. In light of the intolerance expressed by Smith and Holliday and in light of the crude attacks on public education that emanate constantly from Pat Robertson, Jerry Falwell, James Dobson, D. James Kennedy, Tim LaHaye, and their ilk, is it any wonder?

Notes

1. Leo Pfeffer, *Church, State and Freedom* (Boston: Beacon Press, 1953), p. 279.
2. Ibid., p. 376.
3. Ibid., p. 375.
4. Ibid., p. 376.

5. *Board of Education of Cincinnati* v. *Minor*, 23 Ohio St. 211 (1872).
6. *Ring* v. *Board of Education*, 245 Ill. 334 (1910).
7. "School Bible Reading Survey," *Church & State* (January 1960): 5.
8. Boardman W. Kathan, "Prayer and the Public Schools: The Issue in Historical Perspective and Implications for Religious Education Today," *Religious Education* 84, no. 2 (spring 1989): 232–48.
9. *McCollum* v. *Board of Education* 333 U.S. 203 (1948).
10. *Engel* v. *Vitale*, 370 U.S. 421 (1962).
11. Leo Pfeffer, *Church, State and Freedom* (Revised Edition) (Boston: Beacon Press, 1967), p. 466.
12. Protestants and Other Americans United for Separation of Church and State news release, undated.
13. David Barton, *The Myth of Separation* (Aledo, Tex.: WallBuilders Press, 1989), 163.
14. *Abington Township School District* v. *Schempp*, 374 U.S. 203 (1963).
15. Joseph L. Conn, "Reagan Backs Government Sponsored School Prayer," *Church & State* (June 1982): 3.
16. *Board of Education of the Westside Community Schools* v. *Mergens*, 110 S.Ct. 2356 (1990).
17. *Edwards* v. *Aguillard*, 482 U.S. 578 (1987).
18. *County of Allegheny* v. *ACLU*, 492 U.S. 573 (1989).
19. *Lee* v. *Weisman*, 112 S.Ct. 2649 (1992).
20. *Parents*, January 15, 1989.
21. Roddy Stinson, "Now This, Ladies and Gentlemen, Is Just Robertsonesque," *San Antonio Express-News*, December 17, 1992, p. 2A.
22. "Press Reports on 'Playground Bible Bust' Weren't Accurate, Says ABC Reporter," *Church & State* (June 1991): 18.
23. Rob Boston, "American Public Schools: Mission Field USA?" *Church & State* (January 1992): 8.
24. Ibid., p. 11.
25. David Barton, *America: To Pray or Not to Pray?* (Aledo, Tex.: WallBuilders Press, 1988).
26. "The Secular Humanist Witchhunt: Some Burning Evidence," *Church & State* (February 1987): 13.
27. Community Coalition Network press statement, San Diego, Calif., January 1992.
28. Sonia L. Nazario, "Crusader Vows to Put God Back into Schools Using Local Elections," *Wall Street Journal*, June 15, 1992.

6

Government Aid to Religious Schools: A Taxing Issue

The United States, unlike many Western European nations, has long been wary of the idea of using tax dollars to subsidize private religious schools. Throughout our history as a nation, explicit steps have been taken to forbid this type of funding. Until recently, the doctrine of "no direct aid" to religious schools held sway at the Supreme Court. This doctrine has now begun to change, shifting the nation's relationship between church and state.

It would surprise many Americans to learn that the concept of public education for the masses is a relatively recent phenomenon. As the previous chapter indicated, throughout much of the nineteenth century, only wealthy people could afford to educate their children in a formal way. Children in rural areas might receive sporadic education when they were not needed to help with farm work, but there was no widespread, systematic effort to educate the nation's youth.

Even in the first half of the twentieth century, when public education became widespread and was seen as a desirable social goal, dropout rates remained high. For many, a high school education was not necessary. Men could get good-paying jobs in factories, and many women did not work outside the home.

Private education has a long history in the United States. There were private schools before there were public institutions. These schools tended to cater to the upper class. Many undoubtedly offered religious instruction, but they were usually not under the control of specific denominations and did not see imparting religious dogma as their primary reason for existing.

The rise of the Roman Catholic school system in the late nineteenth century began to change that. Catholic schools were different from existing private institutions in several ways: They served a largely immigrant, often poor, population. They were under the complete control of the church hierarchy, and they existed primarily to impart church teachings.

Catholic clergy did not hesitate to pressure local, state, and federal governments for tax assistance. During the Cincinnati "Bible war" of 1869 (see preceding chapter), Archbishop John Purcell, declaring that Catholic parents should not allow their children to participate in Protestant religious exercises in public schools, suggested that one way to solve the problem would be for the Cincinnati School Board to give parents money to offset the cost of private education "as has been done in England, France, Canada, Prussia and other countries."[1]

The country remained divided over what was called the "school question" for a number of years. Some politicians argued that a public school system was required to bring the various immigrant groups together, to teach their children a common language and common customs of the nation. Catholics could chose to remain outside this effort at homogeny, the argument went, but they should not be given public funds to make it easier for them to do so.

President Ulysses S. Grant took a very commonsense view over this issue. Grant understood why Catholics would not want to send their children to public schools infused with Protestant dogma, but at the same time he strongly opposed tax funding of any religious institution. Grant's solution was twofold: remove Protestant worship from public schools, that is, make them religiously neutral, and continue to reserve public funding for public schools.[2]

Unfortunately, Grant's view was too progressive for the times. Although others were beginning to see the dangers of sectarianism in public schools, the drive to weed it out did not take hold until some years later.

By the 1870s emotion was running so high over the "school question" that Congress was pressured to act. James G. Blaine, a U.S. senator from Maine, proposed a constitutional amendment applying the federal religion clauses to the states as well as prohibiting any expenditure of public funds for sectarian schools.

Blaine may have been acting on a proposal from Grant that a new constitutional amendment be adopted. Grant wanted the amendment to do three things: mandate that states maintain public schools, require that those schools be free from sectarian control, and bar any diversion of tax aid to religious schools.

Unfortunately, Blaine's amendment ignored Grant's first two proposals and only barred tax funding of religious schools. The situation was further complicated when the National Reform Association, a type of early Religious Right group that had a good deal of influence at the time, demanded that a provision be put into the amendment protecting Bible reading in public schools and declaring it "nonsectarian."

The amendment failed to pass Congress, though the vote was close. Many states, however, adopted variations of the Blaine amendment and incorporated them into their own constitutions. Many of these state provisions do retain the bar on sectarianism in public schools, as well as the ban on government support to religious education. As a consequence, more than half of the states today have some type of language in their constitutions barring tax aid to sectarian schools. (Not all of these provisions can be traced to Blaine's amendment; some, like Virginia's, were the handiwork of thinkers who came long before Blaine.)

Widespread public wariness over the Roman Catholic Church steadily diminished as the twentieth century progressed. To be sure, there was still bias around. In 1928, Al Smith, the first Catholic to run for president on a major party ticket, was defeated by Herbert Hoover, in large measure due to fantastic and often virulent anti-Catholic propaganda that circulated throughout the nation.

Catholics, however, achieved footholds in several parts of the country. Southern Louisiana, for example, has a strong Catholic tradition dating back to its days as a French territory. Large numbers of Catholics also settled in northeastern states such as Massachusetts, Pennsylvania, and New York.

Early Religious School Aid Cases

As Catholic schools increased in number and Catholics grew politically powerful in some states, it became inevitable that agitation for legislation offering various types of assistance to Catholic schools would escalate.

Louisiana was the site of the country's first parochial school aid court battle, which occurred in 1930 after the state legislature, prodded by populist governor Huey Long, passed a law allowing public money to be used for the purchase of secular textbooks for public and private school students.

Long had campaigned for governor promising free textbooks for schoolchildren in the state. (Parents often had to pay for texts during this period, and in Louisiana the sale was controlled by a cartel, thus driving up the price.) The issue hit home with the voters, although most undoubtedly assumed that the plan would be restricted to public schools.

Supposedly, Long drew up the legislation for free textbooks on the back of a piece of cardboard and presented it to members of his administration. When they saw the language, some of them balked. The plan guaranteed free textbooks to every student in Louisiana, which would include those in Catholic schools.

Louisiana's constitution at the time did not allow government aid to religious schools. Long was undeterred and told members of his administration not to worry. The courts would uphold the plan, he said, because it was designed to aid individual students, not religious schools.[3]

The case eventually reached the Supreme Court, where Long's view prevailed. Ruling in *Cochran* v. *Louisiana State Board of Education*, the High Court said the law was constitutional because it was aimed at benefiting children, not the schools, a legal principle known as the "child benefit theory."[4]

Parochial school aid proponents hoped to use the ruling to secure other types of aid, but it took years for their efforts to bear fruit. In a landmark 1947 ruling, they scored another limited victory when the Court ruled in *Everson* v. *Board of Education* that states could provide public bus subsidies to parochial school children.

Although advocates of religious school aid won bus subsidies in the *Everson* case, the ruling on a whole was a significant loss for them. The High Court seemed to go out of its way to indicate that more expansive aid programs would face tough sledding before the justices. This quickly turned out to be the case.

In ringing language that is some of the High Court's most separationist to date, Justice Hugo Black penned the following: "The First Amendment of the Constitution means at least this: Neither a state nor the federal government can set up a church. Neither can pass laws which aid one religion, aid all religions, or prefer one religion over another. . . . No tax in any amount, large or small, can be levied to support any religious activities or institutions, whatever they may be called, or whatever form they may adopt to teach or practice religion."[5]

The Court's language was a type of prophecy that was soon borne out. Although advocates of parochial school aid won another limited textbook aid program in 1968,[6] after that they faced a series of defeats and continued losing most cases until the late 1980s—when the tide turned decisively in their favor.

1971's *Lemon* v. *Kurtzman* was the first of the high-profile losses. In this case, the Supreme Court struck down laws in Rhode Island and Pennsylvania that allowed the state to pay some portion of parochial school teachers' salaries in subjects deemed "secular."[7]

But in its *Lemon* decision the Court did more than simply strike down parochial school aid plans. The justices also devised a strict three-part test for determining church-state violations. Under what became known as the *Lemon* Test, a law is deemed to violate church-state separation if any one of three conditions are present: The law does not have a secular legislative purpose; the law advances or inhibits religion; the law fosters excessive governmental entanglement with religion.

Since then, the *Lemon* Test has been cited in virtually every major church-state case before the High Court, including several parochial school aid cases. While not always consistently applied by the justices, the test affords a grand measure of protection to religious freedom by making sure that governments adhere to the principle of separation of church and state. Religious Right activists have repeatedly attacked the *Lemon* standard and asked the Court to discard it. Some justices have agreed and criticized the test—notably Antonin Scalia—but so far the Court's findings in *Lemon* remain intact.

Two years after the *Lemon* case was decided, another black day for advocates of religious school aid occurred. The High Court in *PEARL* v. *Nyquist* struck down a series of New York laws offering a package of aid to parochial schools. One segment of the law was a voucher-type plan giving direct state grants to private schools that served low-income families. Another section allowed for state grants to repair and maintain parochial schools. A third section was a plan allowing for private school tuition reimbursement for parents.[8]

In 1975 the High Court struck down yet another parochial school aid plan from Pennsylvania, this one dealing with the loan of audio-visual materials, maps, periodicals, and other materials as well as various "auxiliary services" that the state provided to the schools—guidance counseling, psychological testing, and remedial reading offered by state-paid personnel who came on to the grounds of the parochial schools.[9]

Into the Reagan Era

But in 1983, the High Court, by a narrow 5–4 majority, upheld a Minnesota plan that granted parochial and public school parents a tax deduction for expenses incurred by "tuition, textbooks and transportation."[10] (Since public school parents do not pay for these services, just about all of the program's largess went to private school patrons.)

Two years later, also by a narrow 5–4 margin, the High Court struck down the federal government's plan for implementing "Chapter One" services for private school students needing remedial education. At parochial schools, Chapter One services had been provided by public school teachers on site at the private schools. The Supreme Court said this arrangement entangles church and state.[11] This decision was later overturned in *Agostini* v. *Felton* (1997).

The Court has also seen fit to extend tax assistance to handicapped students attending religious schools under some conditions. In a case from Washington state, the High Court ruled that a blind man could use public funds to attend a seminary.[12] In 1993 the justices ruled 5–4 that it does not violate the First Amendment if a public school chooses to provide a publicly funded interpreter to a deaf student in a sectarian school.[13]

By the late 1980s, it was clear that the High Court was changing course on government aid to religious schools. The Court had already given a stamp of approval to various types of "indirect" aid. Advocates of vouchers believed the time was right for a new challenge.

It took a few years to get a case before the Supreme Court, as no states had operational voucher plans in the late 1980s. Wisconsin passed a limited program in 1990. Aimed at the city of Milwaukee, the plan was at first limited to nonsectarian private schools. When it was expanded to include religious schools, advocates of church-state separation challenged it in the state courts. Wisconsin's Supreme Court eventually upheld the plan, and the U.S. Supreme Court refused to hear another appeal of the case.

In 1995, lawmakers in Ohio passed a voucher plan for the city of Cleveland. This program, which included religious schools from the very beginning, was also challenged in state court and upheld by the Ohio

Supreme Court. Opponents, including Americans United for Separation of Church and State, then filed a new challenge in federal court.

A U.S. District Court and the 6th Circuit Court of Appeals declared the program a violation of the First Amendment. The Supreme Court agreed to hear the case, *Zelman* v. *Simmons-Harris*, during its October 2001 term. The case was argued on February 20, 2002, and a decision was handed down the following June 27.

The case had been closely watched by both sides. In a 5–4 ruling, the majority, led by Chief Justice William H. Rehnquist, upheld the Cleveland plan, arguing that it was not really aid to religion. Justice Sandra Day O'Connor, who provided the crucial swing vote, said in a concurring opinion that religious schools were just one option open to parents and that any aid to religious schools came because of individual choices from parents, not from government action.

Critics noted that the Cleveland plan in reality offered very few choices. More than 80 percent of the private schools taking part in the plan were Roman Catholic, and 96.6 percent of the children in the program were attending religious schools. Suburban public schools had been invited to take part in the program, but all declined. Other options, such as charter schools, were really just alternative forms of public schools. Thus, for the vast majority of parents in the plan, the choice was between a public school and a Catholic school. Nevertheless, the High Court's conservative faction upheld the voucher scheme.

The Court did not say in *Zelman* that other types of government aid to religious schools—such as direct government grants to build new schools—would be constitutional. The majority insisted that its decision was in line with previous rulings. Thus, the majority claimed that it had not explicitly overturned any previous rulings on parochial school aid. The decisions barring direct aid to religious education are still in place, at least until they are tested anew.

Critics asserted that the *Zelman* ruling was a significant departure from previous parochial school aid rulings and said the High Court had opened the floodgates to other types of government aid to religious schools.

This odd state of affairs was probably brought about by the unique role O'Connor plays on the Court. Four conservative justices—Rehnquist, Scalia, Anthony Kennedy, and Clarence Thomas—appear to be ready to approve the idea that government can aid religion directly, as long as it does so on a "nonpreferential" basis. O'Connor does not seem to be willing to go that far. Unable to win over O'Connor, the majority had to craft an opinion that claims to leave prior rulings in place, when it had clearly undercut those decisions.

Unlike religion in public schools, where the High Court has maintained a more or less consistently separationist line, the decisions concerning parochial school aid have been all over the spectrum. As a result, in some states parochial school aid has persistently been a problem. This is only going to increase in light of the ruling upholding vouchers. Legislators in some states have consistently sought to award private sectarian schools as much public money as possible. In light of the *Zelman* ruling, several states are likely to consider full-scale voucher programs, plans whereby a variety of private schools are funded alongside public schools.

Vouchers have an unusual history in America. They were first proposed in the mid-1950s, after the Supreme Court ordered that public schools be desegregated. A number of Southern states actually passed legislation giving tax aid to private, racially segregated schools. These laws were eventually struck down, and voucher plans were forgotten.

The idea was resurrected in the 1970s and early '80s. Ronald Reagan, elected president in 1980 on a platform of "getting government off people's backs," advocated spending public funds on private schools. Reagan was a big fan of privatization generally, and many of his supporters had an automatic bias against government-run services.

Reagan was joined by a new school of economists and would-be education reformers who sought to privatize formerly public institutions—including education. Although Reagan's tuition tax credit proposal failed to pass Congress, the national debate over the issue gave the parochial school aid question new visibility and boosted the movement's supporters.

For the first time, groups other than the Catholic bishops began advocating for voucher plans, tuition tax credits, and other forms of government aid to religious schools. As a consequence, various plans advocating forms of parochial school aid filtered down to the states.

Since then, these plans have been a constant feature in state legislatures. Many never get out of the various committees to which they are assigned, and others die on the floor of the statehouse. But they are bound to increase in light of the High Court's pro-voucher decision. At this writing, only one state besides Ohio and Wisconsin has a publicly funded voucher program—Florida.

Referenda in the States

Opponents of vouchers do have one important weapon at their disposal: Public opposition to vouchers. The public seems to have little desire to see private school aid plans implemented. In recent years, parochial school aid advocates have managed to place voucher questions on several state ballots as referendum questions. The results have not been encouraging for those who favor these types of plans.

Colorado voters, for example, trounced a proposed voucher system by a 2–1 margin in 1992—67 percent against and 33 percent for. Identical results occurred in Oregon two years earlier when a voucher referendum was rejected by voters. In 1988 voters in Utah turned down vouchers by an even bigger margin—70 percent to 30 percent.

More recently, voters in Michigan trounced vouchers 69 percent to 31 percent in 2000. That same year, California voters rejected a voucher referendum, 70 percent to 30 percent.

In fact, since 1967 voters in fifteen states and the District of Columbia have defeated parochial school aid proposals at the ballot box, often by wide margins. Only one plan managed to pass—a limited proposal in South Dakota that allows public schools to "lend" textbooks to private schools. The vote was in 1986.

Who supports parochial school aid these days? Other than the Catholic hierarchy, the idea's most ardent supporters are economic conservatives who believe in a free-market approach to just about everything. This includes activists with the Libertarian Party, a small political movement that wants to do away with most forms of government.

Also jumping on the voucher bandwagon as of late have been various Religious Right leaders such as Pat Robertson, Jerry Falwell, James Dobson, and leaders of the Southern Baptist Convention. The involvement of Protestant fundamentalists marks a reversal of their thinking. Until the Reagan years, many hard-right Christians were wary of accepting any state support for their schools, fearing—rightly so—that government controls would quickly follow. Many conservatives still oppose vouchers for this reason and argue that a fundamentalist academy must pay its own way to be truly independent.

Voucher advocates often assert that African Americans support vouchers, seeing them as a way of getting their children out of poorly performing public schools. The facts do not support this claim. In California and Michigan, where vouchers appeared on the ballot in 2000, black voters rejected vouchers by a slightly higher percentage than white voters. No objective poll has shown African Americans supporting vouchers. There are some polls, paid for by pro-voucher groups, that purport to show blacks supporting vouchers. The questions in these polls are worded in such a way to arrive at a predetermined desired result.

The education group Phi Delta Kappa sponsors a poll every year on the public's attitude toward public schools. This poll, done in conjunction with Gallup, usually asks several questions about vouchers. It has never found majority support for the voucher concept, no matter how the question is worded.

No demographic, socio-economic, religious, or political group supports vouchers. In California, exit polling showed that black, white, Hispanic, and Asian voters rejected vouchers. Democrats, Republicans, and Independents voted against them. Wealthy voters voted against vouchers, as did those from the middle and lower economic classes. Catholic voters were just as likely to reject vouchers as were Protestants, Jews, and the unaffiliated.

Answering Pro-Voucher Arguments

No matter which group is promoting vouchers, the arguments used tend to be the same. Most of them, in fact, are merely the same tired arguments put forth by the Catholic bishops during the first big push for parochial school aid in the late 1940s. As weak as they are, these arguments have become prevalent in the states and are worth responding to in depth. Let's look at some here.

- *Vouchers will promote school "choice."* Voucher advocates' appropriation of the word "choice" to describe their misguided crusade is perhaps their most devious tactic. Choice conjures up all the right images to Americans—primarily freedom.

What the voucher boosters don't point out is that when it comes to private schools, the concept of educational "choice" is meaningless since private institutions remain free to discriminate in admissions. The religious leaders who operate 85 percent of all private schools have the only real "choice" about who gets in and who doesn't. Sectarian and secular private schools have the right to deny admission to or expel students for *any* reason, including concerns over discipline or simply to free up space for other children.

In 1997, a Roman Catholic nun, Sister Mary Angela Shaughnessy, addressed a conference of parochial school administrators in Biloxi, Mississippi, and reminded them that they can dismiss any parent who complains that a child's constitutional rights have been violated.

"You say very politely, 'Ma'am, you don't have any [constitutional rights]. You left them at the door when you walked into St. Mark's or St. Michael's. If you want them back, you'll have to leave.' We determine what the rights are in what is reflected in our handbooks. . . . If they don't like the rules, they don't have to come here."[14]

Fundamentalist Christian schools have expelled students with AIDS. Roman Catholic schools have expelled non-Catholics. A stack of vouchers a mile high and talk of "choice" would not get these children—and others in similar situations—into private schools that do not want them, unless the state required voucher schools to have an open admissions policy, a move religious groups have fought. These schools should not be permitted to discriminate in this manner and still receive public funds.

- *Vouchers will force public schools to improve by making them compete with private schools.* Real competition can never exist between public and private schools because the two systems do not compete on an even playing field. Private schools retain the right to expel any student for whatever reason they please or maintain selective admissions policies. They are not required to offer the special education programs that public schools must provide, and many do not do so. Public schools must by law accept all who apply; private schools do not. Public schools must meet a whole host of state and federal regulations that control every aspect of their operation. Private schools are free from most of these. There can be no competition between two such dissimilar systems. In light of this obvious fact, this argument is rather simplistic.
- *Private school parents are forced to pay taxes twice—once for public schools and once for private.* "Double taxation" does not exist. Private school tuition is *not* a tax; it is an additional expense that some parents have chosen to pay. People should not expect reimbursement for government services that they choose on their own to duplicate. After all, people who build their own swimming pools don't receive a tax break because they don't use municipal pools. People who buy

all of their books from a local store and build an in-house library still have to pay taxes to support the public library.

It is also important to keep in mind that all citizens are expected to support basic public services such as fire departments, police, and public schools, whether they use them or not. After all, an educated populace benefits everyone, not just those with children. That's why childless couples and single people still must pay taxes to support public education.

Ironically, double taxation does result under voucher plans. All Americans will pay first to support public schools—free and open to all—and secondly to support a system of private schools, totally unaccountable to the public, that discriminate on who gets in and teach sectarian doctrines that some may find offensive.

- *The inner-city poor would benefit from a voucher plan and other forms of parochial school aid.* This claim is one of the cruelest frauds perpetrated by voucher advocates. Yearly tuition at a private school can easily run into the thousands. At exclusive private academies, it can be $12,000 or more. Yet most voucher plans offer at most $1,000 to $2,500 in payment or a limited tax break. The poor would have no way of supplying the rest needed to meet private school costs. Vouchers and other forms of parochial school aid would benefit primarily the wealthy and upper middle class—people who can already afford private school fees.

Additionally, most private schools are located in suburbs or small cities. Most would flatly refuse to accept educationally disadvantaged children from inner cities or any child with a discipline problem or difficult learning disability. Even if a few were accepted, the costs of transportation would be prohibitive.

- *Vouchers actually mean more money for public education because fewer students will attend public institutions once voucher aid is made available.* This is another absurd argument. Most voucher plans call for public schools to lose a certain amount of money for every student who leaves and takes a voucher. Yet the public schools find that their fixed expenses do not drop because a few students leave. A teacher who is paid $35,000 a year will not have a salary reduction if her class size drops from twenty-seven to twenty-five. Public schools must pay fixed expenses for utilities, supplies, staff salaries and benefits, special education, and so on that do not drop appreciably just because some students leave the school. Under voucher plans, public schools are expected to do the same job but with less money.

- *Voucher students do better academically in school than public school students.* No objective research supports this claim. At this writing, there were three taxpayer-supported voucher plans operating in the United States: Milwaukee, Cleveland, and Florida. The Milwaukee and Cleveland plans have been studied extensively by researchers, but none have found significant academic improvement among the voucher students.

This last point is worth looking at in some detail. After all, if voucher plans do not deliver what they promise—higher academic achievement—there is no need to allow the plans to proliferate. Unfortunately, what should be a simple matter—testing voucher students to make certain they are doing well—has fallen victim to politics.

Milwaukee's plan originally called for testing the voucher students. After years of test results showing no improvement, legislators there, instead of declaring the program a failure and shutting it down, voted in 1996 to end testing of the voucher students!

Thus, researchers studying the Milwaukee program are forced to rely on old data. It has become impossible to get an accurate picture of what is going on in Milwaukee. In 2001, the federal government's General Accounting Office (GAO) noted this problem in a report it issued about the voucher programs in Milwaukee and Cleveland.

The GAO's bottom line is that the research does not show that voucher students in either city are performing better than their public school counterparts. The report noted that a few studies do show voucher students doing better academically but said these findings are controversial.

"None of these findings can be considered definitive because the researchers obtained different results when they used different methods to compare for weaknesses in the data," concluded the GAO report.

The studies that have found voucher students doing better are controversial because they were undertaken by voucher advocates. In a case from 1996, two researchers at Harvard University claimed that voucher students in Milwaukee were outperforming public school students.

The study was criticized by John Witte of the University of Wisconsin, who had been hired by the state to examine the Milwaukee program. Witte called the study, done primarily by Prof. Paul Peterson, a "confusing, tortured effort" and said Peterson had used a small statistical sample. Other researchers blasted the study as well.

Peterson is a known voucher proponent. In a 1990 article, he compared voucher opponents to Darth Vader, the villain of the *Star Wars* movies. Witte claimed that Peterson and his associates had "set out to reach a conclusion they have held all along."

Voucher supporters have been accused of manipulating data to boost their cause. In 1998, a researcher at Indiana University who had been hired to evaluate Cleveland's program issued a report finding that, after one year of operation, students in the voucher program were performing no better on standardized tests than public school students.

Pro-voucher professors took the data and "re-analyzed" it, issuing a report that showed the voucher students doing better.

Ironically, the Indiana University researcher, Kim K. Metcalf, had not recommended ending the Cleveland program. Metcalf noted no improvement among the voucher students, but said since the program had only been operating for a year, it would be best to leave it alone and test students again later.

Metcalf was not pleased to see his data "re-analyzed." He wrote, "Did the advocates intentionally manipulate the data to get the results they wished? Or, did they unknowingly apply inappropriate research techniques? The members of the team of advocates, though some of them represent prominent institutions, are strong supporters of vouchers and have done much to promote the implementation of voucher programs throughout the country. So, it is possible that they are engaged in a deliberate effort to misrepresent the Cleveland data in order to influence educational policy. We would prefer to believe that scholars would not do such a thing, no matter how strongly they believed in their cause. On the other hand, it is perhaps equally troubling to believe that the advocates were either so uninformed about acceptable standards of educational research that they unknowingly used inappropriate techniques, or they were so arrogant that they believed it unnecessary to follow accepted standards."[15]

In at least one case from Cleveland, researchers did find voucher students performing far worse than public school students. The research team at Indiana University examined a chain of private schools run by industrialist David Brennan. Students at those schools were found to be performing "significantly and dramatically lower" than public school students.[16]

That same study also found that voucher students in schools other than the Brennan academies did slightly better in language skills and science than their counterparts in public schools. Both groups did about the same in math and social studies.

Several privately funded voucher programs also operate in the United States. In 2002, the GAO examined three of these programs, in New York City; Washington, D.C.; and Dayton, Ohio. Again, the GAO found no significant academic difference between the voucher students and the students in public schools.

Voucher advocates promise a lot—better academic performance and better schools. Are they able to deliver? The data currently available does not back up their claims, and voucher boosters in some states seem unwilling to allow the type of testing that could give us the answer. That fact alone is telling. What are voucher supporters afraid of?

Faced with the fact that vouchers do not boost academic improvement, voucher advocates have begun falling back on an unusual argument: They assert that parents of voucher students feel better about the private schools their children attend. The parents having a better attitude about the school somehow supposedly makes up for the lack of academic improvement.

This is a rather patronizing argument to make. Parents of voucher students may indeed feel better about the schools, but that emotional state will not help their children score well on the SAT or get accepted into a college or university. A university admissions officer is unlikely to be persuaded by the argument, "I know Johnny has poor grades and bombed the SAT, but I really feel good about the school he attends, so I'm sure you'll admit him to Yale anyway."

Bottom line: The voucher advocates promised increased academic performance. They said they would get kids out of failing public schools and into schools that work. They have not delivered.

The Problem of Fraud

Aside from the testing debacle, there are other lessons to be learned from the Milwaukee and Cleveland experiment with vouchers. Due to lax oversight, the Milwaukee plan has spawned several examples of fraud. There is no reason to believe that these problems will not surface in other states.

Part of the problem stems from the fact that some private schools want vouchers but don't want any government regulation. Milwaukee lawmakers bought into this philosophy, with disastrous results.

A few years into the program, two schools, Milwaukee Preparatory and Exito Education Center, closed in mid-year amid allegations of financial improprieties. Milwaukee Preparatory claimed to be serving 175 voucher students. In reality, it had about twenty such students and had over-billed the state by claiming to have students who were in fact not attending. After the school collapsed, teachers complained that they hadn't been paid.

One parent told authorities she was pressured to misrepresent the age of her child to qualify for a voucher at Milwaukee Prep. The school also charged her child a $425 "registration fee," then later expelled her child and refused to refund the money. Eventually, authorities issued an arrest warrant for the school's director, who had fled the area.

Exito claimed to have 174 voucher students and 90 nonvoucher students. It really had 124 voucher students and no nonvoucher students. In other words, the school came into existence to cash in on the voucher plan.

After Exito closed, it was reported that its director had issued $47,000 in bad checks. He was also charged with a misdemeanor count of possession of marijuana.

Another Milwaukee choice school, Alex's Academic of Excellence, was headed by a man with a long criminal record. The man, James A. Mitchell, had served time for raping a woman at knifepoint in 1971. He later served time for burglary and telecommunications fraud. In 2000, he was sentenced to six months in prison for tax fraud.

Asked by the Milwaukee *Journal Sentinel* to explain why a convicted rapist should be permitted to work with children, Principal Jerry Gillman responded, "Let me get back to you on that one."[17]

Wisconsin's Department of Public Instruction later issued a report indicating that seven religious and other private schools taking part in the voucher program were not following the rules regarding admissions. The report found that the schools were imposing additional fees above the voucher, a practice forbidden by state law.

Wisconsin's political system has also been tainted by voucher-related scandal. Wisconsin Supreme Court Justice Jon Wilcox, who voted in favor of vouchers at the state high court, was fined $10,000 for election irregularities in 2001 by the state's Elections Board. Wilcox was accused of illegally coordinating his campaign with Citizens for Voter Participation, a pro-voucher front group that poured $200,000 into Wilcox's campaign to pay for last-minute attack ads against his opponent.

The Cleveland voucher program has not been scandal free either. In 1999 the Cleveland *Plain Dealer* reported that a voucher school, the Islamic Academy School of Arts and Sciences, had a convicted murderer on its staff. The man had served ten years in prison for a 1964 barroom shooting and later served eighteen months for selling marijuana. Nevertheless, he was hired to teach history.

The newspaper found that the school was operating out of a rundown building with inadequate heat and no working fire alarms. It had not given students proficiency tests and was late in turning in mandated paperwork. Despite these deficiencies, the Academy received $268,000 in taxpayer money.

A year later it was reported that the Islamic Academy had enrolled fictitious students and billed the state for them, bilking Ohio out of $70,000. The institution shut down in the wake of the revelations.

Another Cleveland school, Golden Christian Academy, was teaching children almost exclusively by having them watch videos. An inspection of the school also found a host of unsafe conditions, including exposed electrical wires.

Asked about the video-based instruction, the school's director, Sharon Golden, replied, "We're the only video school in Cleveland, so I would hate for it to disappear." The school had received $150,000 in tax funds.[18]

An analysis of the Cleveland program by Ohio Auditor Jim Petro found that it wasn't even meeting its primary objective of helping the poor. Petro found that thirty families with incomes between $50,000 to $90,000 were taking part in the program. He also noted that taxi companies used to transport students to and from voucher schools had consistently over-billed the state to the tune of $419,000.

Florida's program has also had its share of problems. In 2000, state officials approved the Philosophical and Spiritual University to receive vouchers, even though the school said it had no students and listed its address as a high-rise building in Sunny Isles Beach.

The "school" said it would charge $1,600 to $3,250 per year for tuition but refused to provide any other financial information to the state. Reporters tried to contact the institution, but their messages were ignored.

The Constitutional Problem

Although the Supreme Court upheld vouchers in *Zelman*, many people still believe that government support for religious schools is a fundamental violation of the right of conscience. These people do not accept the Court's claim that vouchers are aid to parents, not private schools. An estimated 85 percent of all private schools are religious in nature. Since a voucher could be used only to purchase educational services, on average 85 percent of the time tax money taken from the public would be used to subsidize religious institutions.

No public aid should be used to subsidize religion. Just as the government cannot fund churches by funneling the money through individual citizens, it should not be able to fund church schools through like means. Religious schools, as affiliates of the faith groups that sponsor them, are really just one more component of a church's mission. Government has no business paying for any aspect of a church's operation. That is the job of those who believe in what the church stands for.

Any honest religious leader will readily admit that church-related schools exist first and foremost for the benefit of the sponsoring denomination. Leaders of the Catholic Church have been very up front about this, especially in recent years. In fact, many have expressed a desire to increase the schools' Catholic nature and talked about ways to use the schools as instruments of evangelism. This is their right, of course, but clearly a blatantly sectarian goal such as this simply should not be underwritten with state funds in a country that takes separation of church and state seriously.

During a November 1990 meeting of Catholic bishops in Washington, D.C., the church hierarchy lauded its schools as "proven instruments of evangelism." Responding to a suggestion that Catholic schools water down their sectarian flavor to attract non-Catholic parents, Cardinal Anthony J. Bevilacqua of Philadelphia remarked, "We must keep the Catholic identity while reaching out to non-Catholics through evangelism."[19]

But while affirming the religiosity of their schools, the bishops also overwhelmingly approved a policy statement calling for increased public assistance to their parochial schools—a stance the bishops have reaffirmed since then. The bishops, it seems, want it all—a strong network of thoroughly Catholic schools that boost the faith, free from most state regulations and accountable only to church authorities, yet funded with taxpayer dollars drawn from Catholics and non-Catholics alike. The bishops are asking all Americans to pay for their evangelistic efforts. It is easy for most people to see the injustice in this plan—even though the Supreme Court turned a blind eye to it.

Given the Catholic Church's controversial stands on many public policy issues—stands that are taught as absolute truth in its schools—it's no wonder so many Americans remain wary of vouchers. The church has tried repeatedly to cast this opposition as "anti-Catholicism." The charge is offensive to many advocates of church-state separation. Far from being rooted in anti-Catholicism, opposition to vouchers more commonly springs from a desire to protect religious freedom and church integrity. For that reason, the view is shared by a majority of Catholics and non-Catholics alike.

Many Christian fundamentalist academies also teach controversial things as absolute truth. They may teach that women should be subservient to men or that the United States was founded to be a "Christian nation" and that other religions are not as worthy of respect. Of course, no instruction in evolution is offered. Private schools have the right to teach material like this, but they should not have the right to demand taxpayer subsidies for it.

Experiences Abroad

Nevertheless, many advocates of parochial school aid insist they can thwart public opinion and prevail. Some of the more radical ones even assert that the days of the public school system are numbered. Jerry Falwell once remarked that he was looking forward to the day when all schooling in America is run by churches.

To win advocates over to their side, those who favor parochial school aid often point to experiences in other countries where this type of aid is common. Great Britain and Canada are two of their favorite examples.

There are two problems with these types of international comparisons, however. First, neither England nor Canada has a history of civil liberties and church-state separation similar to that found in the United States. Indeed, Great Britain to this day has an established church. Canada, while it does not have an established church, was a British colony for many years and adopted many aspects of the British system.

Second and more important, parochial school aid in these nations has not been implemented as smoothly as voucher advocates would have the American people believe. When the Canadian province of Ontario extended full public funding to the Roman Catholic "separate" school system in 1984, Catholic officials demanded that a number of public school buildings be turned over to them to meet space needs. Many communities were torn apart by the ensuing conflict with citizens divided along religious lines. This conflict continues today.

Furthermore, the extension of public funds to Canadian Catholic schools set in place a competition for funds between the two systems. With tax revenue scarce, many public school parents complain that public schools are being seriously underfunded.

In addition, religious leaders in other denominations are now arguing that the province's policy of funding only Catholic schools violates Canada's antidiscrimination laws and have gone into court to seek public funding for their own schools. In the end, Ontario may end up with a system of education fragmented along sectarian lines and a budget busted by an influx of new sectarian schools seeking handouts. After all, why not build some schools if the government is willing to foot the bill?

England has suffered similar problems. There, the country's Muslim minority demanded that public assistance be extended to its schools alongside those of the Anglican and Catholic churches. Many opposed this move, increasing interfaith tensions. In addition, English religious leaders have lost a measure of control over their schools thanks to parochial school aid. Under the country's laws, a majority of a given school's parents can vote to "opt out" of the local education system and become "independent" (though still receiving government funding). This action can effectively sever a private school's denominational ties.

New Zealand has also experimented with voucher-style programs. The country had to modify the plans when the schools became stratified along socio-economic lines.

Despite the problems that other nations have encountered with parochial school aid, U.S. voucher boosters continue to point to them as models for America to follow. Voucher boosters waited patiently for one state to break the logjam. Wisconsin did so in 1990 and Ohio followed suit a few years later. They knew if they could push a voucher plan through somewhere and have it declared constitutional by the Supreme Court, other states might quickly follow.

The parochial school aid boosters' approach overlooks one key fact: Many state constitutions explicitly bar any diversion of public funds to sectarian schools. And, even if more plans are passed, disgruntled parents whose children are denied admission to the private school of their "choice" are sure to file lawsuits. These legal efforts may in turn open the door to state control of parochial and other private schools, leading to the day when parochial schools become mere adjuncts to the existing public school system. Robbed of their independence, the schools would be no different from the system church leaders originally sought to escape from.

The Church College Example

The issue of state control is put into stark perspective by looking at the history of church-related universities. In the 1970s, the Supreme Court upheld government assistance to church-related colleges and universities, provided they were not "pervasively sectarian." That is, the institutions, founded for religious purposes, can get public money as long as they are not too religious or refrain from being serious about it.

Most church colleges today are completely secularized and maintain only loose affiliations with the churches that founded them. In some cases, church leaders have lost the ability to have a say in the religious lives of students and have had to permit student groups to operate on campus that espouse doctrines at odds with church teachings. Only church colleges that eschew all public funding have been able to remain truly independent.

In light of the experience of church-related colleges, parochial school aid boosters would do well to be careful of what they ask for. They just might get it.

Notes

1. Leo Pfeffer, *Church, State and Freedom* (Boston: Beacon Press, 1953), p. 379.
2. Jean Edward Smith, *Grant* (New York: Simon & Schuster, 2001), pp. 569–70.
3. T. Harry Williams, *Huey Long* (New York: Bantam Books, 1970), pp. 322–23.
4. *Cochran* v. *Louisiana State Board of Education*, 281 U.S. 370 (1930).
5. *Everson* v. *Board of Education*, 330 U.S. 1 (1947).
6. *Board of Education* v. *Allen*, 392 U.S. 236 (1968).
7. *Lemon* v. *Kurtzman*, 403 U.S. 602 (1971).
8. *Committee for Public Education and Religious Liberty* v. *Nyquist*, 413 U.S. 756 (1973).
9. *Meek* v. *Pittenger*, 421 U.S. 349 (1975).
10. *Mueller* v. *Allen*, 463 U.S. 388 (1983).

11. *Aguilar* v. *Felton*, 105 S.C. 3237 (1985).

12. *Witters* v. *Washington Dept. of Services for Blind*, 474 U.S. 481 (1986).

13. *Zobrest* v. *Catalina Foothills School District*, 61 LW 4641 (1993).

14. "Parochial Potentates: Sister Mary Angela Explains It All for You," *Church & State* (January 1998): 14.

15. Kim K. Metcalf, "Advocacy in the Guise of Science," *Education Week*, September 23, 1998.

16. "Catholic Schools Take Wisconsin Tax Money, but Hope to Skip Regulations," *Church & State* (January 1999): 15.

17. "Wisc. Voucher School Had Convicted Rapist on Staff," *Church & State* (June 2000): 16.

18. "Convicted Murderer Working on Staff of Ohio Voucher School," *Church & State* (September 1999): 190–91.

19. Rob Boston, "Parochial Concerns," *Church & State* (January 1991): 4.

7

Polygamy, Pledges, and Peyote: Free Exercise Disputes

The First Amendment consists of just forty-five words. Of those, only the first sixteen concern religious freedom and separation of church and state. About half of those sixteen deal with the free exercise of religion.

Those few words have had a powerful impact on American society. The right to practice religion freely—or to refrain from participating in religion at all—is one of the most cherished rights of the American people. When asked to describe what makes America unique, many people are quick to respond "freedom of religion."

But over the years, Americans have squabbled incessantly over what religious freedom means and how far the principle should be extended. The United States, lacking an established religion, quickly became a haven for those seeking the right to religious freedom. In the fertile soil of freedom new religious movements took root—and continue to do so today. Unfortunately, these new movements sometimes came into conflict with government policy. The scope of those sixteen words has been central to the debate.

What Is a Religion?

Generally speaking, government agencies are reluctant to attempt to define religion. The Internal Revenue Service, for example, grants tax exemption automatically to religious groups, unlike secular nonprofits, which must apply for it—and can be turned down. The IRS will not allow individuals to engage in fraud under the guise of religion—such as calling what is clearly a for-profit business a church and demanding no taxation on the profits—but the agency normally adopts a hands-off attitude toward churches. Federal law greatly restricts the IRS's ability to audit houses of worship.

Courts have also been leery of attempting to define religion. But because courts must in some cases deal with allegations of fraudulent or illegal activity conducted under the guise of religion, they are required to make determinations from time to time. The closest the Supreme Court ever came to attempting to define religion was in 1944. In the case *United States* v. *Ballard*, the High Court held that in cases of criminal fraud levied against religious groups by law enforcement agencies, the only question that really matters is whether the adherent accused of fraud believed his or her claims to be true or deliberately lied in order to swindle people. If the former, such individuals cannot be convicted of fraud.

The *Ballard* case centered on an esoteric religious movement called "I Am," founded by Guy W. and Edna W. Ballard. Guy Ballard claimed to have made contact with the "Ascended Master Saint Germain" in 1930 while hiking on Mount Shasta in northern California. The Ballards stood accused of using the mail to defraud people by claiming to have various supernatural powers, such as the ability to heal the sick and injured. When the case went to the jury, the district judge told the panel that they were not to consider the fantastic claims made by the Ballards. All that mattered was if the Ballards sincerely believed their claims to be true. If they did, they could not be found guilty of fraud.

The Supreme Court upheld this rule, asserting that in a secular state, people have the right to believe in religious concepts that "might seem incredible, if not preposterous, to most people."

Wrote Justice William O. Douglas, "Heresy trials are foreign to our Constitution. Men may believe what they cannot prove. They may not be put to the proof of their religious doctrines or beliefs. . . . If one could be sent to jail because a jury in a hostile environment found those teachings false, little indeed would be left of religious freedom."[1]

For many of the same reasons, courts have been reluctant to intervene in internal church controversies. Several cases have reached the Supreme Court involving divided churches or squabbling congregations whose members fight over church property and buildings. The court's normal practice is to defer to the sponsoring denomination and its rules.[2] In one early case, 1872's *Watson* v. *Jones*, the High Court declared that federal courts must refrain from trying to interpret church dogma and doctrine because "the law knows no heresy, and is committed to the support of no dogma, the establishment of no sect."

Testing the Boundaries

The boundaries of religious freedom are not usually tested by a country's mainstream faiths. Instead, it is the new, unorthodox religions that often push up against the limits. This has certainly been the case in the United States. Religious minorities were the first to test the boundaries of the First Amendment. Many of the early free exercise cases were brought by members of three religious minorities—Mormons, Seventh-day Adventists, and Jehovah's Witnesses.

Because of their efforts, by the 1970s religious freedom in America was expanded and the First Amendment was interpreted by the federal courts to offer its widest extent of protection in U.S. history. Although many critics say recent Supreme Court rulings have reversed the trend and curtailed religious freedom, there is no denying that during a relatively short period of time the country took several giant steps forward in the area of religious free exercise.

With the exception of the Church of Jesus Christ of Latter-day Saints, (the Mormons) most American religious groups have not experienced direct, government-sponsored efforts to eradicate their beliefs. It's true that a certain degree of interreligious tension has always existed in America, and it has flared in ugly ways at different points in our history. But generally speaking, after 1800 even small religious groups were safe to meet for worship without worrying about their doors being kicked in by the local constable.

The main free exercise problems, then, did not stem from government's outright attempts to stamp out certain religious beliefs but rather from conflicts stemming from the specific practices of certain religions. Throughout U.S. history some believers have felt compelled by faith to engage in certain activities the state had declared illegal. The opposite also occurred, of course. Some believers felt compelled by faith to refrain from engaging in certain activities that are mandated by government.

A good example of the former that also provides a brief overview of the free exercise debate is the unusual practice of snake handling. Although most mainstream Christians view this activity as quite bizarre, it is still practiced today by small pockets of dedicated believers, mostly in the rural South. (For an interesting overview of the practice, see Dennis Covington's 1995 book, *Salvation on Sand Mountain: Snake Handling and Redemption in Southern Appalachia.*)

Snake handlers insist they have a sound biblical basis for the activity and point to a passage in the New Testament Book of Mark that refers to the practice (see Mark 16:15–18). But obviously handling poisonous snakes—and drinking strychnine, as some snake handlers also do—can be extremely dangerous. Accordingly, most states have laws on the books making it a crime to handle poisonous snakes during religious services.

On its face, this would seem to be a classic church-state free exercise controversy, and some may see it as an open and shut case. Since the First Amendment means that government has no authority to tell religious groups what they can and can't do in church, the snake handlers must prevail, right?

Wrong. In this case there is an additional factor that makes all the difference: People have died from handling rattlesnakes and copperheads in church (and from drinking poison). The government, the argument goes, has an obligation to safeguard human life that in this case overrides religious freedom. Courts, therefore, have ruled consistently that states and communities have the right to ban snake handling and the consumption of poison in church.

As the example about snake handling shows, no sixteen words, no matter how eloquent or well crafted, can answer every conflict over religious freedom that will arise in a modern, growing, religiously diverse society that seeks to maximize religious liberty. This means that the courts have been forced to hammer out guidelines for determining what types of religiously motivated activities may be curbed by the government and under what conditions they may be curbed. And therein lies the difficulty.

Mormons and Polygamy

For a long time after the Constitution was ratified, the federal courts were loath to adjudicate church-state disputes. Church-state cases dealing with the free exercise of religion were a rarity before the federal courts in the nineteenth century. The first few to bubble up to the Supreme Court centered on the Mormons.

Many people today see Mormons as just other members of America's religious community, known for their theologically conservative views, large families, and worldwide missionary efforts. Most people have encountered young Mormon missionaries on street corners or at their front doors, and, while some Americans dislike this form of proselytism, most people these days see the Mormons as innocuous.

That was not the case in the nineteenth century. Many Americans at that time held a much different view of the Mormons. The group, then just getting off the ground, was a despised religious minority viewed by many as threatening to the American way of life. The chief reason for this vituperation was polygamy.

At that time, some Mormons practiced plural marriage. Although few rank-and-file Mormons engaged in the practice, church leaders, including founder Joseph Smith and Brigham Young, one of his top lieutenants, each had numerous wives. (Smith had forty-nine wives; Young ultimately married twenty-seven women.) Plural marriage was alien to America, and its adoption by Mormons led to conflict and tension that forced the members of the new religion to flee westward, from state to state, seeking safe haven.

It should be pointed out that Smith is not entirely innocent in this drama. There are indications that he may have been involved in fraudulent banking scams early on in his career as a religious leader. Whatever the case, a mob killed him in Nauvoo, Illinois, in 1844, and Young led most of Smith's followers further west into what is today Utah, where they settled. Young, who became governor of the territory, officially named polygamy as a church tenet in 1852. Ten years later, Congress passed the Morrill Act, legislation designed to stamp out polygamy in the western territories.

Federal agents began arresting Mormons living in polygamous households. One of those arrested was George Reynolds, a secretary to Young. Reynolds, facing trial in a territorial court, argued that the Morrill Act could not be applied to Mormons because they were religiously compelled to practice polygamy.

Reynolds lost the case in territorial court and appealed to the U.S. Supreme Court. On January 4, 1879, the High Court issued a unanimous opinion upholding the lower court. The High Court, never before asked to rule on such a matter, formulated what is known as the "belief-action" standard, holding that while the First Amendment makes freedom to believe absolute, it does not similarly protect all actions based on those beliefs.

Declaring that "Polygamy has always been odious among the Northern and Western Nations of Europe," the Supreme Court deemed the Morrill Act constitutional and opened the door for further prosecutions of Mormons engaging in polygamy.[3]

Authorities with the federal government, believing they had the blessing of the Supreme Court, continued to vigorously prosecute Mormons for the next twelve years. In 1890 another Mormon case reached the Supreme Court. In *Davis* v. *Beason* the Court—again unanimously—ruled that an Idaho Mormon who practiced polygamy could be prosecuted for falsely swearing that he did not believe in plural marriage.[4] (The oath was part of the Idaho territory's voting regulations.)

Later that year, the High Court upheld a federal law designed to reduce the power of the Mormon church in Utah by turning church lands over to the government.[5] Realizing that they were outgunned by the federal government, church officials in 1890 issued an executive order banning polygamy. Six years later, Utah was admitted to the union under a constitution that specifically bans plural marriage.

Jehovah's Witnesses

Following the Mormon cases, the free exercise front was quiet at the Supreme Court for nearly fifty years. But beginning in the late 1930s and early '40s, a series of cases went before the Supreme Court concerning yet another unpopular religious group, the Jehovah's Witnesses.

The Witnesses, founded in Pennsylvania in 1872, are known to most Americans for their aggressive proselytism and criticism of other faiths. Though disliked by many, this small group—U.S. membership is less than one million—has not been reluctant to stand up for its rights in federal court. As a result, Jehovah's Witnesses are responsible for a series of High Court rulings that expanded religious freedom for all Americans.

For instance, in a string of early Witness cases the Supreme Court invalidated a succession of state and local laws designed to place unreasonable curbs on groups seeking to distribute literature door to door. Short-sighted politicians had ignored the dangers such statutes could pose to civil liberties at large. If the state were to gain the power to stamp out one religion's message merely because it is deemed unpopular, a dangerous precedent would be set. Many religious and civic groups at the time may not have been supportive of the Witnesses, but they are today thankful for their efforts on this front.

The literature distribution cases were important victories for religious liberty, but perhaps the most important case the Witnesses were involved in was 1940's *Cantwell* v. *Connecticut.* This landmark legal dispute got under way after police in New Haven, Connecticut, arrested a Witness and his son who were broadcasting a virulently anti-Catholic record on public streets. The two were charged with failure to obtain a "certificate of approval" from state authorities, a document that allowed "bona fide" charitable and religious groups to solicit for funds.[6]

The Supreme Court, ruling unanimously, threw out the conviction as well as the Connecticut law requiring a "certificate of approval" to present religious messages. More importantly, the High Court for the first time made it clear that the religion clauses of the First Amendment—and by extension the entire Bill of Rights—are applicable to the states through the Fourteenth Amendment, a doctrine known as "incorporation." As has been noted in previous chapters, incorporation gave Americans greater access to the federal courts in seeking redress of church-state grievances and increased the number of religious liberty disputes before the High Court.

In 1943, the Supreme Court ruled in *Martin* v. *Struthers* that an Ohio town's ordinance making it unlawful to distribute handbills door to door was unconstitutional. Although the High Court decided the case on the grounds of freedom of speech, not religious freedom, the dispute had obvious church-state overtones. (Fifty-nine years later a similar case reached the Supreme Court. The High Court ruled 8–1 in *Watchtower Bible & Tract Society* v. *Village of Stratton* that an Ohio town's ordinance requiring door-to-door canvassers to get a permit from the city and identify themselves to municipal authorities was unconstitutional. Once again, the Court based the ruling on free speech grounds, not religious freedom.)

The Witnesses have not won every case they have brought. In another important case involving Jehovah's Witnesses, the Supreme Court ruled in 1944 that free exercise of religion rights do not overrule child labor laws. The case arose in Massachusetts after a group of Witnesses, who often used children to distribute literature for long hours at night, challenged state statutes regulating the hours children may work.

Observed the High Court in *Prince* v. *Massachusetts*, "The right to practice religion freely does not include liberty to expose the community or the child to communicable diseases or the latter to ill health or death."[7]

Medical Treatment Controversies

In recent years, the ruling in *Prince* has been cited as precedent in some cases involving forced medical treatment for minors. Some religious groups, primarily Christian Scientists and some Pentecostal Christian groups, do not believe in seeking medical care for any reason, holding that religious faith alone can cure disease. (This is true more of Pentecostals; Christian Science theology holds that disease is an illusion that can be overcome by prayer and other spiritual means.)

While adults have a right to refuse medical treatment for any reason, courts have tended to rule that this right does not extend to children, who are considered too young to make an informed decision about health care. As a result, children belonging to these groups in some states have been inoculated or been given medical treatment against parents' wishes.

In other cases, parents whose children died because they received no medical treatment for serious illnesses have been charged with manslaughter or endangering the welfare of a child. State court rulings in this area have produced a mixed bag of opinions. Some parents have been found guilty (generally receiving probation, not prison sentences), while others have been acquitted. It should also be noted that forty-five states have laws on the books shielding parents who use spiritual healing from criminal prosecution. Recently, some medical authorities have begun calling for the repeal of these laws. The issue of the legality of spiritual healing for children is emotional and complex, involving a host of parental rights concerns aside from the church-state dimension.

Proselytism and Flag Salutes

Jehovah's Witnesses, who refuse blood transfusions, have also been involved in some of the medical treatment cases. But most of the court rulings they sparked deal with activities related to religious proselytism in public places. In 1943, for example, the Supreme Court handed down an important decision dealing with the right of religious groups to distribute literature. In a narrow 5–4 vote, the High Court struck down a Pennsylvania statute requiring that groups wishing to distribute literature pay a special tax.[8]

These rulings were grudgingly accepted by the American people, but public sympathy for the Jehovah's Witnesses did not run high. Witnesses had a habit of making nuisances of themselves, and undoubtedly many Americans saw the efforts to curb the group's evangelical fervor through government action a good thing. But given the benefit of forty-five years of hindsight, it is easy to see how dangerous the anti-Witness statutes were and how destructive to religious and political freedom they could have become if they had been permitted to stand. Being forced once in a while to shut the door in the face of an aggressive religious proselytizer is a small price to pay for complete religious freedom for all.

In the midst of these rulings another issue concerning Jehovah's Witnesses ended up in the federal courts. This issue, more emotional than any previous case involving Witnesses, focused on the Pledge of Allegiance.

Jehovah's Witnesses do not believe in earthly allegiances. Their only duty, they say, is to God. They do not participate in secular government. They will not hold office or vote in elections. Also, they steadfastly refuse to recite oaths of any kind—including the Pledge of Allegiance—or salute the flag. Saluting flags, they say, is a form of idolatry.

In 1940 the United States was on the brink of entering World War II, and a heightened sense of patriotism ran through the population. Many states had laws mandating the recitation of the Pledge of Allegiance and flag salute every day in public schools. Children of Jehovah's Witnesses, who refused to participate in the exercises, were frequently expelled from school or otherwise punished.

It is important to note that the Witnesses did not object to the flag salute because it contains the phrase "under God." At the time, the Pledge did not contain those words. "Under God" was added to the Pledge by an act of Congress in 1954. The Witnesses objected to flag salutes generally. (And back then, people did literally salute the flag with a stiff-armed salute. The practice faded away during World War II, as it looked uncomfortably similar to the Nazi salute.)

Although their timing could not have been worse, the Witnesses took the pledge matter into federal court in the late 1930s. In 1940 the Supreme Court issued one of its worst church-state opinions ever and held by an 8–1 vote that a Pennsylvania law requiring recitation of the Pledge of Allegiance in public schools was constitutional, declaring that schools had no obligation to exempt Jehovah's Witnesses or other objectors.[9]

The High Court's ruling in *Minersville School District* v. *Gobitis* was followed by an outbreak of violence against Jehovah's Witnesses across the country. Although the Witnesses lost the case, just the fact that they had dared to bring it outraged millions of Americans. What followed is one of the darkest and most disgraceful periods in American church-state history.

In Richwood, Virginia, the chief of police rounded up a group of Jehovah's Witnesses, forced them to drink castor oil and paraded them through the streets before running them out of town. In Jackson, Mississippi, members of a local veterans' organization attacked a trailer park where many Witnesses were known to live and drove several from their homes.

The list gets worse: A Witness in Nebraska was lured away from his house and castrated by a mob. In Rockville, Maryland, local police assisted a marauding crowd that attacked a Witness church (called a Kingdom Hall) to break up a church meeting. In Kennebunk, Maine, an unruly mob charged the local Kingdom Hall and set it on fire, burning it to the ground.[10]

One week after the ruling in the flag salute case, the U.S. Justice Department had received hundreds of reports of attacks on Jehovah's Witnesses. When schools went back into session that fall, some zealous teachers and principals stepped up their efforts to expel Witness children and even threatened to imprison the children in juvenile homes unless they recited the Pledge.

By 1943 the Supreme Court had realized its mistake. Changes had occurred on the Court by then. Some justices had retired, and others had changed their minds about the *Minersville* case. The High Court accepted a new case dealing with mandatory flag salutes in public schools—this one from West Virginia—and issued a decision strongly upholding religious freedom.

Speaking for the 6–3 majority in *West Virginia State Board of Education* v. *Barnette*, Justice Robert Jackson penned some eloquent words, declaring, "If there is any fixed star in our constitutional constellation, it is that no official, high or petty, can prescribe what shall be orthodox in politics, nationalism, religion, or other matters of opinion, or force citizens to confess by word or act their faith therein."

Continued Jackson, "The very purpose of the Bill of Rights was to withdraw certain subjects from the vicissitudes of political controversy, to place them beyond the reach of majorities and officials and to establish them as legal principles to be applied by the courts. One's right to life, liberty, and property, to free speech, a free press, freedom of worship and assembly, and other fundamental rights may not be submitted to vote; they depend on the outcome of no elections."[11]

Sadly, many Americans apparently do not agree with that reasoning. During the 1988 presidential race, George Bush attacked Democratic nominee Michael Dukakis because Dukakis, as governor of Massachusetts, had in 1977 vetoed a bill requiring recitation of the Pledge in the state's public schools. Dukakis, pointing to the *Barnette* ruling, noted that the measure was clearly unconstitutional. In the resulting furor, Bush accused Dukakis of being opposed to the Pledge, and one opinion poll showed a majority of Americans favoring mandatory recitation of the Pledge of Allegiance in public schools, even if some religious groups or individuals object.

Similarly, a number of states passed or tried to pass laws mandating recitation of the Pledge of Allegiance after the horrific terrorist attack of September 11, 2001. In Minnesota, Gov. Jesse Ventura was criticized for vetoing one of these bills. Defending his action, Ventura pointed out that the law was clearly unconstitutional.

Conscientious Objection to War

A separate line of Supreme Court cases deals with conscientious objection to war. Certain religious denominations espouse pacifism and on principle oppose all wars. Quakers are one example. As early as 1789 James Madison proposed a constitutional amendment that, among other things, would guarantee that "no person religiously scrupulous of bearing arms" would be compelled to serve in the military. Madison's proposal was never adopted, and the issue remained dormant for many years, as the nation relied on volunteers for the army and state militias.

The outbreak of the Civil War brought the nation's first draft laws. In the North, the federal law that established conscription allowed any member of a religious denomination with an article of faith against bearing arms to pay for a substitute or accept duties as a noncombatant. The Confederacy had a similar law.

New draft laws were passed when the United States entered the First World War. The law exempted any member of a "well-recognized religious sect or organization at present organized and existing and whose existing creed or principles forbid its members to participate in war in any form." In practice, however, the law was construed a little more broadly by the War Department, and exemptions were granted to anyone who had "personal scruples against war." The law was challenged by one conscientious objector who refused to even register for noncombatant duty and who argued that the language in the law favored certain churches over others, but the Supreme Court upheld the act.

Meanwhile, a related issue arose in the courts: Could immigrants who were pacifists be forced to swear an oath pledging to defend the United States under arms as a condition of citizenship? In a pair of cases, the Supreme Court said yes.[12] Extending this logic, the High Court even upheld the suspension of several young men, members of the Methodist Episcopal Church, who had refused to take mandatory military training classes at the University of California.[13]

In 1946 the High Court changed course. In *Girouard* v. *United States* the Court, by a 5–4 vote, held that a lower court erred in ruling against a Seventh-day Adventist who refused to swear to bear arms as a condition of naturalization.

The conflict in Vietnam reopened the issue some decades later. In *United States* v. *Seeger*, the Supreme Court ruled in favor of three men who sought conscientious objector status but who argued that their beliefs came from a nontheistic system. Congress tried to amend the draft laws to require objectors to base their claims on theistic beliefs, but the Supreme Court declared the act unconstitutional.

Finally, in 1971, the High Court seemed to resolve the issue. An eight-member majority declared in *Gillette* v. *United States* that Congress had the right to grant conscientious objector status to those persons who said they opposed wars for any reason. This policy, the Court ruled, kept the government out of the tricky business of judging which religions required pacifism and which did not.

The Zenith of Free Exercise

Aside from conscientious objection, another important line of Supreme Court free exercise cases deals with workers' rights. Jehovah's Witnesses and another religious minority, Seventh-day Adventists, have been involved in some of these cases. Seventh-day Adventists, who hold Saturday as the Sabbath, have a special interest in this area of free exercise law. Because devout Adventists refuse to work on Saturday, they have had frequent problems with employment laws and have been forced to go to court several times to assert for their rights. In doing so they expanded religious freedom for all Americans—at least until recently, when the High Court overturned previous rulings and stepped away from awarding free exercise adequate protection.

A series of four cases from 1963 through 1989 set down a basic principle that workers cannot be penalized for refusing to work on their Sabbath. The earliest case, 1963's *Sherbert* v. *Verner*, dealt with a Seventh-day Adventist who was fired for refusing to accept Saturday employment at a textile mill.[14] When the woman, Adell Sherbert, applied for unemployment benefits, she was rejected. In reversing that finding, the Supreme Court ruled 7–2 that Sherbert could not be compelled by the state to choose between her religious beliefs and her livelihood. In a 1989 case, *Frazee* v. *Department of Employment Security*, the High Court unanimously extended the principle to cover Sabbath keepers unaffiliated with any specific church.[15]

Sherbert and the cases that followed it established a broad principle of free exercise law known as the "compelling state interest" test. Under this standard, government may not restrict a person's free exercise of religion unless it can first prove a compelling interest on the part of the state and show that no less restrictive means are available to achieve the state's goals.

The Supreme Court used the standard again in a 1972 case dealing with the Old Order Amish. Members of this community protested Wisconsin's compulsory education law and refused to send their children to school beyond the eighth grade. The Amish argued that sending children to school beyond this level would expose them to corrupting and "worldly" ideas that would conflict with the Amish's simple, religious lifestyle.

In a 7–0 decision (two justices did not participate), the High Court ruled in favor of the Amish, declaring that Wisconsin's interest in educating youngsters was compelling, but that an exception should be made for the Amish so they would not be forced to violate their sincerely held beliefs. The Court's ruling in *Wisconsin* v. *Yoder* was the high-water mark of free exercise rights at the Supreme Court.[16]

Later Free Exercise Rulings

Things quickly went downhill from that point. With the exception of a few minor cases related to employee rights, in the years following *Yoder* the Supreme Court seemed to give only passing acknowledgement to the "compelling state interest" standard, and religious groups began losing free exercise cases. In a surprising 1990 ruling, the High Court scrapped the "compelling state interest" test altogether in a case from Oregon known as *Employment Division* v. *Smith*.[17]

The *Smith* opinion, written by arch-foe of separation of church and state Justice Antonin Scalia, threw free exercise jurisprudence into a state of flux from which it has yet to recover. Fallout from the case is still being felt. Basically, the High Court, by a 5–4 majority, declared that the government no longer must meet a "compelling state interest" in regulating religion. All that matters, said the Court, is that laws that might infringe on religious belief be "neutral and generally applicable."

In other words, any law that is neutral on matters of religion will be considered constitutional, even if its practical effect is to eviscerate a given religious belief. Under this reasoning, religious groups have begun losing a steady stream of free exercise cases in the federal and state courts. Autopsies can now be performed on those who die in accidents, even if family members object for religious reasons. Church leaders can literally lose control of their buildings if the facilities are deemed historic by municipal governments. Policies of church confidentiality have been placed in jeopardy. Things have gotten so bad that some state court judges, frustrated by the Supreme Court's new doctrine, have begun extending protection to religious freedom under state constitutions.

What shocked so many religious groups about the *Smith* ruling was the extent of its reach. The High Court had not been asked to reformulate its free exercise case law and gave no indication that it would do so. The facts of the case, though somewhat exotic, did not lend themselves to such a sweeping decision: Two American Indians in Eugene, Oregon, had been fired from their jobs as substance abuse counselors because they ingested small amounts of peyote, a mild hallucinogenic, during rites of the Native American Church. When the two applied for unemployment benefits, they were turned down by state officials.

The High Court not only rejected the two men's claim, but used the occasion to refashion free exercise law and scrap the old "compelling state interest" standard. Critics of the *Smith* ruling—and they came from both liberal and conservative camps—said the High Court could have denied the Indians' claim without throwing out the "compelling state interest" test. (Justice Sandra Day O'Connor made much the same argument in her opinion, although she agreed with the majority's ultimate conclusion denying the men the benefits.)

Perhaps the most shocking feature of the *Smith* ruling, however, was that Scalia brazenly based portions of the decision on the loathsome *Gobitis* decision, the first flag-salute case from 1940. Civil libertarians were shocked that a Supreme Court justice had based a key church-state ruling on a case that had been expressly overturned and discredited by the Court in 1943. The decision clearly leaves the rights of minority religions in the hands of state and local lawmakers and fosters majoritarianism. The Court had hit another low mark in church-state jurisprudence.

Smith was such an unpopular ruling that it sparked a move in Congress to mute its effects through legislation. The proposed bill, known as the Religious Freedom Restoration Act, gained support from both liberal and conservative civil liberties and religious groups but for two years was unable to pass Congress when it became bogged down in an unfortunate dispute over abortion. The bill eventually passed both chambers and was signed into law by President Bill Clinton in November 1993. In June 1997, however, the Supreme Court declared the Religious Freedom Restoration Act unconstitutional.[18]

After that 6–3 ruling, some of the backers of the Religious Freedom Restoration Act decided to try again. They successfully lobbied Congress to pass a new law, the Religious Land Use and Institutionalized Persons Act. This law is more limited in scope and mainly deals with issues such as zoning and the religious freedom rights of prisoners. It too has been challenged in the federal courts, and several cases were in the pipeline as this book went to press.

Two years after the *Smith* ruling, the Supreme Court agreed to hear another free exercise case, this one from Florida. The facts in the dispute were even more unusual than those in *Smith*, centering on whether communities may pass laws banning the practice of animal sacrifice.

The issue arose in south Florida in a suburb of Miami named Hialeah. Here an estimated 50,000 followers of an Afro-Cuban religion known as Santeria reside. Members of the faith, which blends animism and Roman Catholicism, practice animal sacrifice during certain feast days. The animals sacrificed, often small creatures such as chickens and goats, are usually consumed afterward.

Shocked at the activities, officials in Hialeah passed four ordinances designed to outlaw animal sacrifice for religious purposes. Opponents of the laws argued they were unconstitutional even under the new *Smith* standard since they were aimed specifically at a religious practice and thus were not "generally applicable." Hialeah officials responded that they have the right to ban religious practices that pose a threat to the community.

In June 1993, the High Court ruled unanimously that the Hialeah ordinances had gone too far and struck all four down. The opinion, written by Justice Anthony M. Kennedy, declared that the intent and effect of the laws was to suppress the Santeria religion. Observed Kennedy, "Our review confirms that the laws in question were enacted by officials who did not understand, failed to perceive, or chose to ignore the fact that their official actions violated the Nation's essential commitment to religious freedom."

Elsewhere Kennedy wrote in the *Church of the Lukumi Babalu Aye* v. *City of Hialeah* decision, "The Free Exercise Clause commits government itself to religious tolerance, and upon even slight suspicion that proposals for state intervention stem from animosity to religion or distrust of its practices, all officials must pause to remember their own high duty to the Constitution and to the rights it secures. Those in office must be resolute in resisting importunate demands and must ensure that the sole reasons for imposing the burdens of law and regulation are secular. Legislators may not devise mechanisms, overt or disguised, designed to persecute or oppress a religion or its practices."[19]

The *Church of the Lukumi* decision, while it was a victory for religious liberty, left the findings of *Smith* intact, although three justices criticized *Smith* in concurring opinions. This left religious freedom advocates with at least the hope that in time, with new appointments, a court majority could arise opposed to the new rule announced in *Smith*.

Free Exercise in Transition

What is to be made of all this? First of all, that free exercise law at the Supreme Court is in transition. Ironically, this came about because of the new, conservative appointments to the High Court in the 1980s and early '90s. Many Religious Right leaders eagerly supported these appointees, hoping they would reinterpret the Establishment Clause and pave the way for the return of state-sponsored religious exercises in public schools. Not only has that not happened, but the new right-leaning majority has turned the full force of its judicial attack on the Free Exercise Clause and severely restricted its protections.

A few years after *Smith*, Justice Scalia, speaking at a church-state conference at Baylor University, asserted that the High Court should look to society's historical traditions when dealing with church-state controversies. In the case of the free exercise of religion, he said, societal majorities will decide which religiously motivated activities should receive special protection from government's reach.

Such an approach should send a chill down the spine of all advocates of religious freedom. "Societal tradition" is most assuredly *not* an appropriate guideline for determining constitutional rights. For a long time in the United States, the "tradition" was majority rule in religious matters. If the majority decided to force its religious exercises on all students in the public school, that practice became "tradition," and minority rights were trampled.

Scalia's views underscore one of the greatest dangers facing religious liberty advocates today: the majoritarian and statist bent at the Supreme Court. Contrary to Scalia's assertions, the First Amendment is not a blueprint for the majority to run roughshod over the minority or for the government to always have its way in church-state conflicts over free exercise. Yet under his reasoning, that is exactly the result to be expected.

As I stated earlier, sixteen words cannot possibly be expected to answer every question about religious liberty that will arise in a modern society marked by expanding religious pluralism. Until recently, the Free Exercise Clause was seen as a command that government give religion every benefit of the doubt and as much leeway as possible in seeking to resolve these disputes. As the federal courts move away from this ideal, religious freedom is placed in jeopardy. The first to feel the hit, as usual, are religious minorities.

Phony Free Exercise Claims

Before leaving the discussion of free exercise, one more important point should be covered: Religious Right activists like to play up the supposed tension that exists between the Free Exercise Clause and Establishment Clause. Actually, no such tension exists. Interpreted properly, the two clauses complement one another and don't clash. The problem occurs in the way the Religious Right interprets "free exercise."

All Americans have the right to worship as they see fit within the bounds of the law. But no American has the right to expect the government to endorse or promote his or her religious beliefs or to demand the power of the state for help in spreading sectarian messages. The understandable refusal of the government to support religion is often what the Religious Right means when they talk about "free exercise problems."

For example, Religious Right groups often complain that teachers cannot pray with students in public schools and labels this a free exercise problem. As usual, they have distorted the facts. Teachers have the right to pray on their own, but they do not have the right to abuse the authority of the public school, a government-owned institution, to promote their personal religious beliefs or encourage students to adopt new or different beliefs. The government is not inhibiting any teacher's free exercise rights by demanding that the public school system remain neutral on religious matters.

Religious Right activists expect the government to provide them with religious freedom *and* a public forum that enables them to spread their message far and wide to win new converts. This makes perfect sense to many of them, since they believe their message is the "true" one. But obviously the government is under no obligation to provide that forum and is, in fact, constitutionally forbidden to do so.

Consider the following analogy: Every American has the right to express his ideas, but that does not mean the government has to buy each of us a printing press to more efficiently spread those views. It is ludicrous to assert that the government is "discriminating" against anyone for refusing to provide him or her with a ready-made forum for the expression of their views, be those views religious, political, or whatever.

Advocates of parochial school aid sometimes make a similarly contorted argument when they contend that they cannot practice their religion fully unless the government pays for parochial school tuition. Again, the logic fails. The government has no obligation to assist anyone in practicing religion. Indeed, the government should be forbidden from taking on this role. This argument is analogous to asserting that one is not free to practice religion unless the government provides Bibles, choir robes, candles, prayer books, and other religious items free of charge. The state can only make sure that religious freedom is not infringed upon by bureaucrats or burdened with undue regulation. From that point you're on your own.

Another argument along these same lines is the claim that the religion clauses of the First Amendment are really only one clause. This assertion is most closely identified with conservative Roman Catholic priest

Richard John Neuhaus. Neuhaus argues that the overriding purpose of the First Amendment's religion sections is to promote religious freedom. He insists that the "establishment" provision should be subservient to the "free exercise" goal.

Nothing in the historical record of the development of the First Amendment supports this view. The writings of the founders show that many of them were concerned with the dangers of officially established, state-supported religion. They wanted to put an end to that evil.

Giving Neuhaus the benefit of some doubt shows where his argument has gone off track. For argument's sake, let's accept the claim that the free exercise of religion was the overriding goal of the religion clauses. Can an American have religious freedom if he or she is forced to pay a church tax or subsidize churches in other ways? Are parents free to exercise their faith if their children are being force-fed religious views that are alien to the family in public schools? Doesn't a government-sponsored religious oath infringe on religious freedom?

A guarantee of free exercise is not enough to safeguard religious liberty. There must be some mechanism to ensure that the government does not impose religion on its people—because that imposition is in itself a serious violation of free exercise. That is why our First Amendment contains two key concepts—no establishment and a guarantee of religious free exercise. One does not work without the other.

Phony arguments aside, the concept of religious free exercise faces serious threats today. It is no exaggeration to say that the situation is critical as the Supreme Court continues to turn a deaf ear to legitimate claims of church-state abuses, and Congress is unwilling or unable to help.

There is one bright spot: As I stated at the beginning of this chapter, religious freedom is a cherished right of the American people. If government tampers with it too much, a backlash is inevitable. That backlash may be building now. Unfortunately, the country may have to travel through some difficult periods—periods especially troubling for minority religions—until its full impact is felt.

Notes

1. *United States* v. *Ballard*, 322 U.S. 78 (1944).
2. See *Watson* v. *Jones* (1872) and *Kedroff* v. *Saint Nicholas Cathedral* (1952).
3. *Reynolds* v. *United States*, 98 U.S. 145 (1879).

4. *Davis* v. *Beason*, 133 U.S. 333 (1890).

5. *Church of Jesus Christ of Latter-Day Saints* v. *United States*, 136 U.S. 1 (1890).

6. *Cantwell* v. *Connecticut*, 310 U.S. 296 (1940).

7. *Prince* v. *Massachusetts*, 321 U.S. 158 (1944).

8. *Murdock* v. *Pennsylvania*, 319 U.S. 105 (1943).

9. *Minersville School District* v. *Gobitis*, 310 U.S. 586 (1940).

10. Leo Pfeffer, *Church, State and Freedom* (Boston: Beacon Press, 1953), p. 523.

11. *West Virginia Board of Education* v. *Barnette*, 319 U.S. 624 (1943).

12. See *United States* v. *Schwimmer* (1929) and *United States* v. *Macintosh* (1931).

13. *Hamilton* v. *Regents of the University of California* (1934).

14. *Sherbert* v. *Verner*, 374 U.S. 398 (1963).

15. *Frazee* v. *Department of Employment Security*, 489 U.S. 829 (1989).

16. *Wisconsin* v. *Yoder*, 406 U.S. 205 (1972).

17. *Employment Division, Department of Human Resources* v. *Smith*, 494 U.S. 872 (1990).

18. *City of Boerne* v. *Flores*, 117 S.Ct. 2157 (1997).

19. *Church of the Lukumi Babalu Aye* v. *City of Hialeah*, 113 S.Ct. 2217 (1993).

8

Symbols and Sunday Laws: Other Types of Church-State Problems

Disputes over parochial school aid, religion in public schools, and the free exercise of religion account for the bulk of America's church-state controversies. However, there are other issues in the church-state field that should not be overlooked. Many of these issues have been litigated in state and federal courts, adding much to the body of church-state law. This chapter will review some of these controversies.

Religious Symbols on Public Property

Every year around Christmastime people in communities across the nation squabble over religious symbols on public property. Some years see outbreaks of these types of disputes in cities big and small in every corner of the country. These fights mar the holiday season every year for some people.

The Supreme Court and lower federal courts have wrestled with this issue, and, in a line of decisions, some general guidelines have emerged. If followed, these rulings could give city officials a good idea of what is constitutional and what is not regarding religious displays. Unfortunately, few members of municipal government, it seems, are willing to wade through the rulings. Or, more likely, they simply choose to ignore them and put the symbols up, hoping no one will complain. These same folks then turn around and label as "grinches" those who speak out against government display of the symbols.

Through all the High Court rulings on religious symbols, one fact is clear: Government may not sponsor displays of religious symbols standing alone at government sites. Creches put up by the city council on the steps of the city hall with no other symbols or material present are not constitutional.

The government may, however, include nativity scenes, menorahs, and other religious symbols as part of larger holiday displays that also contain secular holiday symbols (such as Christmas trees, figures of Santa Claus, or reindeer).

Also, private groups—the Jaycees, religious organizations, etc.—may display sectarian symbols on public property *provided that* the property has been open to other free speech activities in the past. A public park, for example, that has been the site of demonstrations or political rallies can be used by private groups to display religious symbols. But even then, the symbols cannot be erected permanently. And, once that area is opened up to displays of these types, all groups in the community have a right to use it.

Confused? It's really not that complex. Generally speaking, the government should stay out of the business of erecting, maintaining, or encouraging the display of sectarian symbols on public property. If government officials insist on doing so, they should add a generous mix of secular symbols to abide by the so-called plastic reindeer rule.

In a nutshell, that is the policy the Supreme Court has articulated. Whether or not it makes sense is open to debate. Many advocates of church-state separation believe the "plastic reindeer" rule is a dodge at best and argue that the presence of secular symbols does not mute the inherent religiosity of creches and menorahs. There is much to be said for this argument.

Conversely, a lot of religious folks argue that mixing the secular and the sacred is offensive to the devout and ought to be avoided. Again, this is a valid argument.

The tragedy of the religious symbols cases is that every year someone's holiday is ruined by often mean-spirited fights that simply aren't necessary. It doesn't have to be that way. There is an obvious solution to this annual seasonal tussle: Let the churches and other faith groups in a given community sponsor religious displays. Keep the government out of it entirely.

Even most small towns have at least one large house of worship occupying space on a prominent thoroughfare. There is no reason why the creches and menorahs could not be erected on the front lawns of these facilities. Better yet, each house of worship could erect its own display, thus increasing the number and variety of religious symbols for citizens to see.

Such an approach has worked in Pittsburgh, site of a major battle over religious symbols at the courthouse and city-county building in the late 1980s that reached the Supreme Court. Weary of the annual fight, Mayor Sophie Masloff in 1990 asked that religious symbols be displayed across the street from the government buildings on private property.

Court intervention or not, disputes over religious symbols tied to Christmas or Hanukkah eventually blow over when the holiday season passes. But recently in some parts of the country battles have broken out over permanently erected crosses on public property.

The problem seems especially bad in California. In the San Diego area, church-state separation activists sued to have two large crosses removed from public property. A federal judge ruled in 1991 that the crosses violate the California constitution's "no preference" religion clause, a decision that was later upheld by the U.S. 9th Circuit Court of Appeals. Meanwhile, a group of state lawmakers launched a drive to amend the state constitution in the event the decision survived further appeals. That attempt failed, and litigation continued to drag on.

Richard John Neuhaus, a Catholic priest and frequent critic of church-state separation, argues that efforts like this to remove religious symbols from public property result in a "naked public square" and encourage government hostility toward religion.[1]

Neuhaus and those who make this and similar arguments overlook several salient points. First of all, the "public square" is more than just a physical place, it is also an intellectual forum where various ideas are advocated, defended, and exchanged. Under this definition, church leaders in the United States have most certainly not been excluded from the public square. Religious groups enjoy absolute freedom to enter the public square and contend for various issues that are important to them. Some people may not like it when churches undertake such a role, but it is perfectly legal and appropriate under our Constitution.

A multitude of religious groups maintain lobbying offices in Washington, D.C., and the state capitals. Collectively they enjoy significant influence over the political system—influence many secular political action committees (PACs) would like to have. Religious leaders, in fact, continually make pronouncements on the burning issues of the day. In Neuhaus's own tradition, one need look no further than the pastoral letters often issued by the U.S. Conference of Catholic Bishops. Such a grand measure of freedom hardly sounds like a system that seeks to silence the voice of religion.

When looking at the public square solely as a physical place, it must be pointed out that the government allows certain public forums to be used by religious groups on an equal basis with nonreligious organizations. True, religious groups do not enjoy monopoly power over the public square, but clearly they have no right to expect such exaggerated influence.

Thirdly, the government must represent people of divergent backgrounds and faiths. No American should be made to feel like an outsider because of his or her religious beliefs. In light of that obvious fact, it is clearly inappropriate for the "public square" to be taken over by the government and filled with sectarian messages that only divide our people.

If the "public square" is really a "government-sponsored square," then it should be a forum for messages that unify us—not tear us apart and suggest that some citizens are more favored by the government than others. Alternately, it should be a place where all citizens and groups have the right to make their say—including religious groups—but not a place where religion receives special favors, which is what Neuhaus and his crowd really mean when they talk about "hostility toward religion" and access to the "public square."

Addressing the symbols issue during a church-state conference in Philadelphia in 1991, Marvin E. Frankel, a retired federal judge, made some wise observations. The effort to flood the public square with sectarian symbols is offensive to many, he pointed out. "The demand is no less and no more than an attempt by some people to show who's boss," Frankel remarked. "It says, 'This is a Christian country. If you don't like it, you know what you can do.'"[2] He is exactly right.

The problem of religious symbols on public property may seem trivial to some, but to those involved in litigation such as that described above, it is a very important issue. Obviously the display of a 103-foot Latin cross on government-owned property, maintained with public funds, sends a signal that Christianity occupies a special place in the eyes of the government. These symbols, which are overt and often impossible to avoid, are the best example of the "in your face" school of church-state thought. To religious minorities they send a clear message of who the majority is and suggest that this majority enjoys special status in government—a status religious minorities clearly do not share. Obviously, this is an inappropriate message for the government to send.

But it is not only religious minorities who are offended by such displays. Often Christians oppose them, too. Many Christians believe that the cross, as the sacred symbol of Christianity, ought not to be appropriated by the state for any reason. They are offended to see a religious symbol, to which they attach deep significance, wedded to the naked power of the government—or junked up by being paired with tacky plastic elves and cheap Christmas tinsel.

Symbols do have meaning, and the infusion of sectarian symbols with government symbols reeks of the worst kind of two-bit theocracy. These displays cheapen both the church and the state. For all involved, it is best that they be removed at once. If that is absolutely not practical, then the land the symbols stand on should be sold to private groups, with all maintenance costs shouldered by voluntary contributions.

In the late 1990s, a number of disputes occurred around the country dealing with government displays of the Ten Commandments. Several Religious Right groups launched projects designed to prod local governments to display the Decalogue, not bothering to point out that litigation would likely follow. It did, and in a number of cases, federal courts struck down the displays. The Supreme Court refused to hear these cases, leaving the counties and cities that had approved these displays stuck with large legal bills.

In Alabama, the chief justice of the state supreme court, Roy Moore, erected a two-ton Ten Commandments display in the lobby of the Judicial Building in Montgomery. Moore had won election to the top judicial slot in 2000 with backing from the Religious Right. He had become a hero to them when, as a local judge in Etowah County, he refused to remove a hand-carved Ten Commandments plaque from his courtroom.

Civil liberties groups asked Moore to remove the display at the state high court, but he refused. Moore seemed to relish his status as a Religious Right poster boy. He traveled the country, speaking before Religious Right groups and insisting that the United States was founded to be a Christian nation. He also entered into an alliance with TV preacher D. James Kennedy, who began raising money in case Moore was sued.

On October 30, 2001, Americans United for Separation of Church and State and the ACLU teamed up to sue Moore on behalf of several Alabama residents, demanding removal of the Ten Commandments monument. The case was pending in federal court as this book went to press.

Civil Religion

In American society, religious leaders are generally looked upon more favorably than government officials. Civic leaders, perhaps hoping to capitalize on some of religion's good public image, often seek the prestige of religion. Many government officials see cloaking themselves in religion as one sure way to boost their poor public persona.

But there is a catch: Religion that is promoted in the public arena by politicians must be sufficiently "nonsectarian" so as not to offend any constituent. For this reason, chaplains who appear before legislative bodies usually end their prayers "in God's name," not "in Jesus' name." Prayers are usually addressed to "Our Lord," "God," or something vague like "the one who watches over us."

Civil religion—religious practices performed for the benefit of government agencies or the type of generalized religion pushed by politicians—is therefore a bland exercise that sometimes offends the devout with its watered-down flavor. Nevertheless, civil religion is definitely on the upswing in the United States. From city halls and school boards to the White House and Congress, government officials are clamoring for religious leaders to open their sessions with invocations and prayers.

A 1983 Supreme Court decision upheld the concept of legislative chaplains and may have sparked the new drive for every school board, city council, and sewer authority in the country to find a preacher for its monthly gathering. In the case *Marsh* v. *Chambers*, the High Court ruled 6–3 that states may hire chaplains and even pay them out of public funds to open governmental sessions with prayers.[3]

The justices were clearly afraid to make the ruling that the First Amendment demands—mainly that state-paid religious ministers do not square with separation of church and state. Under the Court's own precedents the state-paid chaplains should have been struck down, but the justices, perhaps believing such a ruling would be too unpopular, decided to dodge precedent. They ruled that government chaplains have a long history in the United States and are thus "traditional." The majority pointed out that the first U.S. Congress had appointed state-funded chaplains, and thus no constitutional violation was found.

Justice William Brennan, pointing out that founding father James Madison opposed state-funded legislative chaplains, concluded that the practice had been unconstitutional all along and has not saved by its long history. He argued that the first Congress had acted more out of political concerns than respect for the Constitution some of them had helped draft.

But the damage was done. The decision has since been cited by municipal bodies of every sort to justify their premeeting prayers. Few other courtroom challenges on this issue have seen the light of day. In 1999, a federal appeals court ruled that the Cleveland Board of Education must stop opening its sessions with overtly Christian prayers, in part because public school students often attended the meetings.

And certainly municipal prayers have not always gone off without a hitch. Just the opposite is true. In many cases, citizens have criticized the prayers or their content. In 1990 an atheist in San Diego was arrested for protesting during prayers at a meeting of the San Diego Board of Supervisors. The following year, two school board members in the San Diego area challenged the board president's practice of opening the meetings with overtly Christian prayers. One board member said he would prefer a moment of silence because, "That does not offend anybody."[4]

Less commonly, members of government themselves are offended by the content of legislative prayers. In 1989 a guest minister offering a prayer before the Florida House of Representatives used the occasion to launch an anti-abortion tirade, angering pro-choice members of the delegation. The state representative who had invited the minister later apologized for the incident.

A similar incident occurred in Maryland in 1998, when a guest minister who had been invited to give the daily invocation by three lawmakers delivered a prayer that ended in the name of Jesus and criticized legal abortion. After some legislators complained, House Speaker Casper R. Taylor Jr. sent a letter to all House members, reminding them that House guidelines call for "inclusive, non-sectarian" prayers that are "carefully planned to avoid embarrassments and misunderstandings."

In 2000, legislators in Minnesota squabbled over legislative prayers in the House of Representatives after Republicans took control of the chamber and dropped a rule that the prayers must be "nondenominational." Some lawmakers began to express concerns over prayers that ended in Jesus' name or included other Christian references.

Battles over legislative prayers sometimes put units of local governments in difficult positions. In September 2000, a Wiccan leader in Dallas requested permission to give the invocation before a city council meeting, a job normally handled by a guest clergy member.

Council members at first agreed but then cancelled the invitation after religious conservatives complained. When the media publicized the snub, Mayor Ron Kirk reversed again and invited the Wiccan, Bryan Lankford, to offer the invocation. Lankford did so at a meeting on October 4. He addressed his prayer to "Mother Goddess, Father God." One council member, Donna Blumer, refused to acknowledge the prayer and would not bow her head.

Although prayers may be common before legislative bodies such as state senates, it does not follow that state-sponsored prayers can intrude on other branches of government. A county judge in North Carolina, for instance, was sued by the ACLU in 1990 after he refused to stop opening sessions with vocal prayers. The federal 4th Circuit Court of Appeals ruled against the judge, and the U.S. Supreme Court later refused to hear the case. The lower court said the prayers violated the religious neutrality of the courtroom, an essential feature of the secular legal system.[5]

Aside from prayers, the biggest church-state problem in the civil religion field today centers on ceremonial proclamations. Every year lawmakers in Congress, state legislatures, and city councils pass thousands of these resolutions. Most are inoffensive, marking, for example, occasions like National Dairy Goat Week or National Cauliflower Appreciation Day. But sometimes resolutions that deal with religious themes create controversy. Specifically, proposals put forth in many communities to designate 1990 the International Year of Bible Reading led to church-state problems.

In the California town of Benecia, Mayor Marilyn C. O'Rourke refused to sign a Year of the Bible resolution that had been passed by the town council on a 3–2 vote because it described the Bible as "the Word of God." Mayor O'Rourke argued that it was no business of the government to tell people when to pray or what religious texts to consult. Benecia's city council, O'Rourke insisted, should not take it upon itself to decide which religious texts qualify as "the word of God."

To buttress her argument, O'Rourke asked a local Catholic priest, David K. O'Rourke (no relation), to examine the resolution and offer an opinion. The Reverend O'Rourke offered some keen insights that are worth repeating here.

"If this proclamation is inconsequential—another National Asparagus Week or Year of the Grandfather—none of us, I suspect, is going to care one way or the other," observed the Reverend O'Rourke. "If it is intended as a serious action, and I gather it is, then I don't think it is the sort of thing that the council should be involved in. It is neither a good idea, nor a constitutional practice, for the government to tell people how to pray, the form of prayer to use, who to pray to, when to pray or even that they should pray. Our parishioners may call us to task on any of these areas, but for constitutional reasons the city council should not."

Continued the priest, "Every religious group in the United States is a minority group. Some may be unhappy with this status and wish they had official standing. I am not unhappy with it. The Catholic Church, the largest of these minorities, has prospered greatly in this country where we separate church and state."[6]

Courts do occasionally declare sectarian proclamations a violation of church-state separation. This occurred in Arizona in 1998, when a federal judge blocked Gov. Jane Hull's plan to designate a "Bible Week." The court ruled that endorsing the resolution did not have a secular purpose.

In Gilbert, Arizona, a compromise was struck. Rather than go to court, attorneys on both sides of the issue agreed that the mayor could issue a proclamation recognizing Bible Week but would refrain from urging residents to read the Bible or plan city-sponsored events to mark the occasion.

In matters of civil religion, government officials would do well to remember the voluntary principle. A moment of silence before a meeting would afford everyone an opportunity to pray, meditate, or simply clear the mind in preparation for the business at hand. Moments of silence avoid the divisiveness and acrimony that often occur during debates over civil religion. And best of all, they exclude no one. In a free country, no one should be made to feel that they have better standing before the government because they belong to the "favored" religion. Conversely, no one should be made to feel like an outsider on account of religious belief or lack thereof.

Before leaving this topic, it is important to look at two related issues that are continually cited by Religious Right activists who dislike separation of church and state. These are the motto "In God We Trust," which appears on U.S. currency, and the Religious Right's reliance on the phrase "Judeo-Christian heritage."

The argument that America is a Christian nation because "In God We

Trust" appears on the money is very weak. To begin with, this practice is not long rooted in our nation's history. The phrase first began appearing on coins sporadically in 1864 as the result of a pressure campaign by some ministers in the North who believed that the Civil War was God's punishment on the nation for not mentioning him in the Constitution.

President Theodore Roosevelt actually proposed removing "In God We Trust" from the coinage in 1905, but public outcry was so strong that Roosevelt not only backed off, he agreed to sign legislation mandating that the phrase appear on all coins. As paper money became more popular, a campaign got under way to make certain that "In God We Trust" would appear on notes as well. President Dwight D. Eisenhower signed legislation in October 1957 mandating that the phrase appear on all paper money.

Eisenhower also signed legislation designating "In God We Trust" as the country's official motto. He signed the bill on July 30, 1956. The legislation was in part a reaction to hysterical fears of creeping Communism that swept the United States during the heyday of Wisconsin senator Joseph McCarthy, a notorious, Red-baiting demagogue. Two years earlier, the words "under God" were inserted into the Pledge of Allegiance after a campaign spearheaded by the Knights of Columbus.

Arguments that the United States has a "Judeo-Christian heritage" are even less persuasive. ("Judeo" was added only recently, in a feeble attempt at ecumenism.) There is no consensus on what this term means among American religions. Consider the commandment, "Thou shall not kill," which is said to be part of this heritage. (Some versions of the Bible list it as "Thou shall not murder"—an important difference.) Some U.S. Christians and Jews interpret this as a mandate for pacifism, that is, a statement that all killing is wrong. Others do not extend it that far and say the commandment only forbids certain types of killings, carving out exemptions for self defense, war, and the death penalty for crimes. Compounding the situation is that certain great ethical principles—such as the Golden Rule to do unto others as you would have them do unto you—appear in some guise or another in all the world's religious and philosophical systems, thus negating any Judeo-Christian claim of a monopoly on them.

Christianity and Judaism are, to be sure, religions found in abundance in America. But when a Religious Right activist says something like, "The country must return to our great Judeo-Christian heritage," it is important to remember that his interpretation of that heritage is likely to be colored by sectarian and/or political bias. It certainly is not something all American religions agree on.

In sum, references to the United States' "Judeo-Christian heritage" are meaningless. More often than not, they are simply semantic devices used by fundamentalists who really mean, "The country should adopt my far-right Christian principles."

Mandatory Sunday-Closing Laws

Religious Right activists often accuse the Supreme Court of "legislating from the bench" or of forcing policies on the American people that the people do not want. This accusation is levied especially often in controversial church-state issues. But the issue of mandatory Sunday-closing laws proves that some church-state controversies can be resolved in a manner favorable to the separation principle without court mandates.

As chapter 4 indicated, mandatory Sunday-closing laws were typical in many states until well into the twentieth century. Despite their clear religious basis, Sunday-closing laws were often not considered a church-state problem. The statutes, also known as "blue laws" in many communities, simply *were*. Shops did not open on Sunday because it had always been that way.

Jews were early protesters of mandatory Sunday-closing laws. In some cities, Jewish shop owners argued that forcing them to close on Sundays created economic hardships. Observant Jews, who hold Saturday as the Sabbath, were forced to close two days out of the week.

Some Christians who also keep a Saturday Sabbath joined Jews in this protest, notably Seventh-day Adventists and Seventh-day Baptists. Finally, some shop owners who just wanted to make more money by opening on Sundays joined the cause

By 1961—the year the Supreme Court decided its first contemporary blue law case—some states had begun to relax their Sunday-closing laws a bit. At one time, the laws outlawed absolutely all business transactions on Sunday, but gradually certain exemptions were permitted. Medicine and other health-related goods, for example, could be sold on Sunday. Some states allowed food to be sold. Other states permitted small shops, the "mom and pop" type groceries, to open but ordered that large department stores remain closed.

The result was a crazy patchwork of laws in some states governing which items could be sold and which could not. The lists seemed to have little relationship to logic. Some states, for example, allowed frozen food to be sold but not canned food.

This type of confusion only increased cries for reform. In states where legislators did not take action, the courts were invited to step in. The first major legal battle started after employees at a discount store in Anne Arundel County, Maryland, were charged with selling the following items, all illegal to purchase on Sunday: a loose-leaf binder, a can of floor wax, a stapler, and a toy submarine. (The mind boggles at the planning that must have gone into this undercover police sting!) Attorneys representing the store argued that Maryland's blue law, which limited Sunday sales to foodstuffs, medicine, gasoline, and newspapers, violated the Establishment Clause of the First Amendment.

The Supreme Court consolidated the case with a similar dispute involving a department store in Allentown, Pennsylvania, and ruled 8–1 that mandatory Sunday-closing laws do not violate the Constitution. In one of the High Court's lowest church-state moments, the justices put the First Amendment aside in the *McGowan* v. *Maryland* ruling and lamely asserted that blue laws, though they indeed originally had a religious purpose, had become secularized over the years. Their only purpose now, the Court declared, was to provide a "day of rest" for weary retail workers.[7]

But even the Court's poor logic could not save blue laws. Their days were clearly numbered. Even as the Maryland case awaited decision before the Supreme Court, lawmakers in that state were taking steps to make the state's blue law less restrictive. Other states were taking similar actions.

Eventually, strict blue laws began to fade away. The public wanted to shop on Sundays (as evidenced by the fact that many shoppers would cross county or state borders to do so), and retailers, eager to increase their profits and keep dollars in state, urged state and local lawmakers to change or scrap the laws. Politicians, always attentive to the needs of business and cognizant of the economic boost brought by Sunday shopping, did not require much persuading.

As to be expected, there was some opposition to this liberalization, mostly from religious leaders who argued that Sunday shopping violates the "sacredness" of the day. But public will could not be thwarted, and most people apparently found the arguments of religious leaders unpersuasive. Store owners opened their doors on Sunday, and people came to shop.

The Religious Right has always found it difficult to accept that blue laws died a natural death and were not blasted out of existence by the Supreme Court. In his 1991 book *The New World Order*, television evangelist Pat Robertson falsely accuses the High Court of having struck down mandatory Sunday-closing laws in the *McGowan* case. To the Religious Right, it is inconceivable that some people might not want a state-imposed "day of rest."

For the most part, the blue law issue is mostly a dead letter today, but occasionally a dispute flares up somewhere in the country. In 1991 the North Dakota legislature repealed what was probably the nation's strictest blue law after efforts by shopkeepers to have it declared unconstitutional at the state Supreme Court failed. The vote in the state House of Representatives was not even close at 72–33, and Gov. George Sinner immediately signed the measure into law.

Weird blue laws also continue to plague certain parts of New Jersey. In Prospect Park, council members were forced to scrap an extremely strict blue law in 1991 after the American Civil Liberties Union threatened a lawsuit. The law was so severe it forbade even *leisure* activities outdoors on Sundays, and police occasionally told children riding bicycles outside to go home. A resident of a nearby town threatened to sue over the law after he was cited by police for fixing a broken radiator hose on his van while visiting his daughter one Sunday. In response, the town council modified the law to bar loud noises on Sunday.[8]

But these types of stories are exceptions. Most states and communities ditched blue laws years ago, and today department stores and other shops across the United States are open on Sundays, albeit often with curtailed hours. Disputes that do arise these days tend to revolve around issues unrelated to commerce. For example, Virginia and West Virginia lawmakers have in recent years deliberated the question of lifting Sunday hunting bans in those states. In May 2002, referenda questions to allow Sunday hunting appeared on the primary ballots in thirty-five of West Virginia's fifty-five counties. Voters in each county rejected the proposal, retaining the Sunday hunting ban.[9]

Religious leaders still occasionally pine for the old days. In recent years, Pope John Paul II has spoken out against Sunday commerce several times. Addressing French bishops in 1992, the pope bemoaned the fact that more people now work on Sundays, charging that today, "The traditional function of Sunday, day of the Lord, tends to be truncated."

The pope has even gone so far as to recommend that governments reinstate blue laws. In an encyclical issued in 1991, John Paul called for governments to recognize Sunday as a day of rest, calling the position "a human right, which is based on a commandment."[10] John Paul has also urged the leaders of the European Economic Community to impose blue laws—a move that has met with some success.

Some American bishops have picked up on the pope's crusade. In 1991 and 1993 Cardinal Bernard Law of Boston wrote to Massachusetts Gov. William Weld in opposition to Weld's proposal to allow stores to open at 9 A.M. on Sundays instead of noon.

"In the Christian tradition we are reminded that man was not made for the Sabbath, the Sabbath was made for man," wrote Law. "As a society, as families, as individuals, we need the quiet, the change of pace, the worship that a communal day of rest affords. Rather than a further erosion of what is a common good, we encourage the governor and the legislators to help our society restore a sense of the Sabbath."[11]

But as full mall parking lots indicate, the public does not necessarily believe it needs quiet or peace of mind on Sunday. Most don't share the view of Robertson, the pope, or Cardinal Law and favor Sunday shopping. As Americans work longer and longer hours during the week, they seem to need an extra day to run their errands. For the time being at least, this is one church-state issue that appears to be settled.

Churches and Taxation/Churches and Politics

Because the issues of churches and taxes and church involvement in politics are closely related, I will consider the two together in this section.

Religious groups, like other not-for-profit organizations, enjoy tax-free status. That is, they do not have to pay taxes on the donations they receive and are usually exempt from state income tax on the goods they purchase and the land they own. (Individual clergy members, however, must pay federal and state income taxes.)

Occasionally the suggestion is made that churches ought to be taxed. Religious groups, some say, have amassed great wealth and if we tax them we can balance the budget.

Theoretically, no legal barrier to taxing churches and other religious groups or nonprofits exists. In a landmark 1971 ruling in the case *Walz* v. *Tax Commission of the City of New York*, the U.S. Supreme Court declared that it is not unconstitutional for states to give houses of worship tax exemption. The High Court did not say, and has never said, that the federal government or states are *obligated* to give churches tax exemption. They said merely that it does not violate the separation of church and state for government to choose to do so.[12]

But no state, of course, has seriously entertained the notion of directly taxing churches. Many states do tax religious groups if they happen to run for-profit ventures unrelated to their religious mission, but otherwise, the general tax exemption afforded to churches is pretty safe.

One reason that churches stay free from taxation is that most offer a wide array of social services. Government believes these services provide a valuable safety net for society and reduce some of the burden on the state. In other words, if a church runs a homeless shelter, that's one less the government must open. The government does not want to discourage the social mission of houses of worship by slapping them with burdensome taxes.

There is also a fear that taxing churches would require the government to get intimately involved in churches' affairs and private matters, fostering entanglement between church and state.

Finally, the public seems to have little interest in taxing houses of worship. In 1996, advocates of church taxation in Colorado succeeded in getting a proposal on the ballot that would have required most houses of worship, religious nonprofit groups, and other type of nonprofits to pay property taxes. The proposal was easily defeated, 83 percent against to 17 percent for.

But the issue of taxing churches is not without controversy. In order to remain tax free, churches must refrain from getting too heavily involved in politics. For instance, groups awarded nonprofit, 501 (c)(3) status by the Internal Revenue Service—a designation that includes houses of worship and ministries—may not endorse or oppose candidates for public office. Therein lies the gray area. Some churches are known for their political activism, and many have been accused of going too far in their political activities.

In 1980 an abortion-rights group based in New York sued the IRS in an effort to force the tax agency to revoke the tax-exempt status of the Catholic Church over the bishops' anti-abortion activities. To bolster their case, the New York group pointed to several Catholic parishes where candidates for state and federal office had been openly endorsed in church bulletins.

It took nine years, but the Supreme Court ultimately decided that the abortion-rights group lacked the authority to sue the IRS in this manner. The case was dismissed due to lack of "standing"—a legal term meaning the right to sue—and the central issues it raised were never dealt with by a court.[13]

But the case might have had some positive fallout. Just before the

1988 presidential election, the U.S. Catholic Conference issued a twelve-page memo to churches warning clergy not to endorse candidates, form political action committees, or distribute campaign literature. Church lawyers have continued to issue bulletins like this every election year since. Other religious groups have issued them as well.

Many people think of the IRS as a fierce bureaucracy, determined to get every dime of tax revenue owed the government. This image may be accurate for private citizens, but when it comes to churches the IRS has tended to play the game a little softer. In fact, the IRS has traditionally given houses of worship wide berth. Houses of worship, for example, receive tax exemption by virtue of their very existence. They don't have to apply for it, as a secular nonprofit would. Federal law also makes it very difficult for the IRS to audit a house of worship. A secular nonprofit can be audited at any time.

There are signs, however, that the tax agency intends to enforce the no-partisan politicking rule. In 1991 the IRS conducted a lengthy investigation of television preacher Jimmy Swaggart and found him guilty of violating IRS rules by twice endorsing Pat Robertson for president during the 1988 campaign. Swaggart received no monetary fine but was ordered to sign a statement promising to refrain from intervening in future political campaigns.

The IRS's action, to be sure, was a slap on the wrist. However, it was a sign of things to come. By going after Swaggart, who by then was down on his luck due to sex scandals, the IRS might have been sending a not-so-subtle warning to religious groups about the dangers of mixing religion and politics: Next time it could be you.

Sure enough, in 1993 the IRS struck again and fined televangelist Jerry Falwell $50,000 after determining that his nonprofit *Old Time Gospel Hour* had illegally channeled money into a political action committee that gave money to conservative congressional candidates. The IRS also revoked the *Old Time Gospel Hour*'s tax-exempt status retroactively for the years 1986 and 1987.

In March 1998 the IRS announced that it had reached a settlement with Pat Robertson's Christian Broadcasting Network (CBN) over allegations of illegal political campaign activities related to Robertson's abortive presidential campaign in 1988. Under the settlement, the IRS revoked CBN's tax-exempt status retroactively for the years 1986–1987 and required the ministry to make what was called a "significant payment" to the IRS.

In the mid-1990s, the IRS announced that it was investigating a Binghamton, New York, fundamentalist church that ran an ad in *USA Today* just before the November 1992 election telling people that voting for Bill Clinton was a sin. The church, known as the Church at Pierce Creek, actually lost its tax-exempt status. After investigating the matter, the IRS pulled the church's tax-free status in 1995. (It has been reported that the IRS offered to let the church off with a warning if its leaders would promise to refrain from partisan political activity in the future; they refused.) The church, backed by TV preacher Pat Robertson's American Center for Law and Justice, sued to get its tax exemption back.

In court Robertson's attorneys argued that the Church at Pierce Creek had been the victim of selective enforcement. Other churches that engaged in political activity, they argued, had not been punished. Attorneys for the IRS countered that no other church had undertaken such a blatant act of politicking by placing a full-page ad attacking a candidate in a national newspaper and then soliciting tax-free donations to run more ads.

Robertson's attorneys also argued that the provision in the IRS Code barring churches for endorsing or opposing candidates was unconstitutional. These arguments were not persuasive. A federal district court and later the U.S. Court of Appeals for the District of Columbia ruled for the IRS and upheld the "no-politicking" provision. Robertson's legal team didn't even bother to ask the Supreme Court to review the case.

In March 1996, Americans United for Separation of Church and State announced the formation of "Project Fair Play," a national effort to examine the issue of illegal politicking by churches. Americans United announced that it would report instances of blatant politicking by houses of worship and religious nonprofits to the IRS. The group made it clear that its efforts would be bipartisan and that it would report houses of worship for endorsing or opposing Democrats, Republicans, and third-party candidates. The group urged Americans to send in evidence of this type of political activity in churches.

Several Religious Right groups went into an immediate frenzy over the project. Seven years later, Americans United had reported thirty-eight houses of worship and religious nonprofits for inappropriate political activity. Religious Right organizations were so outraged that they persuaded a Republican congressman, Walter B. Jones of North Carolina, to introduce legislation in the House of Representatives that would repeal the sections of the IRS Code that prohibit church endorsements. The legislation was rejected by the House of Representatives in October 2002.

Aside from incurring the wrath of the IRS, religious leaders who choose to get involved in partisan politics run other risks. Members of the denomination, for instance, may object. Many religious people still believe politics to be a dirty business that the church should be above. Some groups, like the Jehovah's Witnesses and some fundamentalist-oriented denominations, take this position to an extreme and refrain entirely from getting involved in politics. Their members don't even vote.

The Roman Catholic bishops run an almost constant risk of sparking a backlash from American Catholics over the issue of abortion. In recent years, some conservative bishops have suggested that Catholic lawmakers who refuse to toe the church's severe anti-abortion line be excommunicated. But support for this position among Catholics in general is very low. Indeed, a majority of American Catholics, polls consistently indicate, are pro-choice. In light of that, the hierarchy wrestles with how far they can take this issue.

Political activity by church leaders can polarize denominations. In the early 1980s, conservative forces in the Southern Baptist Convention (SBC) orchestrated an effort to seize control of the denomination's leadership. Having done so, they immediately reversed the denomination's historic stands in favor of separation of church and state. The group's leadership is now solidly antiseparationist.

In the process of switching from proseparation to antiseparation, the SBC fell into line with the Republican Party. Top Republican officials regularly address SBC gatherings and maintain close ties with church officials. In the early 1990s, both President George Bush and Vice President Dan Quayle appeared before Southern Baptist meetings.

The close ties between the SBC and the GOP has split the denomination. A dissatisfied splinter group of members who still favor church-state separation, known as "moderates," have slowly been building their own institutions and working to keep their ideas and the denomination's traditional views on church and state alive. Some observers believe the moderate wing will eventually branch off and form a separate denomination or will align with more moderate Baptist bodies already in existence.

As the SBC experience shows, religion and politics make for a volatile mixture. Across the country, extremely conservative, antiseparationist forces are launching carefully planned campaigns to win local offices. Much of this activity is coordinated by Pat Robertson's old group, the Christian Coalition, and other Religious Right groups. They have been successful in some parts of the country because of low voter turnout.

Robertson's forces have focused their efforts almost exclusively on the Republican Party. In the 1990s they managed to take control of state Republican parties in more than half of the states. Alarmed moderate Republicans tried to fight back, but their efforts were too little too late. The ongoing battle has alienated many socially moderate Republicans. Some political observers believe it has driven large number of women in the suburbs away from the GOP.

Conservative Christians have every right to participate in politics, of course. They can run for office and register voters just as any other American can. Religious Right activists often claim that their rights to do these things are somehow suppressed when efforts are made to expose their narrow agendas. Nothing could be further from the truth.

Anyone who runs for public office should be prepared to accept thorough and ongoing scrutiny of his or her views. In California in the early 1990s, Religious Right activists ran a variety of "stealth candidates." These people ran low-key campaigns based in several large fundamentalist churches in a given area, making few if any public appearances at voter forums. Many won local races due to low voter turnout. Alarmed citizens organized their own efforts, and many of those candidates were not returned to office. The "stealth" strategy became more difficult to use as the 1990s went on.

Exposing candidates who have narrow, sectarian agendas that run counter to democracy is not bigoted. It is not "anti-Christian." Providing information to voters about candidates is the American way. The Religious Right fears it because so often when this information is released, their people are soundly rejected. Why else would they run "stealth campaigns" in the dark?

One other point needs to be made before we leave this issue: When a church or religious leader speaks out on a controversial issue of the day, the cry is occasionally heard, "He can't do that! What about separation of church and state?"

These types of complaints are misguided. The church leader *can* do that, and separation of church and state has nothing to do with it. Clergy have a broad right to speak on moral issues of the day. However, they do not have the right to expect that their pet theological notions be written into law for all to follow. They must persuade people that their view is the correct one, not seek obedience through the power of the state. Also, members of the clergy who speak out on political issues must expect that others will disagree with them, and some will do so in public. This is how the American system works. Spirited opposition should not be confused with an attempt to censor.

Finally, it is not illegal for members of the clergy to run for and hold public office. Years ago, the state of Tennessee had a law barring "Ministers of the Gospel, or priests of any denomination whatever" from holding public office. In the 1978 case *McDaniel* v. *Paty* the Supreme Court struck the law down by a unanimous vote.[14] The High Court's action was appropriate. In a free society, everyone should have the right to run for public office. If the voters are upset at the thought of clergy running for office, they can make their feelings known at the ballot box.

U.S.–Vatican Diplomatic Ties

Near the end of Ronald Reagan's first term, the president surprised the religious community with the announcement that he would establish full diplomatic ties with the Vatican. An ambassador-elect, William Wilson, was named, and the U.S. Senate was asked to confirm the nominee.

Reagan's action created an uproar in some segments of the American religious and civil liberties communities. In a rare display of ecumenism, mainline Protestants, represented by the National Council of Churches, joined more conservative elements on the spectrum of American theological thought in opposing the move.

The idea of a formal diplomatic relationship between the U.S. government and the Holy See was nothing new. In fact, an ambassadorial exchange had been proposed in 1951 by President Harry S. Truman. Truman was prepared to name Gen. Mark Clark Vatican ambassador, but the plan was derailed by widespread public outcry. Letters deluged the White House and Capitol Hill, and religious leaders denounced the move from pulpits across the nation.

The 1984 protest lacked much of that vigor. While many religious denominations went on record in opposition to the move, they seemed to lack the spirit for an aggressive fight to block the exchange of ambassadors. The Senate Foreign Relations Committee held hearings on the matter, but in the end the Senate voted overwhelmingly to approve Wilson's appointment, 81–13.

A coalition of religious and civil liberties groups, led by Americans United for Separation of Church and State, filed suit in federal court to block the move as a violation of church-state separation. The court, however, dismissed the suit on grounds of "lack of standing," holding that Americans United and the other groups did not have the authority to challenge Reagan's action. The central issue of the lawsuit—whether or not the establishment of diplomatic relations with the Vatican transgresses separation of church and state—was not addressed by the court.[15]

Since then, five men and one woman—all Roman Catholics—have held the ambassadorship. The last ambassador under George Bush, Thomas P. Melady, a former university administrator, is a member of the Knights of Malta, an international Catholic chivalric order with about 2,000 members in the United States. (Melady's two predecessors, Wilson and Frank Shakespeare, were also members of the group.) Bush's son, George W. Bush, named James Nicholson, a former chairman of the Republican Party, to the post.

Although the issue is rarely discussed today, it is clear from a constitutional perspective that U.S.–Vatican ties violate the First Amendment. The Vatican may claim to function as an independent foreign state, but clearly it is a nation in name only. The Vatican, which is only 108 acres in size, exists solely to serve as the world headquarters of the Roman Catholic Church. The United States government, as a secular entity bound by law to treat all religions equally, should not have a special relationship with one church. Such an action gives Catholicism a favored status with the United States government that other religions can never hope to achieve.

Wilson himself acknowledged the religious nature of U.S.–Vatican ties in a 1985 speech, calling the relationship "a quest for morality" on the part of the U.S. government. To say the least, this is a highly questionable motive for establishing diplomatic ties.

Vatican ambassadors have tried in vain to draw some distinction between the Vatican as a religious entity and as a state. Frank Shakespeare once remarked, "We don't have an ambassador to the church. We have an ambassador to the Holy See, which is a legal, juridical state. That's important. We have an ambassador for the same reason that 117 other countries do. It's in our national interest."[16]

But since the Vatican itself makes no such distinction between the sectarian and secular, Shakespeare's assertion is meaningless. The pope is first and foremost the spiritual leader of the world's estimated one billion Roman Catholics. Any action the Vatican takes in world affairs or U.S. policy is first put through a sectarian filter. The United States should no more have an official diplomatic relationship with the Vatican than it should with the Church of England, the Southern Baptist Convention, or the United Methodist Church.

Indeed, the creation of formal ties between the two entities, critics say, has given the church yet another avenue to lobby the U.S. government for political goals favored by the Catholic Church, most relating to social issues such as birth control and abortion and aid to parochial schools.

In 1992 former Vatican ambassador Wilson told *Time* magazine that U.S. officials teamed up with the Vatican in the early 1980s to destabilize Poland's Communist government. As part of the deal, Reagan agreed to help implement the Catholic Church's narrow policy on birth control worldwide by sharply curtailing U.S. involvement in promoting family planning overseas. As a result, U.S. aid was cut off to international family planning agencies that fund birth control and abortions.[17] Subsequent Republican presidents have kept the ban in place.

The special relationship has also given Vatican officials immunity under U.S. law. In 1990, Bishop A. James Quinn told a conference of priests schooled in Roman Catholic Church law that the Holy See's diplomatic status could come in handy under certain conditions, such as when church officials are dealing with charges of clergy misconduct and accusations of child molestation by priests.

Noting that international law prevents police in host countries from searching embassies, Quinn pointed out that subpoenaed files may not be tampered with or destroyed, but added, "If there's something there you really don't want people to see, you might send it off to the Apostolic Delegate [another name for the Vatican Ambassador] because they have immunity. . . . Something you consider dangerous, you might send it there."[18]

It should be noted that Quinn's recommendation was not endorsed by the hierarchy of the church. In fact, a Roman Catholic lawyer-priest warned against such an action in a 1985 report to church officials, pointing out that sending sensitive material to the Vatican embassy could "insure that the immunity of the nunciature would be damaged or destroyed by the civil courts."[19] Still, the suggestion that church officials could exploit U.S.-Vatican diplomatic ties to cover up wrongdoing is chilling, especially in light of the child-abuse scandal that rocked the Catholic Church in 2002.

Critics have also argued that the diplomatic relationship gave the Catholic Church, which has become increasingly conservative under current pope John Paul II, opportunities to team up with rightist elements in the Reagan and Bush administrations to meddle in world politics. The Knights of Malta, for example, have been active in funding various covert operations in Latin America ostensibly designed to subvert Communism. The Knights' close ties to the Republican-appointed Vatican ambassadors have undoubtedly facilitated these actions.

When Democrat Bill Clinton was elected president in 1992, separationists urged him to leave the Vatican ambassador slot vacant. But Clinton ignored the advice and appointed Boston mayor Raymond Flynn to the post. Flynn was the fourth Roman Catholic to hold the position. When Flynn resigned, Clinton named another Catholic, Corinne "Lindy" Boggs, to the position. In 2000, President George W. Bush appointed another Catholic, Nicholson, to the slot. There seems to be something like a "religious test" to be U.S. ambassador to the Vatican—you have to be a Roman Catholic.

In summary, then, although the establishment of diplomatic ties between the United States and the Vatican raised serious church-state questions that remain unanswered to this day, the action did not raise sufficient concern among the American people to warrant serious examination of the issue by the Senate. This is unfortunate. Now that the relationship is entrenched, it is unlikely to be undone.

Unfortunately, official U.S.–Vatican ties are probably here to stay—much to the detriment of both church and state in this country.

Notes

1. Richard John Neuhaus, *The Naked Public Square* (Grand Rapids, Mich.: William B. Eerdmans Publishing, 1984).

2. Rob Boston, "Religious Liberty at the Crossroads," *Church & State* (July–August 1991): 4–7.

3. *Marsh* v. *Chambers*, 463 U.S. 783 (1983).

4. "School Boards Struggle with Sex Ed. Classes, Distribution of Condoms," *Church & State* (April 1991): 17.

5. *North Carolina Civil Liberties Union* v. *Constangy*, 90-1880, 90-1881, U.S. App. 4th Cir. (1991).

6. "Bible Reading, Prayer and City Hall: Don't Make Anybody an Outsider!" *Church & State* (July–August 1990): 21.

7. *McGowan* v. *Maryland*, 366 U.S. 420 (1961).

8. "New Jersey Town Challenges Sunday Law to Avoid Lawsuit," *Church & State* (October 1991): 3.

9. "Voting Yes, Putnam County Can Hold a Referendum on Sunday Hunting," *Charleston Daily Mail*, September 13, 2002.

10. "New Papal Encyclical Endorses Religious Liberty, Sunday Laws," *Church & State* (July–August 1991): 21.

11. "Cardinal Law Attacks Sunday-Closing Reform in Massachusetts," *Church & State* (June 1991): 19–20.

12. *Walz* v. *Tax Commission of the City of New York*, 397 U.S. 644 (1971).

13. *United States Catholic Conference* v. *Abortion Rights Mobilization*, 487 U.S. 72 (1988).

14. *McDaniel* v. *Paty* 435 U.S. 618 (April 19, 1978).

15. *Americans United for Separation of Church and State* v. *Reagan*, 85-1309 (3rd Cir.) (March 21, 1986).

16. "Vatican, U.S. 'Groping' for Relationship, Ambassador Says," *Church & State* (September 1988): 16–17.

17. Carl Bernstein, "The Holy Alliance," *Time* (February 24, 1992): 28–35.

18. Jason Berry, "Loose Canon," *Church & State* (October 1990): 4–5.

19. Ibid., p. 5.

9

Thy Kingdom Come: Christian Reconstructionism

The Religious Right is not a monolithic movement. Like the mythical Hydra, the Religious Right is multiheaded, with each head representing a different faction. While the various groups that make up the Religious Right may agree on many key issues, they squabble over others—especially issues of theology and its relationship to the political order.

Some groups, like the Christian Legal Society and the National Association of Evangelicals, while theologically conservative and generally favoring closer ties between religion and government, are not unequivocally opposed to the concept of separation of church and state. Some of their supporters may agree that church-state separation is a good idea but argue that the concept has been taken too far in the modern age. (For many years, Sam Ericsson, an attorney with the Christian Legal Society, argued against official prayer in schools, warning evangelicals that coerced religion rarely increases devotion.)

Other Religious Right organizations, such as the Christian Coalition, the Family Research Council, Concerned Women for America, and Jerry Falwell's now defunct Moral Majority, are more vociferous in their attacks on Jefferson's wall of separation, brazenly proclaiming that they see no need for separation of church and state. They often attempt to portray separation as a myth or tie it to Communism or some other distasteful philosophy.

Extreme Antiseparationism

At its most extreme, the Religious Right encompasses a loose conglomeration of organizations that forthrightly call for scrapping the First Amendment and reordering government along the lines of the Bible's Old Testament. This movement is known as Christian Reconstructionism, theonomy, or dominion theology.

Reconstructionism is premised on the idea that people must submit totally to God in all areas of their lives, and that this submission should include the governments people form. At first thought, this may not sound so threatening to many believers. Many religious people in America believe in submitting to God's will. The problem with Reconstructionists is that they believe only *they* have the correct and proper interpretation of "God's will." And their interpretation is quite extreme. In a country where an estimated 2,000 separate religious denominations and communities strive to live together in peace, the problem inherent in the Reconstructionist approach is obvious.

Adding to the difficulty, Reconstructionists believe that the Old Testament contains a blueprint for a model society. Accordingly, they would have the government enforce Old Testament dictates through law. They have no use for democracy as we understand the concept today. They are quick to label those who do not agree with them "apostates," "blasphemers," or even "pagans." The society they burn to create would severely restrict the religious freedom rights of most Americans.

The Reconstructionists' insistence on doctrinal purity has fractured the movement more than once. Despite the infighting, strains of the movement continue to surface in many American churches of various denominations, especially those with a rigid fundamentalist or Pentecostal bent.

Because Reconstructionist ideas are so unusual, there is little threat that the philosophy's adherents will ever have their way in the United States. The primary threat from their ideas stems from the steady and increasing influence they have on conservative Christianity. Some church leaders, while not buying into the entire Reconstructionist package, have adopted portions of the ideology, particularly the movement's opposition to separation of church and state and the idea that the government has some sort of obligation to be run along religious lines. As a result, more and more conservative church leaders are turning away from the idea that separation protects religious liberty and adopting some variation of the notion that the state should enforce religious dictates by law and even asserting that this is what God demands. This is a tragic development. Separation of church and state will not survive unless the religious community supports it.

Even with that newfound support, Reconstructionists have a long way to go before achieving any of their public policy goals. Still, the movement has come a long way in just under forty-five years and should be watched.

R. J. Rushdoony

The best known proponent of Reconstructionism in the United States was Rousas John Rushdoony, a writer and theologian who for many years ran a California-based Reconstructionist think tank called the Chalcedon Foundation. In 1959 Rushdoony, who died in 2001, published his first Reconstructionist tome, titled *By What Standard?: An Analysis of the Philosophy of Cornelius Van Til*. Van Til, a Dutch theologian, is considered the movement's godfather.

Going back even further, Reconstructionists trace their ideas to John Calvin (see chapter 2), the French theologian who called for governments to purge "idolatrous practices" from the lands and advocated church-state union. As was indicated, Calvin's Geneva was a harsh theocracy that suppressed religious liberty. Nevertheless, Geneva under Calvin remains the Reconstructionists' model society.

The Reconstructionist Agenda

What do Reconstructionists believe? A complete analysis of the movement is not possible in a few pages. Entire books have been written analyzing the philosophy. A survey of the movement's views, however, shows that a reconstructed society would bear little resemblance to the religiously neutral, pluralistic American society of today.

The first thing to understand about Reconstructionists is that they consider "pluralism" to be a dirty word. By their thinking, anyone espousing theological error—that is, anyone who fails to agree with them totally on religious matters—has no right to religious freedom and may have his or her actions curtailed by the government. Such people, the Reconstructionists argue, are a threat to the moral order of the state. Religious toleration, a system whereby various faiths contend for members and public voice in an open dialogue, is anathema to the Reconstructionists because it affords people an opportunity to be exposed to theological error. As Rushdoony once put it, "In the name of toleration, the believer is asked to associate on a common level of total acceptance with the atheist, the pervert, the criminal, and adherents of other religions as though no differences existed."[1]

Virginia-based Reconstructionist Byron Snapp was even harsher in his analysis of the dangers of religious toleration and pluralism. Writing in *The Counsel of Chalcedon*, a Reconstructionist journal, in 1987, Snapp observed, "The Christian must realize that pluralism is a myth. God and His law must rule all nations. . . . At no point in Scripture do we read that God teaches, supports or condones pluralism. To support pluralism is to recognize all religions as equal. Such a recognition denies God glory that belongs uniquely to Him. Clearly our founding fathers had no intention of supporting pluralism for they saw that the Bible tolerates no such view."[2]

From this starting point, Reconstructionists go on to formulate a reordered society that would strip away most forms of government, leaving citizens accountable to local church authorities. Taxes would be replaced with mandatory tithing, and social services would be provided by church groups. Security and police services would be provided by local militias.

Reconstructionists advocate the death penalty for a variety of offenses, and some observers have noted that the scope of punishable offenses is so great that if a reconstructed society is ever implemented in the United States, few will be left to live in it!

Reconstructionists go beyond advocating the death penalty for criminal acts such as murder and rape and would apply it to a variety of "offensive" acts, some of which are religious in nature. A partial list of offenses meriting the death penalty under Reconstructionism includes striking or cursing a parent, adultery, incest, bestiality, homosexuality, "unchastity," witchcraft, juvenile delinquency, blasphemy, propagation of "false doctrines," and sacrificing to "false gods."

Commenting on this list, Rushdoony observed, "To the humanistic mind these penalties seem severe and unnecessary. In actuality, the penalties, together with the Biblical faith which motivated them, worked to reduce crime. Thus, when New England passed laws requiring the death penalty for incorrigible delinquents and for children who struck their parents, no executions were necessary: the law kept the children in line."[3]

In an article that appeared in the Reconstructionist journal *Chalcedon Report* in January 1999, the Rev. William Einwechter argued that incorrigible juvenile delinquents should be stoned to death. He cited Deuteronomy 21:18–21 to buttress his argument. "Properly understood," the Pennsylvania pastor argued, "it displays the wisdom and mercy of God in restraining wickedness so that the righteous might flourish in peace. It is those who reject this case law that should be embarrassed, for they have cast reproach on God and his law, cast aside the testimony of Christ and substituted their own imaginations for the blessed word of God."[4]

Gary North

Despite its extreme views, Reconstructionism has attracted a small core of followers, many of whom are prolific writers. One of them is Gary North, an economist who became one of Rushdoony's first disciples. North later married Rushdoony's daughter, but the two men had a falling out over an obscure theological point some years ago and remained estranged until Rushdoony's death. Rushdoony, if asked, would not acknowledge North and other theonomists outside his sphere of influence as real Reconstructionists.

North's bespectacled appearance hides an aggressive theocratic personality. In his books and newsletters, he blasts popular culture and lambastes those who do not espouse his version of Christianity. He also has a strong paranoid streak and is fond of predicting the eminent demise of American society. When the AIDS crisis erupted in the early 1980s, North asserted that the disease would become so widespread that hospital beds would be exhausted by the end of the twentieth century.

For many years North was based in Tyler, Texas, where he ran something called the Institute for Christian Economics. In the late 1990s, convinced that the "Y2K" crisis was going to cause the collapse of society, North relocated to an isolated compound in rural northwest Arkansas. North spent more than a year urging people to get out of cities, stockpile food, and buy guns. When the collapse failed to come about, North issued a brief statement acknowledging that he had overestimated the extent of the problem.

Like Rushdoony, North also has little use for democracy and once wrote, "The modern world has been threatened by the rise of mass democracy, the politics of one man, one vote."[5] And when it comes to implementing the death penalty for various religious "crimes," North outdoes Rushdoony. North's preferred method is stoning. To North, stoning has a nice biblical ring to it. North has researched the issue extensively and once listed five reasons why stoning is the method of choice for executing today's idolater: (1) Stones are plentiful and available at no cost; (2) No single blow can be traced to one person, thus reducing feelings of guilt; (3) Stoning displays the collective responsibility for crime prevention; (4) Executions should be public events; and (5) Stoning is symbolic of God's crushing the head of Satan as prophesied in Genesis 3:5.[6]

Reconstructionist Connections

Scholars H. Wayne House and Thomas D. Ice examined Reconstructionism in an interesting book published in 1989 called *Dominion Theology: Blessing or Curse?* (The two side with "curse.") House, a theology professor at Dallas Theological Seminary, and Ice, a Baptist minister who once followed Reconstructionist teachings, make a good case that the movement is increasing power in ultraconservative fundamentalist Christian churches.

House and Ice say Reconstructionists are becoming more and more willing to put aside doctrinal differences and work with other conservative religious groups. They hope to draw into their network ultra-Calvinist strains of Presbyterianism, Baptists, and assorted charismatic Christians.

Some of these groups, hearing only part of the Reconstructionist message, are falling for it. Oddly enough, the new alliance includes some charismatics, Christians who believe in a "spirit-filled" theology often marked by speaking in tongues, faith healing, and loud, spontaneous worship services. Naturally, Reconstructionists don't tell the charismatics that under a "Reconstructed" government, such forms of worship would be considered unlawful and might warrant the death penalty.

Rushdoony himself blasted charismatics in a 1982 book titled *Law and Society*. Wrote Rushdoony, "The mindless, meaningless babble of such worship is common to paganism, ancient and modern, where it is often associated with spiritistic possession. It is in any form alien to the

Biblical faith. It is a form of the 'abomination' condemned by Biblical law. It is not found with any faithful and consistent affirmation of the sovereignty of God and a full trust in the atoning blood of Christ."[7]

Strong words. But when Rushdoony was asked by *Church & State* magazine in 1988 to explain how he expects to build bridges to charismatics after writing a denunciation this harsh, his response was rather lame: "I am not [charismatics'] judge," he said. "The Lord Jesus Christ is. Too many Christians feel they have been called to sit in judgment of everyone."[8] (This from a man who advocates the death penalty for those propagating "false doctrines"!)

The real answer is that the Reconstructionists don't intend to tell charismatics what they think of their worship. They are only interested in whatever support they can cull from this group. They simply hope charismatic leaders won't bother to do the research necessary to uncover statements like Rushdoony's.

The Coalition on Revival

The Reconstructionists have tried on a few occasions to launch a political arm. Their first effort was called the Coalition on Revivial (COR). Based in California, the COR was headed by Dr. Jay Grimstead, who founded the group in 1982. Through the organization denied that it was Reconstructionist, some of its views fall more or less into lockstep with adherents of that philosophy.

At one time, COR's steering committee list read like a virtual who's who in Religious Right circles. The Rev. Donald Wildmon, head of the pro-censorship American Family Association, was a member. Other Religious Right luminaries who claimed membership included televangelist D. James Kennedy; Robert Dugan of the National Association of Evangelicals; the Rev. Tim LaHaye of the Traditional Values Coalition; former U.S. Rep. Mark Siljander, a Michigan Republican whose congressional comeback effort in Virginia failed in 1992, and Ed McAteer of the Religious Roundtable. (Gary North is also a steering committee member.)

Unhappily for COR and its sympathizers, the group's militant agenda, which called for abolishing public education, forming county-wide "militias," and dismantling the Federal Reserve, began to leak out in the late 1980s and early '90s.[9] In the wake of the disclosures, the more prominent Religious Right leaders began scurrying away from the group;

several hastily resigned from the steering committee. Wildmon went so far as to sue an official with the National Endowment for the Arts who attributed some of COR's ideas on capital punishment to him.

COR soldiered on. The group issued a series of "Worldview" documents and a list of theological tenets called the twenty-five articles. Investigative reporter Frederick Clarkson, who often writes about militant elements of the Religious Right, reports that one article reads in part, "We deny that anyone, Jew or Gentile, believer or unbeliever, private person or public official, is exempt from the moral and juridical obligation before God to submit to Christ's Lordship over every aspect of his life in thought, word, and deed."[10] Once again the Reconstructionist-type intolerance comes rapidly to the surface. Just who is to determine how to interpret "Christ's Lordship"? Could it be Jay Grimstead?

Grimstead himself seemed to think so. In December 1991 Grimstead became infuriated when Bill Allen, a conservative Republican in California, decided to run in a primary election for a U.S. Senate seat. Grimstead was angry because he wanted all California far-right forces to throw their support behind former U.S. representative William E. Dannemeyer, an ultraconservative ally of the Religious Right. Allen's candidacy, he feared, would split the Religious Right vote.

COR activists drafted a harshly worded letter to Allen warning him of the consequences if he did not drop out of the race. Although the letter was never mailed to Allen, a copy somehow got to him. Allen was appalled by the strident tone it took.

Grimstead said three things would occur if Allen did not drop out. First, Christian activists would work to "expose to our Christian network the foolishness and destructiveness of your efforts and encourage them to see your campaign for what it truly is—a political abortion which can only aid, indirectly, the forces of darkness." Second, the letter said, Allen's future political plans would be jeopardized. Last and most ominously, Grimstead warned, "We suspect that God Himself will take efforts to discipline you and judge this action of yours however He sees fit. Any of us who have been disciplined by our Heavenly Father can tell you He can deal very forcibly with us."[11]

Although the actual letter sent to Allen was softer in tone and deleted the reference to divine reprisal, the candidate took the original threat seriously and asked state officials to investigate. The California Attorney General's Office declined to do so. (In the end, both Allen and Dannemeyer were trounced in the primary.)

COR did not intend to limit its activities to the political sphere. A COR document issued in 1990 contained a twenty-four-point action plan that covered virtually all aspects of life, including the arts and popular culture. To counteract what they saw as the negative effect of the television, COR called for producing a Reconstructionist version of *Saturday Night Live*![12]

Other COR goals relating to film and television were not so amusing. Dr. Theodore Baehr, a COR steering committee member who heads the Christian Film and Television Commission, has called for implementation of a restrictive film code that would ban, among other things, "lustful kissing" and "dances that suggest or represent sexual actions" in movies. The code also declares that "No movie shall be produced that will lower the moral standards of those that see it," a guideline so loose it would give COR censors what they really wanted: veto power over all films.[13]

Baehr's code was originally endorsed by Cardinal Roger Mahony of Los Angeles, an archconservative Roman Catholic who in 1992 called on the motion picture industry to voluntarily adopt the Baehr standards. If the industry refuses, Mahony said, the government should intervene. When reporters exposed Baehr's ties to Reconstructionism, Mahony quickly broke contact with him and backed away from the code.

COR had big plans but lacked the ability to implement them. By the mid-1990s the group was more or less defunct. COR leaders announced that Grimstead had been working too hard and was going on a long sabbatical. Grimstead eventually returned to lead COR again, but the group's profile has been greatly reduced. Today COR's budget is a measly $78,000 annually—$51,000 of which goes toward Grimstead's salary. COR's main reason for existence these days seems to be to keep Grimstead employed. Even the group's Web site is rarely updated.

COR resurfaced in the media in 2002, when Florida governor Jeb Bush appointed Jerry Regier to head the state's Department of Children and Families. It soon came to light that Regier had worked with COR and helped draft a document called "The Christian World View of the Family," which endorsed spanking of children and male supremacy in marriage.

Although Regier served as co-chair of a COR committee that produced the document, he denied he helped write it and tried to distance himself from its conclusions. Regier also said he resigned from COR in 1990, although Grimstead said Regier did not leave until 1994 or 1995.

The Return of the NRA

The collapse of COR led some Reconstructionists to start a new political vehicle. In the late 1990s, a group of Reconstructionist ministers in Pennsylvania and Ohio took over the National Reform Association (NRA), an organization that was originally founded in 1864 with the aim of adding a "Christian nation" amendment to the Constitution. (See chapter 4.)

The NRA's heyday was the latter half of the nineteenth century. After the turn of the century, the organization took up the cause of Prohibition and soon lapsed into obscurity. But the NRA never became officially defunct. It continued to publish a magazine and undertake a few other activities. It was, however, more or less moribund.

The resurrection of the NRA was led by the Rev. Jeffrey A. Ziegler, a Presbyterian minister in Ohio. Like the leaders of COR, Ziegler has great ambitions for political activism. Unlike COR's leaders, he's close enough to the nation's capital to actually implement them. NRA leaders have made several forays into Washington, visiting with congressmen, senators, and their staffs. Organization leaders said they had made inroads with House Majority Leader Tom DeLay (R-Tex.), who had promised to help the NRA organize a session on biblical worldview issues for staffers in Congress. The group eventually hopes to have a full-time lobbyist and a related 501(c)(4) organization.

DeLay seems to have more than a little sympathy for the Reconstructionists' underlying philosophy. In April 2002, he appeared at a conference in Pearland, Texas, run by a group called Worldview Weekend. During his remarks, DeLay praised the idea that a fundamentalist interpretation of Christianity should rule over all areas of life.

DeLay told the crowd,

> Ladies and gentlemen, Christianity offers the only viable, reasonable, definitive answer to the questions of "Where did I come from?," "Why am I here?," "Where am I going?," "Does life have any meaningful purpose?" Only Christianity offers a way to understand that physical and that moral border. Only Christianity offers a comprehensive worldview that covers all areas of life and thought—every aspect of creation. Only Christianity offers a way to live in response to the realities that we find in this world—only Christianity.[14]

Reconstructionism and the Religious Right

At this point, readers might be wondering how Pat Robertson fits into all of this. After all, where there are wild-eyed antiseparationists to be found, Pat Robertson is usually not far behind. But when it comes to Reconstructionists, Robertson at least tries to keep a distance.

Robertson disagrees with a key component of Reconstructionist theology concerning the end of the world. Reconstructionists believe Christians of their stripe will rule over the world *before* the second coming of Christ and perhaps pave the way for His return. This view, common among evangelicals in the nineteenth century but largely out of favor today, is called *postmillennialism*. Robertson, by contrast, is a *premillennialist*. He believes that "born-again" Christians will not rule over the planet until a period of chaos and conflict following Christ's return.

Robertson has said of Reconstructionism, "I admire many of these teachings because they are in line with the scripture. But others I cannot accept because they do not correspond with the biblical view of the sinful nature of mankind or the necessity of the second coming of Christ."[15]

In June 1992 Robertson told *Christianity Today*, "I don't agree with Reconstructionism, although I do believe that Jesus is Lord of all the world. I believe that he is Lord of the government, and the church, and business and education, and, hopefully, one day, Lord of the press. I see him involved in everything. And that's why I don't want to stay just in the church, as such. I want the church to move into the world."[16]

The comments sparked an interesting response from Gary DeMar, a Georgia-based Reconstructionist. In the letters to the editor section of the magazine, DeMar wrote, "I was a bit confused when Pat Robertson claimed that he doesn't 'agree with Reconstructionism' but does believe that 'Jesus is Lord of all the world . . . of the government, and the church, and business and, hopefully, one day, Lord of the press.' This is the heart and soul of Reconstructionism."

Concluded DeMar, "At the very least, Pat Robertson, as I've always suspected, is an operational Reconstructionist."[17]

Although Robertson shuns the title "Reconstructionist" and says he disagrees with the movement over "endtime" theology, that hasn't stopped him from using books by Rushdoony and North at his Regent University. Also, Herbert Titus, former dean of the university's School of Law, once attended a small Reconstructionist-affiliated Orthodox Presbyterian church in Oregon. Titus, however, says he is not a Reconstructionist. Robertson has also spoken openly about receiving a financial newsletter produced by North.

More Reconstructionist Connections

Reconstructionist ideas also influenced John Whitehead, founder of the Rutherford Institute, one of the most active of the Religious Right legal groups. Whitehead says he is not a Reconstructionist, but several of his early books clearly reflect Reconstructionist ideas. Rushdoony wrote the introduction to Whitehead's first book, *The Separation Illusion*, an attack on separation of church and state, and the two appeared at a Washington, D.C., Religious Right conference in 1985. In fairness to Whitehead, it should be noted that he has moved quite a distance away from his earlier views. While he's still no fan of separation, Whitehead has broken with the Religious Right over some issues, such as gay rights.

Also apparently influenced by Rushdoony is John Lofton, a far-right columnist who was fired by the ultraconservative *Washington Times* newspaper (owned by the Rev. Sun Myung Moon, head of the controversial Unification Church). Lofton, who now puts out a far-right newsletter, occasionally writes columns for the Chalcedon Foundation.

More troublesome are the Reconstructionist ties to the Bush administration. Marvin Olasky, a University of Texas journalism professor who served as Bush's guru on "faith-based initiatives," has written several books with Reconstructionist overtones. In one of his books, *Fighting for Liberty and Virtue*, Olasky, writing of slavery, notes that the Bible "does not simply ban all of its modes."[18]

What do these spider-web–like connections mean? How concerned should we be about Christian Reconstructionists?

To begin with, *any* group that advocates policies as radical as the Reconstructionist agenda should be watched. Like hate groups that operate in the United States, the Reconstructionists are a potentially dangerous force that cannot be ignored just because they are currently scarier on paper than they are in real life.

At the same time, Americans must be cognizant of where the real danger lies. There is very little threat that the Reconstructionists will seize power next week and institute their odd ideas. Rather, as has been pointed out, the real danger lies in the influence they have had on some churches and the larger Religious Right movement. Reconstructionists could make this movement more extreme than it already is.

After Rushdoony's death, North commented in the *Los Angeles Times*, "Rushdoony's writings are the source of many of the core ideas of the New Christian Right's political activism."[19] As far back as 1980, Robert Billings, one of the founders of the Moral Majority, commented, "If it weren't for his books, none of us would be here."[20]

Rushdoony may have laid intellectual foundations for the Religious Right, but the goals of these organizations remain extreme. With that thought in mind, the best strategy for fighting Reconstructionism is simply a strong defense of separation of church and state. The Reconstructionist agenda will not appeal to any church leader who sees the value in maintaining a healthy distance between church and state. It needs to be said time and time again, therefore, that separation protects churches and helps them grow. If American church leaders lose sight of this, they are open to being tempted to embrace portions of the Reconstructionist agenda. They won't become theonomists overnight, but they might sign up with a Pat Robertson crusade or agree to show an anti-separationist video at church. Those types of small victories are what the Reconstructionists want—for now.

Fighting the Reconstructionists

The fight against Reconstructionism must be two-pronged. Many mainstream Christian bodies find "dominion" teachings abhorrent and completely antibiblical. These organizations must take the lead in working to persuade their brethren in other theological camps not to fall under the sway of North, the National Reform Association, and other Reconstructionist bodies.

At the same time, secular opponents of Reconstructionism must come to the forefront. While religious communities wage war against Reconstructionism from a theological perspective, secular groups can attack it from a public policy angle.

The majority of Americans do not favor executing children for any reason. Nor do most Americans, even those who believe that the sexual revolution has gone too far, want to see adulterers or fornicators dragged into the streets and stoned.

Americans, by and large, do not believe prosecuting people for blasphemy is a good idea. They also do not want to see the government making judgments about which religious beliefs are "true" and warrant state-sponsored support and which are "false" and warrant state persecution.

Some Reconstructionists are now making feeble attempts to portray themselves as "moderates" on the religious scene, but few are fooled by this stance. Reconstructionists are radicals who would impose a religious state on America. They want to line those who disagree with them up against a wall and stone them to death. They favor mandatory tithing to churches and executions for blasphemy. No matter how one tries to cover it up, this is what Reconstructionism is about. These are not moderate positions, and they are not positions that Americans—even conservative Americans—want to see implemented. Exposing these facts should be enough to cut Reconstructionism off at the knees.

Some Reconstructionist leaders are clearly uncomfortable defending the more extreme views of the movement. Gary DeMar, who runs a group near Atlanta called American Vision, spends most of his time promoting a mythical "Christian nation" view of U.S. history. Yet DeMar is a Reconstructionist and, when once forced by the Atlanta *Journal-Constitution* to say whether gays should be executed, he began to squirm and dissemble.[21] Reconstructionsts know how strange their ideas are to the average American. That's why they often don't discuss them before the general public.

We can learn a lesson from the fate of COR. Unlike the Reconstructionists, COR does not advocate stoning or the death penalty for a variety of "religious crimes." Their agenda is much more vague, but portions of it were extreme enough to draw support away once examined under the harsh light of media scrutiny. If the stated goals of COR were radical enough to spark desertions like this, the even more extreme agenda of the Reconstructionists should be more than enough to scare away any religious leaders tempted to flirt with the philosophy and still be taken seriously in the American religious community.

Most Reconstructionists can't be argued with or persuaded to return to the more sane folds of American theology. Advocates of church-state separation shouldn't waste too much time on efforts like that. Rather, the emphasis should be on containing the spread of Reconstructionism and isolating it to where it belongs—the lunatic fringe of extreme right-wing Christianity. If successful, this strategy will eventually relegate Reconstructionism to the long list of forgotten ideas in American religious history.

As recently as forty-five years ago some misguided religious leaders in America still preached that segregation of the races was "God's plan." It took a while, but eventually religious leaders came to realize that no worthwhile church would deny membership to anyone based on race or ethnic heritage. Today there are still faith groups that preach racism, but they are few in number and almost universally scorned in the United States. Separationists must work diligently to make sure that the same fate awaits the Reconstructionists.

American religious opinion runs the gamut. Some Americans are deeply devout, others are completely irreligious. Diversity like this keeps our country spirited and lively. It also guarantees, unfortunately, that certain strains of religious fanaticism will always be with us. Religious extremists will never hesitate to equate their twisted political and social notions with the word of God. This is their right in a free society, but that does not mean people should not oppose such views.

While Reconstructionist groups may have the right to exist, they have no right to expect to be taken seriously by the American people. They are, in fact, fair game for exposure and condemnation. In the end, these two powerful weapons may be all we need to spare America the tyranny of the Reconstructionists.

Notes

1. Rob Boston, "Thy Kingdom Come," *Church & State* (September 1988): pp. 6–12.
2. Ibid., pp. 7–8.
3. Rousas John Rushdoony, *The Institutes of Biblical Law* (Vallecito, Calif.: Ross House, 1973).
4. William Einwechter, "Stoning Disobedient Children," *Chalcedon Report* (January 1999): 11–12.
5. Boston, "Thy Kingdom Come," p. 7.
6. H. Wayne House and Thomas D. Ice, *Dominion Theology: Blessing or Curse?* (Portland, Ore.: Multnomah Press), pp. 73–74.
7. Rousas John Rushdoony, *Law and Society* (Vallecito, Calif.: Ross House, 1986).
8. Boston, "Thy Kingdom Come," p. 10.
9. Fred Clarkson, "HardCOR," *Church & State* (January 1991): 9–12.
10. Ibid., p. 11.
11. Frederick Clarkson, "Divine Discipline," *Church & State* (March 1992): 13–14.
12. Clarkson, "HardCOR," p. 11.

13. "Cardinal Teams Up with Fundamentalist Radical to Censor Movies, TV," *Church & State* (March 1992): 19.

14. Rob Boston, "Weekend Warriors," *Church & State* (June 2002): 6.

15. Boston, "Thy Kingdom Come," p. 9.

16. "Robertson Bullish on Family Channel, UPI," *Christianity Today* (June 22, 1992): 51–52.

17. Gary DeMar, "Letters," *Christianity Today* (August 17, 1992): 10.

18. Boston, "Operation Potomac."

19. Ibid.

20. Ibid.

21. Frederick Clarkson, *Eternal Hostility: The Struggle between Theocracy and Democracy* (Monroe, Maine: Common Courage Press, 1997), p. 82.

10

Preserving Church-State Separation in Your Own Community: Suggestions for the Citizen-Activist

The separation of church and state will not survive if it is not defended. It will not survive if people come to believe that the principle is not in the best interests of the nation or that it is hostile to religion.

Religious Right organizations are working to persuade Americans that separation of church and state harms, and does not protect, religious freedom. Unless Americans are educated about the true history behind church-state separation and how the principle defends religious liberty today, they may accept this propaganda.

While the public is being educated, separation of church and state must also be defended in the nation's courtrooms, statehouses, and in Congress. It will not be an easy task. But if it is not done, the results for the country could be disastrous.

People often ask what one individual can do to support church-state separation. The answer is quite a lot. With that thought in mind, here are some specific suggestions for activists who want to defend church-state separation in their own communities:

Stay informed. The first thing to remember is that information is vital. You have to know what's going on in your community, the nation, and the world. Americans are busier today than they have ever been according to some observers who track work trends, but do try to find time to read a daily newspaper or check a reliable news site on the Internet. (The Associated Press' Web site, ap.org, is a good source for this.) You certainly don't have to read every story all the way through, but by reading the top stories you can keep up with what's happening.

Newspapers and TV news will give you general information, but when it comes to church-state issues you'll need something more specific. One way to keep up on the current church-state issues is through *Church & State* magazine, the monthly publication of Americans United for Separation of Church and State. This magazine is the only journal of its type published in the country—a publication for the lay reader that provides news and analysis of the full range of church-state issues. Through guest columns and editorials, the journal provides activists with cogent arguments that make the case for separation. (Americans United also sponsors a listserve for those who want to get regular updates about church-state separation via e-mail. Visit www.au.org to sign up.)

Other organizations that work on church-state issues can serve as outlets for information. The American Civil Liberties Union, for example, is well known for its church-state legal work, although the group works on a whole range of additional civil liberties concerns. Aside from the ACLU, a variety of groups affiliated with religious denominations keep an eye on the church-state scene. Many Baptists who support church-state separation belong to the Baptist Joint Committee on Public Affairs, based in Washington, and read the BJC's publication *Report from the Capital.*

The American Jewish Committee and the American Jewish Congress also monitor church-state developments and often issue bulletins on specific religious liberty issues. The Anti-Defamation League of B'nai B'rith is another good source. The Seventh-day Adventist Church maintains a religious liberty office and publishes *Liberty* magazine, which centers on religious freedom issues.

With all of these resources around, there is really no excuse for not keeping informed.

Be involved politically. Watching the national scene is a good start, but it's not enough. Separationists must advocate at the local level. The Religious Right has done this with great success, focusing on local public schools and libraries. Advocates of church-state separation must learn to parrot that model. Across the country, thousands of Religious Right extremists are pressuring school officials to ban books, introduce creationism into the curriculum, or asking city councils to display the Ten Commandments, among other things. Separationists need to counter these actions.

Local elections are extremely important, and church-state separation activists should keep watch over all of them, no matter how insignificant the office may seem. You must be registered to vote, and you need to show up on election day.

Remember, voter turnout in the United States is often low. Even in presidential elections, only about 50 percent of the registered voters go to the polls. The turnout can be even lower for state and local races. Religious Right activists know this and have enjoyed great success in some parts of the country getting people elected to school boards, as well as to city and county councils, by taking advantage of low turnout. Once seated, these people can create untold mischief.

Leaders of Religious Right groups, especially the Christian Coalition, used to openly brag that they did not need the support of a majority of the voters to win elections. With so many people not even registered to vote and so many who are registered not bothering to cast ballots on election day, a candidate can win with the support of about 15 percent of the adult population. This strategy was sometimes called the "15 percent solution."

Being registered yourself is not enough. You also need to make sure that friends and associates who share your concerns about the Religious Right are registered and voting. Again, this is a strategy perfected by Religious Right groups. The Christian Coalition used to advise supporters to canvass church members and conservative neighbors with the aim of getting them registered and voting. On election day, they would call these people and offer a ride to the polls.

The Religious Right did not invent these techniques. They are time-tested strategies for political success. Candidates win by getting out the vote. It's that simple. Although employed by the Religious Right with great success in some parts of the country, defenders of church-state separation can also use these strategies.

Exposing Religious Right candidates is also important. Attend voter forums and ask candidates some pointed questions. Be wary of any candidate who refuses to attend voters' forums. In years past, Religious Right groups have run "stealth candidates" who make few public appearances but who mobilize a few large fundamentalist churches in town and work to turn out the vote there. They win by banking on the fact that most people do not vote.

Work with the media. Encourage reporters in your area to do full reports on all candidates for local office and list where they stand on a variety of issues. Every candidate for school board, for example, should be required to explain his or her position on two education-related church-state issues: vouchers and state-sponsored religious exercises in public schools.

In small and medium-sized towns, editors and reporters at local papers or radio stations are often quite approachable and open to ideas from readers or listeners. Suggestions for regular "candidate profiles" can bear great fruit. Encourage the local press to investigate candidates who have Religious Right ties. The public has a right to know if a candidate for the school board is in the pocket of Pat Robertson.

Newspapers in large, urban areas can be tougher to crack. If you fail to make headway here, it may be useful to approach a suburban weekly or a smaller paper in the area. These papers often cover local or neighborhood news more closely.

Remember, the Religious Right can win only as long as it is able to keep its agenda in the dark. Experience has shown time and time again that when Religious Right candidates are exposed, they usually lose. Religious Right candidates often depend on the votes of a few large fundamentalist churches as their support base. An informed electorate from the general population can often beat them, but only if people know what is going on and care enough to vote.

Educate the community. Advocates of church-state separation must step up their public outreach efforts. Friends of separation of church and state who have a flair for writing might want to consider letters to the editor. Again, this strategy takes a page from the Religious Right's own playbook: Their activists have flooded daily and weekly papers across the country with their propaganda. These letters should not go unchallenged.

Don't hesitate to respond to such letters. If you are unsure of your writing skills, ask a friend or family member who enjoys writing to help you get your ideas in order. Don't get overly concerned about your writing abilities. You don't have to be a best-selling novelist to write a letter to the editor; you simply need a statement that is as concise and as easy to read as possible.

Remember, the letters to the editor page is one of the most read sections of a newspaper. A proseparation message in this forum can reach tens of thousands of readers.

For letter writers, here is some specific advice:

- Most newspapers and magazines have a letters policy that is usually printed on the editorial or letters page or may be available at the paper's Web site. Read it and learn the newspaper's rules before you write. Some newspapers, for instance, limit the length of letters or the number that a reader can submit in a month. Few papers print anonymous letters, so always be willing to provide your name, address, and telephone number for verification purposes.
- In general, shorter letters are better. They stand a better chance of being published and read. Use short, direct sentences in the active voice. If you are unsure of your writing skills, go to a bookstore and pick up a self-help book on better writing to get some tips.
- Strive to be polite. When responding to an antiseparationist letter or editorial, resist the temptation to engage in name-calling or vituperation. Such letters are rarely printed, and if they are they can damage your credibility.
- Brush up on your grammar, and no matter how good your spelling is, try to find someone to proofread your letter before you mail it. Despite your best efforts, little mistakes can slip by you. (Of course, it won't be a disaster if you do make a grammatical error. Chances are the newspaper's editors will correct it.)
- Mail responses promptly, the same day or the next if possible. (You might want to ask if the paper accepts letters by fax machine or e-mail.) The longer you wait, the less timely the issue becomes and the smaller your chances of seeing the letter in print becomes.
- Check your letter for accuracy. If you are in doubt about any fact, look it up for confirmation in a reliable source. Be prepared to back up anything you say in your letter; remember, you may be challenged by another letter writer. If you make a factual error, you will be vulnerable to attack by other letter writers. A good rule of thumb is, "If in doubt, leave it out."

Speaking of accuracy, it is important to remember that Religious Right activists are often quite loose with the "facts" when they write about church and state. Mistakes and distortions are common because much misinformation about separation of church and state circulates in the Religious Right. Many fundamentalists simply accept these distortions as gospel and don't bother to check them for accuracy. The high rate of errors gives church-state separationists an excellent opportunity to respond to set the record straight.

For example, Religious Right activists are fond of claiming that Communists in the Soviet Union invented separation of church and state.[1] Of course this claim is patently untrue. Its frequent appearance in print provides separationists with an almost guaranteed letter placement to correct the misstatement. Keep a church-state resource handy to attack the Religious Right's historical errors and distortions. (See Appendix 1 for a list of the Religious Right's most common myths about church-state separation and the responses to them. Feel free to use this material—indeed anything in this book—when responding to the Religious Right.)

Form local watchdog groups. Work through the media need not be done alone. Letters to the editor can be handled by a special committee of a local proseparationist organization. It is vital that citizens form such groups across the country to counter existing antiseparationist Religious Right groups that have local chapters in large and small communities across the country. As the church-state controversy escalates, separationists must be willing to go head to head with the Religious Right in every town.

Many people are concerned about the inroads the Religious Right has made in society in the past twenty-five years, and increasingly in various parts of the country activists are coming together to counter extremist forces. Where are these people found? In churches, fraternal organizations, social groups, and so on. Mainline religious leaders may be interested in such an effort. Enlist local teachers, school administrators, and librarians in the effort to protect the religious neutrality of public education and combat religiously based censorship. Talk to your friends, neighbors, and family members. Post notices in community bulletin boards and public places. Look into running free announcements on local cable television access channels.

Religious Right groups frequently attack gay people. Many gays are concerned about the Religious Right and are natural allies in the struggle to maintain church-state separation. The same holds true for advocates of women's rights, members of minority religions (Pagans, Wiccans, etc.), reproductive freedom advocates, and anticensorship proponents.

Exploit everything local Religious Right activists do and turn their activities around to your own advantage. If the local chapter of Pat Robertson's Christian Coalition attacks a book used in the local public school, study the book and consider forming a committee to defend it. Use that incident as a starting point to form a proseparation group that, as part of its activities, keeps an eye on the local Christian Coalition unit.

Handling Church-State Problems

Despite your best efforts to monitor church-state developments in your community, conflict may still erupt in your local public school or city hall. What should you do if a situation arises in your community? How do you handle it? Can one person or a small group of citizens make a difference?

The key to dealing with church-state controversy at a local level is assessing frankly what you are up against and determining what avenues of solution are open to you. You must chose your battles carefully and be patient and polite—but tenacious. If you keep at it, in many cases you can win.

Church-state problems come in varying degrees of intensity. Your first task is to determine exactly what you have on your hands. Assume, for example, that your local city council decides to pass a resolution recognizing the International Year of the Bible and calls on all citizens to read the Bible. While protesting this action is certainly appropriate—after all, it is no business of the city to tell citizens what religious texts to consult—you will probably have to accept the fact that, once your protest is on record, you may not be able to do much else about this. Courts have looked at resolutions like the one described above in the past and ruled that since they are symbolic and don't have the force of law, they pass constitutional muster. In my assessment that opinion is wrong, but this battle may be lost and it's often not worth your time and money to go into court over such a matter.

If you have any doubts about the constitutionality of the issue before you, seek a professional opinion. Contact Americans United for Separation of Church and State, the state branch of the ACLU, or another separationist organization. Officials at these groups can give you a legal opinion and may be able to cite case law from similar situations that have occurred before. Find out if you are standing on firm constitutional ground before you complain.

Of course, there are other types of arguments you can make aside from a constitutional one. In the case of the resolution, you could point out that the wording excludes non-Christians and makes members of religious minorities feel like outsiders. It is insensitive and inappropriate. An argument like this, made directly to the city council, may win you enough support to sink the resolution. Members of a city council, after all, usually take great pains to avoid alienating any member of their constituency.

But what if the issue is not ambiguous and looks to be a clear violation of separation of church and state? What should you do then? As an example, assume that instead of a city council issuing a sectarian proclamation, the problem centers around a public school teacher who is preaching to seventh grade students during math class and reading to them from the Bible in an effort to encourage them to convert to his religion. (Cases like this have actually happened.) Is this situation worth contesting in court if necessary?

Definitely. Such actions are absolutely unconstitutional and have in fact been struck down before by courts. In fact, courts have held that public school officials are within their rights to fire teachers who refuse to stop preaching to students. What's more, if school officials knowingly persist in breaking the law concerning school prayer, they can be held personally responsible for court costs and any damages assessed by the courts.

Chain of Command

Naturally, you don't want to run into court right off the bat. Once you have determined the scope of what you're up against, you should try other ways to solve the problem.

It may be helpful to imagine the school and government officials who will be involved in this case as a pyramid or chain of command. At the bottom of the pyramid or the beginning of the chain rests the teacher involved. At the very top is the court system. You must start at the bottom and work your way up until the problem is resolved at some level.

In the case of our hypothetical example, you should begin with the teacher. Explain that his activities are inappropriate. Tell him that you, as the parent, are solely responsible for your child's religious upbringing. Say you do no want your child exposed to religious beliefs at school that conflict with whatever religious or philosophical system that the child is trained under at home. Make it clear to the teacher that you are willing to discuss this matter with the principal if his activities do not cease at once.

If that doesn't work, follow up on what you told the teacher and go to the principal. Do not assume a conspiracy exists if there is no evidence to point at one. School officials may not be aware that the teacher is proselytizing. A polite letter and complaint listing specific instances to the principal and outlining your discussion with the teacher (with a copy forwarded to the superintendent) may clear up the problem. If you live in a small community and can approach the principal directly for a face-to-face discussion, all the better. But still send a copy of a letter just to get your case in writing. Put a date on every letter and keep copies of every letter you send. Make it clear in your letter that you expect a response within a certain time frame.

If it appears that school officials are aware of the situation but will not do anything about it or have in fact encouraged the teacher's actions, go over their heads. Try the superintendent first, but if that goes nowhere write to the president of the school board and send copies to all the members. If there is still no action or if the response you receive is not satisfactory, request an opportunity to address the board about the issue. Let the school board know that illegal activities are going on.

Before you contact the school board it may be helpful to have a preliminary consultation with a watchdog group such as Americans United for Separation of Church and State or the ACLU. Tell them that at this stage you want to try to handle the matter on your own and request copies of any information they can send you about similar situations that may have been litigated in the past. Tell them you are looking to buttress your argument. If officials at the group can cite a court case for you, mention it in your letter to the school board. That way, they know you've done your homework and are serious about the complaint. (When you contact the cause organization let them know you might be calling back later for more help. Get the name of a contact to deal with and keep a careful record of when you called and what was discussed for your growing file.)

If your protest to the school board fails, write to the education officials in the capital of your state. Explain the situation fully and send copies of all of the correspondence that has been generated so far. (You might want to call first and get the name of the staffer who handles legal affairs.) It might be helpful to follow up with a telephone call in a few weeks if you haven't heard anything. State education departments have staff attorneys who will examine the claim and look for constitutional violations. In some cases, they might contact the school officials and order them to cease and desist.

By this time you might have found some allies in your struggle. If other parents are upset about the activity, have them join your cause with letters of their own. Keep up the pressure. Remember, an individual is easy to ignore, but a group is not. There is strength in numbers.

If all of this fails, if you've contacted everyone from the principal to the director of the state department of education and still have had no satisfaction, it is time to call on the professionals again. Contact Americans United, the local affiliate of the ACLU, or another separationist group and explain the situation, again sending copies of all of the relevant documentation.

Sometimes a letter from an activist group can result in positive change. If local officials see that a national organization with powerful resources is following the situation, they may reverse course. But if all else fails, litigation may be necessary. If the watchdog group is willing to bring suit on your behalf, be sure to let school personnel know. At the prospect of going to court, many public school officials will back down and stop unconstitutional activities. They don't want to waste scarce resources fighting court battles they know they cannot win.

If you decide to enter a church-state fight, you must be prepared for criticism. Lots of people in your community will disagree with what you are doing, and some will want to let you know about that. You can look forward to being attacked in the letters to the editor columns of the local paper as well as receiving hate mail and unpleasant—maybe even threatening—phone calls. Remember, making harassing telephone calls is a crime, and if the problem gets especially bad, contact the phone company and the police. Likewise with mail. If the letters threaten your life, contact the appropriate authorities.

(But don't assume the situation will get this out of hand. While many people who have pursued church-state litigation have been harassed, others have not. Simply be prepared for some ugliness that may come your way. Church-state disputes seem to bring out the worst in some people.)

Accept the fact that your protest will probably find its way to the local media. News like this travels fast, especially in small towns. Consider going to the media first. If your cause is publicized and you are open and sincere about your complaint, it may help you find supporters or bring the newspaper's editorial staff over to your side. Media pressure may even convince the school to back down. Be accessible to reporters and state your case as articulately as possible. Also, dealing with reporters directly greatly enhances the chances of your side being told accurately. Don't let the media piece together your story from secondary sources.

While this model has used a church-state problem in a public school as its example, I hope you can see how it would translate into other areas of government. For instance, if the city council is considering an action that you believe is a violation of church-state separation, start your protest with the council member who made the recommendation and move up from there. Strive to be as open and courteous as possible, and don't threaten a lawsuit right at the beginning. You may be surprised what an open, friendly dialogue can do for you.

Taking a Proactive Stance

With the Religious Right becoming more and more active, local separationist groups must be prepared to not only initiate lawsuits if necessary but fend off those brought by antiseparationists. The number of Religious Right groups that litigate has skyrocketed in recent years. In some cases, these groups believe they can harass and bully local officials into doing things their way with threats of costly lawsuits. Proseparation forces need to be on the lookout at all times for this deplorable tactic and must be ready to defend governmental officials if necessary.

Recently, Religious Right activists have pressured a number of states and local communities to teach creationism in public schools or to water down the teaching of evolution. Advocates of good science education and church-state separation have joined forces to fend off these efforts. In many cases they have been successful.

Had the proseparationist forces remained apathetic, Religious Right groups might have been able to change the school curriculum and thus harm the education of every child in the state or community who attends public schools.

Separationists must be constantly on the lookout for Religious Right activity. Keeps tabs on the local units of government—the school board and the city or county council especially. Attend meetings when possible or tune in if they are televised. If you are wondering if chapters of local Religious Right groups are active in your community, you may be able to find out by checking the Web sites of various Religious Right groups. Many list their chapters.

If there are chapters of national Religious Right groups operating in your community, find out what they are up to by attending their public meetings. Don't try to disrupt their activities or argue with them. Simply gather what useful information you can. If they have a mailing list, get on it. To fight these people effectively, you must first know what they are doing.

Mailings from national Religious Right groups can also be helpful. Many of these groups will put you on their mailing list for free, at least for a few months. Many issue regular e-mail updates and will add your name at no cost. This is an excellent way to get up-to-date information about what Religious Right groups are doing nationally and in your state. Also, be sure to visit the Web sites of Religious Right groups regularly. Most have a section for breaking news or put their press releases online.

If you want to see financial information about Religious Right groups, you can write and request it. By law, the groups must send you a financial statement. The Web site www.guidestar.com is also a good source for this type of information. Financial information is important, as it can help you get a handle on how strong the different Religious Right groups are. An organization with a staff of fifty and an annual budget of $12 million is likely to cause more trouble than a shoestring operation run out of someone's garage on $100,000 a year.

The Religious Right is fond of portraying the current struggle over church and state as a war. In their books and materials, they use battlefield imagery to stir up their supporters in an effort to make them believe they are part of some grand design—most often a war to crush "humanism" or "Satan."

These are unpleasant metaphors, but they can help you understand how the Religious Right views its foes. Remember, the Religious Right is cunning and well organized. Do not underestimate its strength. And remember, Religious Right organizations are not above using sneaky and underhanded tactics done in the dark of night, away from the glare of public view, to achieve their aims. If you are going to take on the Religious Right, you have to be prepared for just about anything. Personal attacks are common. You may be vilified and called names. You can take solace in remembering that hysterical broadsides like this only expose the Religious Right for the mean-spirited movement that it so often is.

Monitoring the Religious Right and keeping an eye on the local school board is important, but some activists might want to take things a step farther. Some people might want to consider running for local office themselves. True, a seat on the local school board or city council can take up a lot of a person's free time, but obviously someone must be willing to make the sacrifices necessary to ensure good government free from sectarian control.

In some small towns, seats on local governance boards go unfilled because no one wants to run. This is the type of power vacuum that fills Religious Right groups with glee. If voters are apathetic and decent candidates don't run, that only makes the Religious Right's job all the easier. Even if you don't run yourself, you must get involved at politics at the local level, including helping locate good candidates who will reject the oppressive agenda of the Religious Right. Voters need a good alternative if they are to reject extremism.

Enlisting Religious Groups

Before closing this chapter, there is one factor about citizen action that must be discussed—participation of churches and other religious groups in the fight against the Religious Right.

Only a small segment of the American religious community opposes church-state separation. Most church leaders realize that separation has been a great boon to religion, a principle that enables various religious bodies to grow and prosper and freely take their messages to the people. Enlist these people on your side. Contact leaders of the mainstream religious groups in your community. Let them know what you are doing and ask for help. Don't let religious differences be a barrier to cooperation. Remember, the battle to preserve separation of church and state benefits everyone—from the deeply devout to the committed atheist. Don't leave anyone who is willing to help out of your coalition. Diversity is a great strength. It shows that your movement is not narrowly focused by sectarian concerns, as Religious Right pressure groups often are. Religious diversity adds to your credibility and can increase your numbers by showing people that yours is a truly open, diverse, and democratic movement committed to the principles that exemplify American freedoms.

Most Americans don't agree with the Religious Right. In fact, polls have continually shown that Americans express a great deal of apprehension over the agenda of these organizations. The only way they can win is if public apathy remains high. Overcoming that apathy and rousing people to action is undoubtedly the greatest challenge advocates of church-state separation face today.

Note

1. David Barton, *The Myth of Separation* (Aledo, Tex.: WallBuilders Press, 1989), p. 45.

11

Final Thoughts: The End of Separation?

Thomas Jefferson excelled as a political leader and architect of religious liberty, but he was a lousy prophet.

Jefferson once predicted that Unitarianism would become the dominant religion in the United States. He also believed the country would remain a largely agrarian society; he never foresaw the rise of sprawling urban metropolises.

What if Jefferson could see America today—a nation of 270 million people, the world's sole remaining superpower? What would he think?

Jefferson might have a lot to say about American foreign policy, economic strategy, and even American popular culture. He would probably also have strong opinions about the state of religious liberty in America. I can't say what he would think about the other issues, but if Jefferson were to look at religious freedom in America today, I believe he would be pleased.

During his lifetime, Jefferson spoke eloquently about the need for religious liberty for all people—not just Christians. He would be delighted to see an America that has welcomed Jews, Muslims, Hindus, Buddhists, Wiccans, nonbelievers, and others. He would be pleased by the diversity among the Christian denominations as well. The Sage of Monticello would be happy to see these groups living side by side in peace.

Jefferson was a strong advocate of the idea that there must never be force or coercion in matters of religion. If you visit the Jefferson Memorial in Washington today, you will see chiseled on the wall a famous quote from Jefferson: "I have sworn upon the altar of God eternal hostility against every form of tyranny over the mind of man."

Jefferson made that statement in reaction against ultraconservative religious leaders in New England who opposed him politically and opposed his views on church-state separation. Any assertion that Jefferson would find common cause with today's Religious Right is laughable. Not only would Jefferson disagree with Religious Right theology, he would adamantly oppose its political views and agenda. Jefferson would recognize today's Religious Right as the spiritual descendants of the narrow-minded clergy he swore "eternal hostility" against so long ago. He would treat the Religious Right with similar disdain.

Unfortunately, too many American political leaders today, while pretending to honor Jefferson's legacy in speeches, labor to tear it down through their actions. Jefferson's wall of separation is under assault—and not just from the Religious Right. Political leaders and judges have joined the attack.

It has also become fashionable lately for academics to assail Jefferson. A spate of books has been produced that attempt to portray Jefferson as a duplicitous, even hypocritical, politician. It's as if Jefferson's stature got so high that some people decided to knock him down a few pegs.

Obviously Jefferson should not be portrayed as a demigod. He was a man with faults and flaws, as we all are. In some ways, Jefferson was very much the product of his time with views shaped and anchored in the prejudices and assumptions of the day. In other ways, his thinking was light-years beyond that of his contemporaries. In the areas of religious freedom and freedom of conscience generally, Jefferson's contribution enabled humanity to take a kind of great leap forward. His thoughts in this area simply cannot be minimized or written off because of shortcomings in his thinking in unrelated areas.

Jefferson was the author of the Declaration of Independence, one of the greatest testaments to human liberty ever penned. More than 220 years after it was written, the Declaration still inspires oppressed people today. If that was all Jefferson had ever done, his name would still ring down through the ages—but of course he did much more: Jefferson served as ambassador to France, governor of Virginia, and president of the United States. He founded the University of Virginia and authored Virginia's Statute for Religious Liberty.

Jefferson was a prodigious thinker with an innate curiosity about the world around him. In his spare time, he invented things—most notably the dumbwaiter, the swivel chair, and a new type of plow. He conducted scientific experiments in botany and took great interest when a nearly complete mastodon skeleton was unearthed near Newburg, New York, in 1801. He engaged in a vigorous correspondence with several people at once on just about every topic imaginable.

Jefferson was a man of keen intellect. Religious freedom undergirded by the separation of church and state is just one of his legacies to the American people.

Attacks on separation of church and state assail the legacy of James Madison as well. Madison is one of the most important founders, but his contributions are often overlooked and tend to be overshadowed by his less-than-successful presidency.

Jefferson could write quite eloquently about religious freedom and the need for church-state separation, but in many ways it was Madison who perfected the concept. Madison's prose in the "Memorial and Remonstrance" is workmanlike and to the point. It's less flowery than what Jefferson would have penned. But Madison's words did the trick and turned back a dangerous bill. In this and other instances, we see with Jefferson and Madison evidence of a powerful partnership—the intellectual prowess of Jefferson paired with the parliamentary skills of Madison. Jefferson drafted the Virginia Statute for Religious Liberty, but it was Madison who pushed it through the legislature and made it law.

As president, Madison put church-state separation into action. He vetoed bills that would have allocated federal aid (in the form of surplus land) and even symbolic support for houses of worship. Madison made his thinking clear: Such government assistance to religion, he believed, violated the First Amendment. In the early days of the republic, with the separation doctrine essentially untested, Madison's actions went a long way toward defining the type of relationship between religion and government that would exist in the new nation.

Given their accomplishments, it is difficult to accept the fact that many in the nation have never fully embraced the wisdom of Jefferson and Madison. Public opinion polls often show majorities of people backing things like state-sponsored school prayer, the teaching of creationism in public schools and government display of religious symbols.

Perhaps most discouragingly, surveys have unveiled an uncomfortably high degree of ignorance about the Constitution and the First Amendment. In the fall of 2002, the First Amendment Center, an arm of the Freedom Forum, polled Americans on their attitude toward and knowledge about the First Amendment.

Religious liberty is the first freedom listed in the First Amendment, but this poll found that only 18 percent were aware that religious freedom is even in that amendment. Few people can list all of the freedoms in the First Amendment; fewer still can actually recite its language. Other polls have shown that people do not understand what the Bill of Rights—the first ten amendments to the Constitution—even is.

When asked about their support for separation of church and state specifically, most people back the concept. However, many seem to have difficulty accepting application of the concept in specific cases.

Also alarming is the fact that some opinion polls have shown that as many as 25 percent—a full quarter of our people—don't agree with the concept of separation of church and state at all. Obviously this is a minority view, but it means that a full quarter of our population, tens of millions of people, don't believe we should separate church and state.

What system, it is fair to ask, are these people prepared to substitute instead? A merger of church and state? Which church? By what mechanism? Unfortunately, public opinion polls are not the proper venue to pose questions like this. Therefore, except for the rantings of extremists like Christian Reconstructionists, who propose a state based on Old Testament law, the questions remain unanswered and we don't know what this 25 percent would do.

Widespread ignorance about the Bill of Rights helps the Religious Right. For example, the Religious Right exploits the low level of knowledge among Americans when it argues that the United States was founded as a "Christian nation." As past chapters indicated, Religious Right groups point to documents like the Northwest Ordinance or even more obscure proclamations that contain religious references. "See!" they say. "This proves America was meant to be Christian!"

What the Religious Right doesn't tell people, and what, tragically, many Americans apparently don't know, is that when it comes to determining what the laws of the United States mean, the only document that matters is the Constitution. The Constitution, a completely secular document, contains no references to God, Jesus, or Christianity. It says absolutely nothing about the United States being officially Christian. The

Religious Right's constant appeals to documents like the Declaration of Independence, which contains a Deistic reference to "the Creator," cloud the issue and make some people believe their rights spring from these other documents. They don't. As important as those other documents are to history, the rights of all Americans are ultimately traced to the Constitution and its amendments, specifically the Bill of Rights. When we talk about separation of church and state and religious freedom, therefore, only one document matters—the Constitution.

In light of this situation—growing hostility to Jefferson's wall and ignorance about the development and meaning of the concept of separation of church and state—it's fair to ask if the idea can survive in the United States.

The short answer is that it is highly likely that the United States will always at least claim to operate under a system of separation of church and state. Assuming that we can continue to fend off school prayer amendments, the First Amendment's religion clauses will not be altered outright or done away with. No official church will be established. Government will never have the power to directly order someone to take part in religion.

The much harder question is determining whether or not the United States will ever adopt a system whereby separation of church and state exists more or less in name only. Under such a system, religion would receive government support for its projects, and government would promote religious belief at every turn. Separation of church and state would be merely a slogan held over from days gone by.

How likely is this to happen? The disturbing answer is that we may be well on the way to it. And, if certain Supreme Court justices had their way, we would already have such a system.

A few examples may be helpful to understand what type of system may be evolving in the United States. Remember, overt forms of church-state union are never likely to prosper in the United States. In Germany, the government deducts money from each worker's wages and turns it over to the religious group of the worker's choosing. Anyone seeking to opt out of the system must appear before a government official and sign a form stating that, for example, he or she is an atheist. A system like this will probably never develop in America. But what's more likely is no better and may in fact be worse.

The Supreme Court has already upheld vouchers for private religious schools. If these plans catch on and spread nationwide, tax money collected from all citizens will be turned over to a select few religious groups. There will be no opt-out mechanism, and the individual taxpayer will be able to do nothing to keep his or her hard-earned dollars from flowing into church coffers. Under such a system, all Americans would pay the equivalent of church taxes.

In Germany, the government is at least up front about what it is doing and offers an out—albeit an inconvenient one—for those who absolutely refuse to participate. In the United States right now, no such out exists to save conscientious objectors from religious taxes in some states. Everyone has to participate.

So-called faith-based initiatives will only compound this problem. Some political leaders have proposed spending billions of tax dollars on aid to houses of worship so they can provide a variety of social services—everything from drug and alcohol abuse counseling to job-training programs. The problem is, many of these church-run programs contain, not surprisingly, large amounts of religion. Participants may be forced to pray, attend religious services, or read religious material as a condition of receiving help. In the past, programs like this were funded with money raised through voluntary contributions from people who believed in the religion being taught. With private funds, these programs could be as religious as they wanted to be.

Now some political leaders want to provide tax aid to these programs—even though the church officials who run the programs may require vulnerable people to participate in religion, even though they may refuse to hire people unless they hold certain religious beliefs and even though the programs may be little more than a Bible study posing as a drug-treatment program.

(Of course, some religiously based treatment programs are effective. But the assumption, common among many politicians today, that religious programs are always more effective and always cheaper to run, is simplistic and not backed by objective research data.)

Not only may Americans now be taxed to support religion, but if the Religious Right and some Supreme Court justices have their way, American children may be coerced to take part in religious exercises in public schools. Prayers read daily over the loudspeaker or during school events are considered "voluntary" by some church-state separation foes, even though all students have to listen. There is nothing "voluntary" about a scheme like this. It is nothing less than forced participation in religion, and it is wrong.

At this writing, at least three justices on the Supreme Court would also like to revisit the High Court's rulings barring government display of religious symbols and religious codes like the Ten Commandments.

On May 29, 2001, the Supreme Court announced that it would not hear a case from Elkhart, Indiana, challenging the display of the Ten Commandments at city hall. A federal appeals court had ruled the display a violation of church-state separation, and High Court's refusal of the case left that decision in place.

Chief Justice William H. Rehnquist dissented. He wanted the Court to hear the case, and he made it clear he would have overturned the lower court. Rehnquist, joined by Justices Antonin Scalia and Clarence Thomas, asserted that the Ten Commandments have played a "foundational role in secular, legal matters" and they can be displayed by government officials in a city to celebrate its "cultural and historical roots" without becoming a "promotion of religious faith."

If Rehnquist, Scalia, and Thomas have their way, communities all over America will be able to display sectarian documents (and even worse, in the case of the Ten Commandments, pick one religion's version of that sectarian document) and post it in a prominent place at taxpayer expense. Somehow, to a significant bloc of the Supreme Court, this is not government promotion of religion. Under the Rehnquist model, one has to wonder how far a community would have to go before it violated church-state separation. Could Utah officially declare itself a Mormon state? Why not—after all, the state's culture and history is steeped in that religion. Such a declaration could be defended as a mere recognition of that.

The judicial attack on separation of church and state is always surreptitious, never direct. Even as they are tearing down Jefferson's wall, judges try to pretend that what they are doing comports with the Constitution.

Other countries don't bother with this ruse. In some Latin American nations, the doctrines of the Roman Catholic Church are written into secular law. For example, divorce and abortion may be outlawed. In some cases, provisions in the law explicitly state that the regulations stem from the country's close ties to Catholicism. Some nations still have special agreements with the Vatican that give the church some say over public policy. These agreements are called concordats.

In the United States, we will not likely see the day when religious leaders stand beside the president and members of Congress signing concordats or special agreements that provide for church-state union. But again, what we might get won't be much better. Rather than seek special favors through treaties, sectarian special interests will simply lobby lawmakers to have their views on social issues written into law—as many are doing now. Courts will later uphold the laws as valid, arguing that they serve some manufactured secular interest of the government.

How a given church's views on social policy get written into law is irrelevant to the church in question. Be it by concordat or lobbying, the result is the same: Citizens are living under laws drafted by religious groups that reflect the beliefs and practices of those groups. The church is telling the state what to do. In America nothing as explicit as a concordat will probably ever exist, but the practical equivalent of this type of agreement very well might.

The tragedy is that even as these types of events unfold, Americans will continue to insist that they have all the protections listed in their Constitution—long after they stop following them. The concept of separation of church and state will remain enshrined in our Constitution and praised by our politicians long after it has been drained of all meaning by the courts.

Is this bleak scenario inevitable? Not at all. But it can only be blocked if the Religious Right is stopped and politicians who parrot the Religious Right's view on church-state issues are not permitted to stack our courts with men and women hostile to real religious liberty.

The Religious Right has never represented the majority of Americans. The only reason antiseparationists have gotten as far as they have is because of apathy. The views held by the Religious Right are minority views. The movement has power only because the Religious Right has successfully filled a vacuum left open by other Americans who have forfeited their voice in public discourse. If enough Americans get back into the game, the tide can easily turn.

Even though public opinion polls might show Americans waffling on specific issues such as crosses on government property, the Religious Right knows that when it comes to the big picture, their view of church-state relations is in the minority. They don't care because they know they can win elections anyway, due to apathy.

The message is clear: Unless Americans wake up, the Religious Right and other antiseparationists will continue to consolidate power.

What can be done to bring about a reversal? Unfortunately, some of the solutions will be difficult to implement because they are tied to certain national trends that have nothing to do with separation of church and state or religious and civil liberties.

For instance, one way to cut the Religious Right off at the knees would be to increase voter participation. Estimates vary, but the Religious

Right probably accounts for at best 15 percent of the electorate. This small group wields such power in politics—especially Republican Party politics—because, generally speaking, Religious Right activists are well disciplined and work together. They know how to get out the vote. Thus, politicians court them. If more Americans voted, the Religious Right's influence would wane. Getting people to vote in this age of dirty politics and TV-driven sound bite campaigns, however, is a challenge.

Another factor that works in the favor of Religious Right is its inordinate degree of influence over the Republican Party. Again, if the Religious Right were stopped here, separation would benefit.

It won't be easy. Pat Robertson and other TV preachers have focused exclusively on the GOP. Robertson, Falwell, and others sought to take over the party from the ground up, starting with precincts and moving up to state and national positions. So far, they have enjoyed great success.

The Republicans have been forced to accommodate the Religious Right because they believe they need them to win elections. This proposition is debatable, and some political analysts believe that the Religious Right drives suburban women away from the GOP. When Bill Clinton was elected in 1992 and reelected in 1996, some GOP strategists blamed the results on the Religious Right and suggested a purge.

But the Religious Right took credit for George W. Bush's narrow victory in 2000, and it's unlikely that national Republican leaders will now seek to expel the Religious Right from the party. Especially in primaries, Religious Right voters tend to be very active.

A better-educated public would also help preserve church-state separation. World history proves conclusively that unions of church and state are detrimental to freedom. But many young people never read about the horrible persecution and tyranny that raged in Europe of the Middle Ages and colonial America. If they are exposed to this material at all, the presentation is often watered down or incomplete.

Educators must realize that history has to be taught "warts and all." It does not honor religion to exclude discussion of the excesses that have occurred in history when governments aligned themselves with religion. A frank assessment of our history as a people will help our youngsters understand and appreciate America's unique system.

The reluctance of some members of the liberal or moderate religious community to defend church-state separation also contributes to the weakening of that concept. As the last chapter pointed out, separationists must work with the religious community to boost support for church-state separation among the worshippers in the pews of America's churches, synagogues, and temples. In fundamentalist churches, ministers frequently rail against separation of church and state. Religious leaders in the so-called liberal, mainline, and right-thinking evangelical communities should tell their flocks the real story behind religious freedom. Religious groups have been the biggest beneficiaries of separation of church and state. Now that the concept is in trouble, it is up to the leaders of these groups to return the favor by standing up for the idea.

Proseparation religious leaders must also keep in mind that it isn't enough to simply talk to their own congregations about the importance of separation. These leaders must be willing to undertake public relations campaigns on behalf of separation in their own communities so everyone can hear the message.

Religious Right activists do not limit their efforts to the already converted. They constantly attack separation on all fronts. They place anti-separation letters in secular newspapers and magazines. They produce videos giving a distorted view of U.S. history and pay to have them aired on local television stations. They buy time on radio stations to broadcast their far-right propaganda. They distribute antiseparationist pamphlets in public places. There is no reason why religious leaders who understand the value of separation should not adopt these strategies to defend church-state separation. If the Religious Right is left unanswered, they win by default.

Religious groups should form coalitions with secular organizations that favor separation—groups like the local PTA, area Humanist organizations, and so forth. The various groups must put their religious and political differences aside and work together toward the common goal of warding off the narrow views of the Religious Right. Anyone or any group willing to play a role should be welcomed as a full partner.

Religious leaders can clear up many common misconceptions about church-state separation. Thanks to a steady stream of propaganda from the Religious Right, separation of church and state has become too closely identified with hostility toward religion in the public mind. When religious figures take the lead in defending the principle, it proves to the public that separation works for everyone—from the deeply devout to the completely nonreligious. No one group, religious or atheistic, can claim exclusive rights to benefits meant for all Americans to share. In other words, separation of church and state, like other great constitutional principles, is for everyone. Its protection extends equally to all Americans, regardless of sex, age, race, or creed.

Strategies for saving separation are important, but in the end the concept will not survive unless the American people decide they want it. Right now, we as a nation are failing to make a positive assertion that we do.

Church-state separation has faced difficult tests before. In the early 1960s, when public hysteria over the Supreme Court's school prayer rulings was running high, misguided lawmakers tried to whip up enough outrage to convince Americans that altering the First Amendment was a smart thing to do. Thankfully, enough Americans looked at the situation without the color of fanaticism and brought that misguided drive to a halt. Cooler heads and calmer minds prevailed.

Separation's current test—its prolonged assault by the various forces of ignorance and extremism that constitute the Religious Right—may be its toughest. Certainly, it has been its longest test. But the fight is by no means over, and the fact that the concept has held up under such sustained and relentless attack is cause for optimism.

Americans are a people in transition, constantly working to improve their society and the way it treats all of its members. Any effort at progress will always face stiff opposition from those who would drag our country back to false images of prior times of perfection. Although these times exist only in the minds of those who conjure them up, their hold on the public mind can be powerful. The belief that vexing social problems can be solved through the imposition of a rigid code of morality and state-enforced orthodoxy seduces many Americans.

More enlightened Americans pierce through the haze of distortion and remind us of the hard truths. They tell us it's not that easy and say the difficulties we face in society today cannot be washed away with quick fixes like school prayer or a swift injection of church into state. Rather, these problems must be confronted, at the roots, one by one with a lot of hard work and a spirit of cooperation from a people determined to make things right.

But the latter is not easy to conjure up, and despite our best efforts often exceeds our grasp. So unfortunately, the quest for the quick fix goes on. Separation of church and state continues to receive the blame for somehow creating a society that seems at times to be falling apart instead of what it rightly deserves: praise for holding together a diverse collection of immigrants, people of many different religious faiths, and helping to sculpt them into the most successful society the world has ever known.

Will we lose separation of church and state? Not if we as a people wake up and understand all that's at stake in the current battle. For more than two decades, aggressive, well-funded Religious Right organizations have assailed the church-state wall. As part of their strategy, they have backed politicians at the local, state, and national level who have disdain for the separation concept. The Religious Right's ultimate goal is to reshape the federal judiciary and overturn a whole host of church-state rulings that protect religious freedom. This effort is taking a toll. The wall has been weakened and needs defenders.

The legacy of Jefferson and Madison is under threat today as never before. Americans who value this legacy and understand all that it has given our nation need to stand up now and respond to the misinformation and propaganda of the Religious Right. Start today. Nothing less than the future of religious freedom is at stake.

For more information about how to defend church-state separation, contact

Americans United for Separation of Church and State
518 C Street, N.E.
Washington, D.C. 20002
(202) 466-3234
(202) 466-2587 (fax)
www.au.org
americansunited@au.org

Appendix 1

Common Myths about Separation of Church and State

Religious Right organizations spread a lot of misinformation about the separation of church and state. They make false claims about history and frequently distort the church-state rulings of the Supreme Court. For quick reference, I have collected some of the most commonly heard myths here along with refutations. Readers should feel free to use this information—and indeed any of the material in this book—to refute the Religious Right in letters to the editor, debates, newspaper columns, and so forth.

MYTH: Separation of church and state is not in the U.S. Constitution.

It is true that the literal phrase "separation of church and state" does not appear in the Constitution, but that does not mean the concept isn't there. The First Amendment's religion clauses read, "Congress shall make no law respecting an establishment of religion or prohibiting the free exercise thereof."

What does that mean? A little history is helpful: In an 1802 letter to the Danbury, Connecticut, Baptist Association, Thomas Jefferson, then president, declared that the American people through the First Amendment had erected a "wall of separation between church and state." (Colonial religious liberty pioneer Roger Williams used a similar phrase 150 years earlier.)

Jefferson, however, was not the only leading figure of the postrevolutionary period to use the term "separation." James Madison, considered to be the Father of the Constitution, said in an 1819 letter, "[T]he number, the industry and the morality of the priesthood, and the devotion of the people have been manifestly increased by the total separation of the church and state." In an earlier, undated essay (probably early 1800s), Madison wrote, "Strongly guarded . . . is the separation between religion and government in the Constitution of the United States."

As eminent church-state scholar Leo Pfeffer notes in his book *Church, State and Freedom*,

> It is true, of course, that the phrase "separation of church and state" does not appear in the Constitution. But it was inevitable that some convenient term should come into existence to verbalize a principle so clearly and widely held by the American people. . . . [T]he right to a fair trial is generally accepted to be a constitutional principle; yet the term "fair trial" is not found in the Constitution. To bring the point even closer home, who would deny that "religious liberty" is a constitutional principle? Yet that phrase too is not in the Constitution. The universal acceptance which all these terms, including "separation of church and state," have received in America would seem to confirm rather than disparage their reality as basic American democratic principles.

Thus, it is entirely appropriate to speak of the "constitutional principle of church-state separation" since that phrase summarizes what the First Amendment's religion clauses do—they separate church and state.

MYTH: Thomas Jefferson's 1802 letter to the Danbury Baptists was a mere courtesy and should not be regarded as important.

Religious Right activists have tried for decades to make light of Jefferson's "wall of separation" response to the Danbury Baptists, attempting to dismiss it as a hastily written note designed to win the favor of a political constituency. But a glance at the history surrounding the letter shows they are simply wrong.

Jefferson clearly saw the letter as an opportunity to make a major pronouncement on church and state. Before sending the missive, Jefferson had it reviewed by Levi Lincoln, his attorney general, and Gideon Granger, the postmaster general. Jefferson told Lincoln he viewed the response as a way of "sowing useful truths and principles among the people, which might germinate and become rooted among their political tenets."

At the time he wrote the letter, Jefferson was under fire from conservative religious elements that disliked his strong stand for full religious liberty. Jefferson saw his response to the Danbury Baptists as an opportunity to clear up his views on church and state. Far from being a mere courtesy, the letter represented a summary of Jefferson's thinking on the purpose and effect of the First Amendment's religion clauses.

Jefferson's Danbury letter has been cited favorably by the Supreme Court many times. In its 1879 *Reynolds* v. *United States* decision, the High Court said Jefferson's observations "may be accepted almost as an authoritative declaration of the scope and effect of the [First] Amendment." In the court's 1947 *Everson* v. *Board of Education* decision, Justice Hugo Black wrote, "In the words of Jefferson, the clause against establishment of religion by law was intended to erect 'a wall of separation between church and state.'" It is only in recent times that Jefferson's observations have come under attack by those who oppose separation of church and state.

MYTH: *Thomas Jefferson wrote in the Danbury letter that the church-state wall is "one-directional" and meant only to protect the church from incursions by the state.*

Nothing like this statement appears in the Danbury letter. It's impossible to say how this myth got started, but it did appear in "Christian nation" propagandist David Barton's 1989 book, *The Myth of Separation*. The evidence is clear that Jefferson believed that church-state separation was good for both institutions. He never, in any of his writings, expressed an opinion like the "one-directional wall" myth.

MYTH: *Separation of church and state is not an American principle but is found in the constitution of the Soviet Union.*

This lie about separation of church and state—still frequently espoused by religious broadcaster Pat Robertson—is perhaps the most offensive to church-state separationists because it attempts to taint a vital American principle with the brush of Communism.

Even a brief review of the facts proves that this statement is nonsense.

The modern Soviet state came into being after the Russian Revolution of 1917. The Soviet constitution was rewritten several times, and more recent versions included American-style guarantees of freedom of speech, press, religion, and assembly. (These provisions, of course, were never enacted by the Soviet government.)

Article 124 of the country's 1947 constitution has been translated by some scholars to read, "In order to ensure to citizens freedom of conscience, the church in the USSR is separated from the state, and the school from the church. Freedom of religious worship and freedom of anti-religious propaganda is recognized for all citizens."

Since Jefferson coined the phrase "wall of separation between church and state" in 1802, a full *145 years* before the Soviet provision was written, it is obviously incorrect to suggest that the Soviets pioneered the separation principle. If anything, the Soviets stole the concept from the United States, in an effort to make their oppressive society appear like America's free society. In any case, what the Soviet constitution said about religious freedom has no bearing on U.S. constitutional provisions. The Soviet document also guaranteed free speech, but no one has labeled freedom of expression a Communist idea.

MYTH: The United States was founded as a Christian nation.

Those who make this assertion confuse the founding of the United States as a political unit with the settlement of North America. It is true that a number of the first Europeans to arrive on our shores were religious dissenters who sought freedom to worship. Many of these people believed they were establishing some type of Christian utopia, and many supported religious liberty only for themselves. Most of the early colonies were theocracies where only those who worshipped according to state orthodoxy were welcome.

Following the American Revolution, political leaders began to construct the new U.S. government. Although a minority clung to European notions of church-state union, a general consensus emerged that the new country should steer clear of officially established religion. States with government-favored religions gradually began moving toward separation also. Massachusetts, the last state to maintain an official religion, disestablished its state church in 1833.

During the Constitutional Convention, a minority faction favored some recognition of Christianity in the Constitution. In a report to Maryland lawmakers, delegate Luther Martin asserted that some delegates had believed that "in a Christian country, it would be at least decent to hold out some distinction between the professors of Christianity and downright infidelity or paganism." But those views were rejected by the convention, and the Constitution was adopted as a secular document.

Further proof that the founders did not intend for the government to be Christian is found in the Treaty of Tripoli, an agreement signed between the United States and the Muslim region of north Africa in 1797 after negotiations under George Washington. The document, which was approved by the Senate under John Adams, states flatly, "[T]he Government of the United States is not, in any sense, founded on the Christian religion." (The assertion remained a part of the agreement for eight years, until the treaty was renegotiated.)

The framers wrote the Constitution as a secular document not because they were hostile to Christianity but because they did not want to imply that the new federal government would have any authority to meddle in religion.

MYTH: *At the urging of Ben Franklin, official prayers took place during the Constitutional Convention.*

Ben Franklin did indeed urge the delegates of the Constitutional Convention of 1787 to open their sessions with prayers, as many Religious Right activists point out. However, the Convention, which had been meeting for a month without invocational prayers, did not concur. The Convention's records show that the delegates voted to adjourn rather than debate the issue. Some delegates feared that if word got out that they had had to resort to prayer to resolve deadlocks, people would fear the session was not going well. The matter was not brought up again when the Convention reconvened.

MYTH: *The Supreme Court has declared that the United States is a Christian nation.*

In the Supreme Court's 1892 *Holy Trinity Church* v. *United States* decision Justice David Brewer wrote, "This is a Christian nation." Brewer's statement occurred in *dicta*, a legal term meaning writing that reflects a judge's personal opinion, not an official court pronouncement that sets legally binding precedent.

Historians debate what Brewer meant by the statement, some claiming that he only intended to acknowledge that Christianity has always been a dominant force in American life. Research by Americans United shows that five years after the *Holy Trinity* ruling, Brewer himself seemed to step away from it in a case dealing with legalized prostitution in New Orleans.

The New Orleans dispute arose when a Methodist church sought an injunction to bar implementation of a city ordinance allowing prostitution in one zone in the city. The Methodists argued the measure would "destroy the morals, peace and good order of the neighborhood."

Citing the *Holy Trinity* decision, church officials insisted that the ordinance encouraged prostitution, an activity inconsistent with Christianity "which the Supreme Court of the United States says is the foundation of our government and the civilization which it has produced."

Writing for a unanimous court, Brewer completely ignored the church's religious argument and upheld the New Orleans law. Brewer's bypass suggests that he did not mean to assert in the *Holy Trinity* case that the United States should enforce Christianity through its laws.

In any case, the *Holy Trinity* decision is a legal anomaly that has been cited by the Court only once since then. And obviously the opinion of one obscure Supreme Court justice does not amount to an official decree that the United States is a Christian nation. If a Christian republic had been the goal of the framers, that sentiment would have been included in the Constitution.

MYTH: Early state constitutions contained language limiting public office to Christians. This is proof that the United States was founded to be a Christian nation.

This is a common argument of "Christian nation" propagandist David Barton. There are several things wrong with it. A number of early state constitutions did limit public office to Christians, Trinitarian Protestants, or those who believed in Heaven and Hell. These provisions are from a more intolerant time in our history when church and state were united in some parts of the country. More enlightened founders considered them an embarrassment. During the Constitutional Convention, Charles Pinckney, a South Carolina delegate, recommended language prohibiting such "religious tests" for federal office. It was adopted, and the provision may be found in Article VI of the Constitution.

In time, as state constitutions were updated, just about every state repealed religious requirements for public office. A handful remained but were not enforced. In 1971, the U.S. Supreme Court in *Torcaso* v. *Watkins* declared such provisions unconstitutional, saying they violated the First Amendment.

People like Barton who favorably cite the religious test language of the old state constitutions are in effect endorsing religious intolerance and prejudice. Limiting office to "Trinitarian Protestants," for example, would rule out Roman Catholics, Mormons, Unitarians, and other groups.

MYTH: *The First Amendment's religion clauses were intended only to prevent the establishment of a national church.*

If all the framers wanted to do was ban a national church, they had plenty of opportunities to state exactly that in the First Amendment. In fact, early drafts of the First Amendment were more limited and could be construed as barring only an official state church. These drafts were rejected as too weak. Following extensive debate, the language found in the First Amendment today was settled on.

The historical record indicates that the framers wanted the First Amendment to ban not only establishment of a single church but also "multiple establishments," that is, a system by which the government funds many religions on an equal basis. This system was common in some colonies, where it had created problems, and the framers did not want to see it replicated on a national level.

A good overview of the development of the language of the First Amendment is found in scholar John M. Swomley's 1987 book, *Religious Liberty and the Secular State*. Swomley shows that during the House of Representatives' debate on the language of the religion clauses, members specifically rejected a version reading, "Congress shall make no law establishing any particular denomination in preference to another." The founders wanted to bar *all* religious establishments; they left no room for "nonpreferentialism," the view touted by some of today's opponents of church-state separation, who argue that government can aid religion as long as it assists all religions equally. (The Senate likewise rejected three versions of the First Amendment that would have permitted nonpreferential support for religion.)

MYTH: *The First Amendment was intended to keep the state from interfering with the church, not to bar religious groups from co-opting the government.*

Jefferson and Madison held an expansive view of the First Amendment, arguing that church-state separation would protect both religion and government.

Madison specifically feared that a small group of powerful churches would join together and seek establishment or special favors from the government. To prevent this from happening, Madison spoke of the desirability of a "multiplicity of sects" that would guard against government favoritism.

Jefferson and Madison did not see church-state separation as an "either or" proposition or argue that one institution needed greater protection than the other. As historian Garry Wills points out in his 1990 book, *Under God*, Jefferson believed that no worthy religion would seek the power of the state to coerce belief. In his writings he argued that disestablishment would strengthen religion, holding that it would "oblige its ministers to be industrious [and] exemplary." The state likewise was degraded by an established faith, Jefferson asserted, because establishment made it a partner in a system based on bribery of religion.

Madison also argued that establishment was no friend to religion or the state. He insisted that civil society would be hindered by establishment, charging that attempts to enforce religious belief by law would weaken government. In his 1785 "Memorial and Remonstrance," Madison stated flatly that "Religion is not helped by establishment, but is hurt by it."

MYTH: *Madison once stated, "We have staked the whole future of American civilization, not upon the power of government, far from it. We have staked the future of all of our political institutions upon the capacity of each and all of us to govern ourselves . . . according to the Ten Commandments of God."*

There is no evidence that Madison ever said or wrote this. The quotation frequently appears in Religious Right publications, but the curators of the Madison Papers at the University of Virginia have been unable to find it in any of Madison's writings. David Barton, a "Christian nation" propagandist who circulated the quote in the early 1990s, has now recommended that people stop using it.

MYTH: Madalyn Murray O'Hair, an atheist, single-handedly removed God, the Bible, and prayer from public schools in 1962.

Atheist leader Madalyn Murray O'Hair played no role in the Supreme Court's school prayer decision of 1962.

In the *Engel* v. *Vitale* case, the U.S. Supreme Court ruled 6–1 against New York's "Regents' prayer," a "nondenominational" prayer state education officials had composed for public school children to recite.

The government-sponsored religious devotion was challenged in court by a group of parents from New Hyde Park—some atheists, some believers. O'Hair was not involved in the case at all.

One year later, a case originated by a Philadelphia-area man named Ed Schempp challenging mandatory Bible reading in Pennsylvania schools reached the Supreme Court. At the same time, Murray O'Hair was challenging a similar practice as well as the recitation of the Lord's Prayer in Maryland public schools. The Supreme Court consolidated the cases and in 1963 ruled 8–1 that devotional Bible reading or other government-sponsored religious activities in public schools are unconstitutional.

The *Engel* and *Schempp* cases were a result of the changing religious landscape of the United States. As religious minorities grew more confident of their rightful place in American society, they came to resent the *de facto* Protestant flavor in many public schools. Litigation was inevitable. The High Court's rulings striking down mandatory prayer and devotional Bible reading in public schools would have occurred if O'Hair had acted or not. The late atheist serves as a convenient villain for Religious Right propagandists who hate religious liberty and church-state separation.

MYTH: It is illegal to pray in a public school.

No Supreme Court ruling has ever stated that truly voluntary devotions by students in public schools are unconstitutional. The rulings of the early 1960s simply prevented the government, through the public schools, from intervening in sensitive religious matters. Prior to those rulings, many public schools used to force children to recite or at least listen to recitation of the Lord's Prayer or verses from the King James version of the Bible. These are sectarian exercises, and some parents objected to their children being required to take part.

Voluntary student religious expression is protected in public schools. Students may pray in a nondisruptive way whenever they like. They may read the Bible or other religious texts during their free time. They may talk to their peers about religion.

In addition, voluntary, student-initiated Bible study and prayer clubs were reaffirmed by the Supreme Court in 1990, when the justices upheld the Equal Access Act, a federal law that permits students to form religion clubs at public high schools under certain conditions.

MYTH: *Public schools cannot discuss religion at all.*

This is simply not true. Public schools are permitted to teach about religion in an objective and academic way, and most do. Students learn about the role of religion in world and U.S. history. They may take courses that deal with religious literature. As long as the approach is objective and fair, the classes are legal.

The rulings from the 1960s are not hostile toward religion, as the justices took pains to point out. In the *Abington* decision, Justice Tom Clark wrote for the court majority, "[I]t might well be said that one's education is not complete without a study of comparative religion or the history of religion and its relationship to the advancement of civilization. It certainly may be said that the Bible is worthy of study for its literary and historic qualities. Nothing we have said here indicates that such study of the Bible or of religion, when presented objectively as part of a secular program of education, may not be effected consistently with the First Amendment."

MYTH: *The school prayer rulings contain no references to prior cases or history and are based on a legal theory invented by the justices on the spot.*

This is another David Barton myth. Anyone who takes the time to read the school prayer rulings—*Engel* v. *Vitale* (1962) and *Abington Township* v. *Schempp* (1963)—will see that this claim is simply false. Both decisions contain multiple references to prior case law as well as an ample review of history. *Abington* contains a lengthy review of church-state history during the colonial period written by Justice William Brennan.

MYTH: *Ever since prayer was removed from schools, public school performance has declined and social ills have increased.*

This argument is a common fallacy of logic known as *post hoc ergo propter hoc*, or, the assumption that if two events occur in sequence, that the first must have caused the second. (The phrase is Latin for "after this, therefore on account of this.")

It is true that some indices of school performance have decreased since 1962, but absolutely no evidence exists linking these developments to the school prayer issue. In fact, the drop has been caused by wholly unrelated factors. SAT scores, for example, are lower today simply because more students from a wider variety of socio-economic backgrounds take the test. In the years preceding 1962, the SAT was taken almost exclusively by upper class, well-educated students from wealthy backgrounds.

The problems experienced in American society today are due to complex socio-economic factors. It is simplistic thinking to blame every societal problem—from the increase in teenage pregnancies to the escalating divorce rate—on a lack of required prayer in schools.

It should also be pointed out that not all indicators of American society have declined since 1962. For example, life expectancy is up, racial discrimination is no longer common, and the average standard of living has increased. Impressive medical advances have occurred in the past forty years, and labor-reducing technologies are commonplace. School prayer advocates are quick to blame every bad thing that has occurred since 1962 on the prayer ruling, but they never mention the positive developments, which, under their premise, must also be a result of the decisions.

The prayer and Bible reading decisions did cause two clear-cut results: Families gained greater religious liberty and the right to decide which religious exercises their children participate in, and church-state separation was strengthened.

MYTH: *School-sponsored prayer and Bible reading took place in all public schools before 1962.*

Several state supreme courts had already removed government-sponsored school prayer and Bible reading from public schools prior to 1962. The Illinois Supreme Court, for example, declared mandatory public school religious exercises unconstitutional in 1910. By the time of the *Engel* decision, public school-sponsored religious exercises were most common in Northeastern and Southern states. Some Western and Midwestern states had already removed the practices.

A 1960 survey by Americans United determined that only five states had required Bible reading laws on the books. Twenty-five states had laws authorizing "optional" Bible reading. Eleven states had declared the practice unconstitutional, and the remaining states had no laws on the subject. The trend was clearly running in favor of a voluntary phase-out of these practices.

MYTH: U.S. law is based on the Ten Commandments.

Religious Right activists frequently make this claim, but it cannot be sustained. Several of the Ten Commandments deal with humankind's relationship to God. These strictures have no counterpart in U.S. law. The Ten Commandments, for example, bar the worship of "false" gods, but U.S. law does not concern itself with which gods are false and which are true. Americans are free to worship any god or gods they like. The Ten Commandments also require people to honor a Sabbath, but again secular law cannot and does not make such a requirement.

Some provisions in the Ten Commandments that bar murder, stealing, and lying may have counterparts in U.S. law. But there is no evidence that these legal provisions were inspired by the Ten Commandments. Most societies in history, regardless of their religious orientation, promulgated laws banning behaviors like these because they are destructive to the larger society and, if not punished, make it impossible for people to live together in peace.

MYTH: The Supreme Court has declared that Secular Humanism is a religion, and Secular Humanism is the established religion of the public schools.

In a footnote to the Supreme Court's 1961 *Torcaso* v. *Watkins* decision, Justice Hugo Black wrote, "Among religions in this country which do not teach what would generally be considered a belief in the existence of God is Buddhism, Taoism, Ethical Culture, Secular Humanism, and others." The *Torcaso* case dealt with religious tests for public office; it had nothing to do with public schools. The justice's comment is far from a finding that Secular Humanism is being taught in the schools.

The Supreme Court and lower federal courts have ruled repeatedly that public schools and other government agencies may not establish "a religion of secularism" any more than they can promote any other religious viewpoint. The courts have decreed that public schools must be religiously neutral. Government neutrality toward religion is not the same thing as government hostility toward religion. They are synonymous only in the view of Religious Right groups that label as hostility any action by government that does not favor their beliefs.

Furthermore, the percentage of Americans who call themselves Secular Humanists is very small. It is not possible that such a minuscule group could take control of the entire public school system, which is highly decentralized and controlled by local school boards chosen by the voters or their representatives. "Secular Humanism" is a bogeyman the Religious Right uses to attack public education.

Appendix 2

Thomas Jefferson's 1802 Letter to the Danbury Baptists

Thomas Jefferson's January 1, 1802, letter to the Danbury, Connecticut, Baptist Association is a seminal document in American church-state history. In the letter, Jefferson used the metaphor of the "wall of separation between church and state," a phrase that, as the Supreme Court once noted, has come to be accepted as an authoritative declaration of the scope and meaning of the First Amendment.

Religious Right groups often spread misinformation about the letter in an attempt to discredit its importance. To set the record straight and understand why the letter is important, it's necessary to read first the Danbury Baptists' letter to Jefferson and understand why they sent it.

Religious Right groups frequently assert that the Baptists wrote to Jefferson because they wanted him to issue a proclamation calling for a day of fasting and prayer or because they were alarmed over a rumor they had heard that a national church was about to be established.

These assertions are not true. The Baptists wrote to Jefferson to commend him for his stand in favor of religious liberty and to express their dissatisfaction with the church-state relationship in Connecticut. (See chapter 3 for the complete story behind the letter.)

Jefferson considered using his reply to explain why he, as president, refused to issue proclamations calling for days of fasting and prayer. Jefferson's attorney general, Levi Lincoln, recommended against this, so Jefferson used the letter to make a statement about the importance of church-state separation.

Below is the transcript of each letter. Original spelling, punctuation, and capitalization have been retained.

The Baptist Address

The address of the Danbury Baptist Association, in the State of Connecticut; assembled October 7th 1801.

To Thomas Jefferson Esq., the President of the united States of America.

Sir,

Among the many millions in America and Europe who rejoice in your Election to office, we embrace the first opportunity which we have enjoy'd in our collective capacity, since your Inauguration, to express our great satisfaction, in your appointment to the chief Magistracy in the United States: And though our mode of expression may be less courtly and pompious than what many others clothe their addresses with, we beg you, Sir to believe, that none are more sincere.

Our Sentiments are uniformly on the side of Religious Liberty—That Religion is at all times and places a Matter between God and Individuals—That no man ought to suffer in Name, person or effects on account of his religious Opinions—That the legitimate Power of civil Government extends no further than to punish the man who *works ill to his neighbour*: But Sir our constitution of government is not specific. Our antient charter, together with the Laws made coincident therewith, were adopted as the Basis of our government at the time of our revolution; and such had been our laws & usages, & such still are; that Religion is considered as the first object of Legislation; & therefore what religious privileges we enjoy (as a minor part of the State) we enjoy as favors granted, and not as inalienable rights: and these favors we receive at the expense of such degrading acknowledgements, as are inconsistent with the rights of freemen. It is not to be wondered at therefore; if those who seek after *power & gain* under the pretence *of government* & *Religion* should reproach their fellowmen—

should reproach their chief Magistrate, as an enemy of religion Law & good order because he will not, dares not assume the prerogative of Jehovah and make Laws to govern the Kingdom of Christ.

Sir, we are sensible that the President of the united States is not the national Legislator & also sensible that the national government cannot destroy the Laws of each State; but our hopes are strong that the sentiments of our beloved President, which have had such genial Effect already, like the radiant beams of the Sun, will shine & prevail through all these States and all the world till Hierarchy and Tyranny be destroyed from the Earth. Sir, when we reflect on your past services and see a glow of philanthropy and good will shining forth in a course of more than thirty years we have reason to believe that America's God has raised you up to fill the chair of State out of that good will which he bears to the Millions which you preside over. May God strengthen you for the arduous task which providence & the voice of the people have cal'd you to sustain and support you in your Administration against all the predetermin'd opposition of those who wish to rise to wealth & importance on the poverty and subjection of the people.

And may the Lord preserve you safe from every evil and bring you at last to his Heavenly Kingdom through Jesus Christ our Glorious Mediator

Signed in behalf of the Association,
Neh'h Dodge — The Committee
Eph'm Robbins
Stephen S. Nelson

Jefferson's Reply

To mess. Nehemiah Dodge, Ephraim Robbins, & Stephen S. Nelson, a committee of the Danbury Baptist association in the state of Connecticut.

Gentlemen

The affectionate sentiments of esteem and approbation which you are so good as to express towards me, on behalf of the Danbury Baptist association, give me the highest satisfaction. my duties dictate a faithful & zealous pursuit of the interests of my constituents, & in proportion as they are persuaded of my fidelity to those duties, the discharge of them becomes more and more pleasing.

Believing with you that religion is a matter which lies solely between Man & his God, that he owes account to none other for his faith or his worship, that the legitimate powers of government reach actions only, & not opinions, I contemplate with sovereign reverence that act of the whole American people which declared that *their* legislature should 'make no law respecting an establishment of religion, or prohibiting the free exercise thereof,' thus building a wall of separation between Church & State. adhering to this expression of the supreme will of the nation in behalf of the rights of conscience, I shall see with sincere satisfaction the progress of those sentiments which tend to restore to man all his natural rights, convinced he has no natural right in opposition to his social duties.

I reciprocate your kind prayers for the protection & blessing of the common father and creator of man, and tender you for yourselves and your religious association, assurances of my high respect & esteem.

Th. Jefferson
Jan. 1. 1802.

Appendix 3

James Madison's 1785 Memorial and Remonstrance against Religious Assessments

James Madison's "Memorial and Remonstrance against Religious Assessments" was written in 1785 in opposition to a proposal by Patrick Henry that all Virginians be taxed to support "teachers of the Christian religion." (See chapter 3 for the full story.)

To this day, the "Memorial and Remonstrance" remains one of the most powerful arguments against government-supported religion ever penned. This is the full text of the document. Original spelling and punctuation have been retained.

To the Honorable the General Assembly of the Commonwealth of Virginia

We the subscribers, citizens of the said Commonwealth, having taken into serious consideration, a Bill printed by order of the last Session of General Assembly, entitled "A Bill establishing a provision for Teachers of the Christian Religion," and conceiving that the same if finally armed with the sanctions of a law, will be a dangerous abuse of power, are bound as faithful members of a free State to remonstrate against it, and to declare the reasons by which we are determined. We remonstrate against the said Bill,

1. Because we hold it for a fundamental and undeniable truth, "that religion or the duty which we owe to our Creator and the manner of discharging it, can be directed only by reason and conviction, not by force or violence." The Religion then of every man must be left to the conviction and conscience of every man; and it is the right of every man to exercise it as these may dictate. This right is in its nature an unalienable right. It is unalienable, because the opinions of men, depending only on the evidence contemplated by their own minds cannot follow the dictates of other men: It is unalienable also, because what is here a right towards men, is a duty towards the Creator. It is the duty of every man to render to the Creator such homage and such only as he believes to be acceptable to him. This duty is precedent, both in order of time and in degree of obligation, to the claims of Civil Society. Before any man can be considered as a member of Civil Society, he must be considered as a subject of the Governour of the Universe: And if a member of Civil Society, do it with a saving of his allegiance to the Universal Sovereign. We maintain therefore that in matters of Religion, no man's right is abridged by the institution of Civil Society and that Religion is wholly exempt from its cognizance. True it is, that no other rule exists, by which any question which may divide a Society, can be ultimately determined, but the will of the majority; but it is also true that the majority may trespass on the rights of the minority.

2. Because Religion be exempt from the authority of the Society at large, still less can it be subject to that of the Legislative Body. The latter are but the creatures and viceregents of the former. Their jurisdiction is both derivative and limited: it is limited with regard to the co-ordinate departments, more necessarily is it limited with regard to the constituents. The preservation of a free Government requires not merely, that the metes and bounds which separate each department of power be invariably maintained; but more especially that neither of them be suffered to overleap the great Barrier which defends the rights of the people. The Rulers who are guilty of such an encroachment, exceed the commission from which they derive their authority, and are Tyrants. The People who submit to it are governed by laws made neither by themselves nor by an authority derived from them, and are slaves.

3. Because it is proper to take alarm at the first experiment on our liberties. We hold this prudent jealousy to be the first duty of Citizens, and

one of the noblest characteristics of the late Revolution. The free men of America did not wait till usurped power had strengthened itself by exercise, and entangled the question in precedents. They saw all the consequences in the principle, and they avoided the consequences by denying the principle. We revere this lesson too much soon to forget it. Who does not see that the same authority which can establish Christianity, in exclusion of all other Religions, may establish with the same ease any particular sect of Christians, in exclusion of all other Sects? That the same authority which can force a citizen to contribute three pence only of his property for the support of any one establishment, may force him to conform to any other establishment in all cases whatsoever?

4. Because the Bill violates the equality which ought to be the basis of every law, and which is more indispensable, in proportion as the validity or expediency of any law is more liable to be impeached. If "all men are by nature equally free and independent," all men are to be considered as entering into Society on equal conditions; as relinquishing no more, and therefore retaining no less, one than another, of their natural rights. Above all are they to be considered as retaining an "equal title to the free exercise of Religion according to the dictates of Conscience." Whilst we assert for ourselves a freedom to embrace, to profess and to observe the Religion which we believe to be of divine origin, we cannot deny an equal freedom to those whose minds have not yet yielded to the evidence which has convinced us. If this freedom be abused, it is an offence against God, not against man: To God, therefore, not to man, must an account of it be rendered. As the Bill violates equality by subjecting some to peculiar burdens, so it violates the same principle, by granting to others peculiar exemptions. Are the Quakers and Menonists the only sects who think a compulsive support of their Religions unnecessary and unwarrantable? can their piety alone be entrusted with the care of public worship? Ought their Religions to be endowed above all others with extraordinary privileges by which proselytes may be enticed from all others? We think too favorably of the justice and good sense of these denominations to believe that they either covet pre-eminences over their fellow citizens or that they will be seduced by them from the common opposition to the measure.

5. Because the Bill implies either that the Civil Magistrate is a competent Judge of Religious Truth; or that he may employ Religion as an engine of Civil policy. The first is an arrogant pretension falsified by the contradictory opinions of Rulers in all ages, and throughout the world: the second an unhallowed perversion of the means of salvation.

6. Because the establishment proposed by the Bill is not requisite for the support of the Christian Religion. To say that it is, is a contradiction to the Christian Religion itself, for every page of it disavows a dependence on the powers of this world: it is a contradiction to fact; for it is known that this Religion both existed and flourished, not only without the support of human laws, but in spite of every opposition from them, and not only during the period of miraculous aid, but long after it had been left to its own evidence and the ordinary care of Providence. Nay, it is a contradiction in terms; for a Religion not invented by human policy, must have pre-existed and been supported, before it was established by human policy. It is moreover to weaken in those who profess this Religion a pious confidence in its innate excellence and the patronage of its Author; and to foster in those who still reject it, a suspicion that its friends are too conscious of its fallacies to trust it to its own merits.

7. Because experience witnesseth that ecclesiastical establishments, instead of maintaining the purity and efficacy of Religion, have had a contrary operation. During almost fifteen centuries has the legal establishment of Christianity been on trial. What have been its fruits? More or less in all places, pride and indolence in the Clergy, ignorance and servility in the laity, in both, superstition, bigotry and persecution. Enquire of the Teachers of Christianity for the ages in which it appeared in its greatest lustre; those of every sect, point to the ages prior to its incorporation with Civil policy. Propose a restoration of this primitive State in which its Teachers depended on the voluntary rewards of their flocks, many of them predict its downfall. On which Side ought their testimony to have greatest weight, when for or when against their interest?

8. Because the establishment in question is not necessary for the support of Civil Government. If it be urged as necessary for the support of Civil Government only as it is a means of supporting Religion, and it be not necessary for the latter purpose, it cannot be necessary for the former. If Religion be not within the cognizance of Civil Government how can its legal establishment be necessary to Civil Government? What influence in fact have ecclesiastical establishments had on Civil Society? In some instances they have been seen to erect a spiritual tyranny on the ruins of the Civil authority; in many instances they have been seen upholding the thrones of political tyranny: in no instance have they been seen the guardians of the liberties of the people. Rulers who wished to subvert the public liberty, may have found an established Clergy convenient auxiliaries. A just Government instituted to secure & perpetuate it needs them not. Such

a Government will be best supported by protecting every Citizen in the enjoyment of his Religion with the same equal hand which protects his person and his property; by neither invading the equal rights of any Sect, nor suffering any Sect to invade those of another.

9. Because the proposed establishment is a departure from the generous policy, which, offering an Asylum to the persecuted and oppressed of every Nation and Religion, promised a lustre to our country, and an accession to the number of its citizens. What a melancholy mark is the Bill of sudden degeneracy? Instead of holding forth an Asylum to the persecuted, it is itself a signal of persecution. It degrades from the equal rank of Citizens all those whose opinions in Religion do not bend to those of the Legislative authority. Distant as it may be in its present form from the Inquisition, it differs from it only in degree. The one is the first step, the other the last in the career of intolerance. The magnanimous sufferer under this cruel scourge in foreign Regions, must view the Bill as a Beacon on our Coast, warning him to seek some other haven, where liberty and philanthropy in their due extent, may offer a more certain repose from his Troubles.

10. Because it will have a like tendency to banish our Citizens. The allurements presented by other situations are every day thinning their number. To superadd a fresh motive to emigration by revoking the liberty which they now enjoy, would be the same species of folly which has dishonoured and depopulated flourishing kingdoms.

11. Because it will destroy that moderation and harmony which the forbearance of our laws to intermeddle with Religion has produced among its several sects. Torrents of blood have been spilt in the old world, by vain attempts of the secular arm, to extinguish Religious discord, by proscribing all difference in Religious opinion. Time has at length revealed the true remedy. Every relaxation of narrow and rigorous policy, wherever it has been tried, has been found to assuage the disease. The American Theatre has exhibited proofs that equal and compleat liberty, if it does not wholly eradicate it, sufficiently destroys its malignant influence on the health and prosperity of the State. If with the salutary effects of this system under our own eyes, we begin to contract the bounds of Religious freedom, we know no name that will too severely reproach our folly. At least let warning be taken at the first fruits of the threatened innovation. The very appearance of the Bill has transformed "that Christian forbearance, love and charity," which of late mutually prevailed, into animosities and jealousies, which may not soon be appeased. What mischiefs

may not be dreaded, should this enemy to the public quiet be armed with the force of a law?

12. Because the policy of the Bill is adverse to the diffusion of the light of Christianity. The first wish of those who enjoy this precious gift ought to be that it may be imparted to the whole race of mankind. Compare the number of those who have as yet received it with the number still remaining under the dominion of false Religions; and how small is the former! Does the policy of the Bill tend to lessen the disproportion? No; it at once discourages those who are strangers to the light of revelation from coming into the Region of it; and countenances by example the nations who continue in darkness, in shutting out those who might convey it to them. Instead of Levelling as far as possible, every obstacle to the victorious progress of Truth, the Bill with an ignoble and unchristian timidity would circumscribe it with a wall of defence against the encroachments of error.

13. Because attempts to enforce by legal sanctions, acts obnoxious to so great a proportion of Citizens, tend to enervate the laws in general, and to slacken the bands of Society. If it be difficult to execute any law which is not generally deemed necessary or salutary, what must be the case, where it is deemed invalid and dangerous? And what may be the effect of so striking an example of impotency in the Government, on its general authority?

14. Because a measure of such singular magnitude and delicacy ought not to be imposed, without the clearest evidence that it is called for by a majority of citizens, and no satisfactory method is yet proposed by which the voice of the majority in this case may be determined, or its influence secured. "The people of the respective counties are indeed requested to signify their opinion respecting the adoption of the Bill to the next Session of Assembly." But the representation must be made equal, before the voice either of the Representatives or of the Counties will be that of the people. Our hope is that neither of the former will, after due consideration, espouse the dangerous principle of the Bill. Should the event disappoint us, it will still leave us in full confidence, that a fair appeal to the latter will reverse the sentence against our liberties.

15. Because finally, "the equal right of every citizen to the free exercise of his Religion according to the dictates of conscience" is held by the same tenure with all our other rights. If we recur to its origin, it is equally the gift of nature; if we weigh its importance, it cannot be less dear to us; if we consult the "Declaration of those rights which pertain to the good

people of Virginia, as the basis and foundation of Government," it is enumerated with equal solemnity, or rather studied emphasis. Either then, we must say, that the Will of the Legislature is the only measure of their authority; and that in the plenitude of this authority, they may sweep away all our fundamental rights; or, that they are bound to leave this particular right untouched and sacred: Either we must say, that they may controul the freedom of the press, may abolish the Trial by Jury, may swallow up the Executive and Judiciary Powers of the State; nay that they may despoil us of our very right of suffrage, and erect themselves into an independent and hereditary Assembly or, we must say, that they have no authority to enact into the law the Bill under consideration. We the Subscribers say, that the General Assembly of this Commonwealth have no such authority: And that no effort may be omitted on our part against so dangerous an usurpation, we oppose to it, this remonstrance; earnestly praying, as we are in duty bound, that the Supreme Lawgiver of the Universe, by illuminating those to whom it is addressed, may on the one hand, turn their Councils from every act which would affront his holy prerogative, or violate the trust committed to them: and on the other, guide them into every measure which may be worthy of his blessing, may redound to their own praise, and may establish more firmly the liberties, the prosperity and the happiness of the Commonwealth.

Index